Michael Ondaatje

LEE SPINKS

Manchester University Press

Manchester and New York

distributed exclusively in the USA by Palgrave

Published by Manchester University Press
Oxford Road, Manchester M13 9NR, UK
and Room 400, 175 Fifth Avenue, New York, NY 10010, USA
www.manchesteruniversitypress.co.uk

Distributed exclusively in the USA by
Palgrave, 175 Fifth Avenue, New York, NY 10010, USA

Distributed exclusively in Canada by
ubc Press, University of British Columbia, 2029 West Mall, Vancouver, bc, Canada v6t 1z2

British Library Cataloguing-in-Publication Data
A catalogue record for this book is available from the British Library

Library of Congress Cataloging-in-Publication Data applied for

ISBN 978 0 7190 6632 0 *hardback*
ISBN 978 0 7190 6633 7 *paperback*

First published 2009

18 17 16 15 14 13 12 11 10 09   10 9 8 7 6 5 4 3 2 1

Typeset in Aldus
by Koinonia, Manchester
Printed in Great Britain
by Bell & Bain, Glasgow

Contents

Acknowledgements

My principal debt is to Claire Colebrook, whose careful reading of successive drafts of the manuscript rescued me from many errors and infelicities. While writing the book I was particularly grateful for the encouragement and intellectual companionship of Andrew Taylor, Penny Fielding, James Loxley, Miriam Nabarro, Michelle Keown and Jonathan Wild. I am also grateful to the Department of English Literature, Edinburgh University, for a period of teaching remission that enabled me to complete this book, to the staff at both Edinburgh University Library and the National Library of Scotland for their courtesy and efficiency, to the students of my Modern Poetry seminar for their continuing interest in Ondaatje's poetry, to Professor John Thieme for inaugurating the project in the first place, and to Alison Kelly at Manchester University Press for her meticulous copy-editing of the manuscript. This book is dedicated to my mother, Paula.

Series editor's foreword

Contemporary World Writers is an innovative series of authoritative introductions to a range of culturally diverse contemporary writers from outside Britain and the United States or from 'minority' backgrounds within Britain or the United States. In addition to providing comprehensive general introductions, books in the series also argue stimulating original theses, often but not always related to contemporary debates in post-colonial studies.

The series locates individual writers within their specific cultural contexts, while recognising that such contexts are themselves invariably a complex mixture of hybridised influences. It aims to counter tendencies to appropriate the writers discussed into the canon of English or American literature or to regard them as 'other'.

Each volume includes a chronology of the writer's life, an introductory section on formative contexts and intertexts, discussion of all the writer's major works, a bibliography of primary and secondary works and an index. Issues of racial, national and cultural identity are explored, as are gender and sexuality. Books in the series also examine writers' use of genre, particularly ways in which Western genres are adapted or subverted and 'traditional' local forms are reworked in a contemporary context.

Contemporary World Writers aims to bring together the theoretical impulse which currently dominates post-colonial studies and closely argued readings of particular authors' works, and by so doing to avoid the danger of appropriating the specifics of particular texts into the hegemony of totalising theories.

Abbreviations

AG   *Anil's Ghost* (London: Picador, 2001)

BTK   *The Collected Works of Billy the Kid* (London: Marion Boyers, 1981)

CTS   *Coming Through Slaughter* (London: Picador, 1984)

DM   *The Dainty Monsters* (Toronto: Coach House Press, 1967)

EP   *The English Patient* (London: Picador, 1993)

H   *Handwriting* (London: Picador, 2000)

ISL   *In the Skin of a Lion* (London: Picador, 1988)

RF   *Running in the Family* (London: Picador, 1984)

RJ   *Rat Jelly and Other Poems* (Toronto: Coach House Press, 1973)

SL   *Secular Love* (Toronto: Coach House Press, 1984)

TMWST *the man with seven toes* (Toronto: Coach House Press, 1975)

Chronology

1943   Philip Michael Ondaatje born (12 September) in Kegalle, Ceylon; son of Philip Mervyn Ondaatje and Enid Gratiaen Ondaatje.

1945   Ondaatje's parents divorce.

1948   Ceylon wins independence from Britain and is reborn as Sri Lanka.

1949–52   Attends St Thomas College, Colombo.

1952   Follows mother, brother and sister to London.

1952–62   Attends Dulwich College, London.

1962   Immigrates to Montreal, Canada.

1962–4   Student at Bishops University, Lennoxville, Quebec; takes BA General Arts degree, majoring in English and History; wins President's Prize in English; marries artist Kim Jones (two children from this marriage; subsequently dissolved).

1965   Completes BA at University of Toronto; receives Ralph Gustafson Award for poetry.

1965–7   Completes MA in English at Queens University, Kingston, Ontario.

1966   First poems published in major new anthology *New Wave Canada*; produces and acts in David Secter's film *The Offering*; receives the Norma Epstein Award for Poetry.

1967   *The Dainty Monsters* published in Toronto; takes up teaching position at University of Western Ontario; wins President's Medal at Western Ontario for poem 'Paris'.

1968   *the man with seven toes* performed in Vancouver as a dialogue for voices.

1969   *the man with seven toes* published in Canada.

1970   *Leonard Cohen,* a critical study, and *The Collected Works of Billy the Kid: Left Handed Poems* published in Canada; completes short film *Sons of Captain Poetry*; editor for Coach House Press.

1971   *The Collected Works of Billy the Kid* wins the Governor General's Award; a dramatic reading of *Billy the Kid* is performed in Toronto; denied tenure at University of Western Ontario and takes up a teaching position at Glendon College, York University, Toronto; *The Broken Ark: A Book of Beasts* published in Canada.

1972   Makes two short films, *Carry on Crime and Punishment* and *The Clinton Special,* a documentary record of the Theater Passe Muraille Farm Show

1973   Fourth volume of poems, *Rat Jelly,* published in Canada; play of *Billy the Kid* performed in Stratford, Ontario; Chalmers Award finalist for *Billy the Kid.*

1976   *Coming Through Slaughter* published in Canada and New York.

1977   Edits *Personal Fictions: Stories by Mumro, Wieve, Thomas and Blaise.*

1978   *Elimination Dance* published in Canada; makes his first return visit to Sri Lanka since leaving as a child.

1979   *There's a Trick with a Knife I'm Learning to Do* published in Canada and New York and subsequently wins the Governor General's Award; *Claude Glass* published in Canada; edits *The Long Poem Anthology*; collapse of his marriage to Kim Jones.

1980   *Rat Jelly and Other Poems* published in London; makes second return trip to Sri Lanka; accepts one-year Creative Writing post at University of Hawaii at Manoa; meets Linda Spalding; receives the Canada-Australia Literary Prize; play of *Coming Through Slaughter* performed in Toronto.

1981   Lives for a year in Australia as the recipient of an Exchange award.

1982   *Running in the Family* published in Canada and New York; *Tin Roof* published in Canada; wins first-prize category of CBC Radio's Annual Literary Competition for 'The Passions of Lalla'; Professor of English at Glendon College.

1982   Outbreak of Sri Lankan civil war.

1983   *Secular Love* published in Canada.

1984   Contributing editor of *Brick: A Journal of Reviews*.

1985   *Two Poems* published by Woodland Pattern Press.

1987   *In the Skin of a Lion* published in Canada; finalist for Ritz Paris Hemingway Award (no award given).

1988   Receives Order of Canada; receives Literary Festival of Arts Award; wins Best Paperback in English Award.

1989   *The Cinnamon Peeler: Selected Poems* published in the UK; edits *Brushes with Greatness: An Anthology of Chance Encounters with Greatness* with Russell Banks and David Young.

1990   Edits *From Ink Lake: An Anthology of Canadian Stories* edits *The Faber Book of Contemporary Canadian Short Stories*; Visiting Professor at Brown University in Rhode Island; co-writes short film *Love Clinic*.

1991   Edits *The Brick Reader* with Linda Spalding.

1992   *The English Patient* published in Canada and New York; wins the Booker Prize, the Governor General's Award and the Trillium Award.

1994   Edits *An H in the Heart: A Reader* with George Bowering.

1996   Première of *The English Patient*, with a screenplay based on Ondaatje's novel.

1998   Publication of *Handwriting* in Canada.

2000   *Anil's Ghost* published in Canada and New York; wins the 2000 Giller Prize, the Prix Médicis and the Governor General's Award.

2001   Co-edits *Lost Classics*.

2002   Co-edits *Brick: A Literary Journal Number 69* with Linda Spalding.

Contexts and intertexts

Philip Michael Ondaatje was born in 1943 in Kegalle, Ceylon, a town about fifty miles west of the capital Colombo.[1] He was the second son of Mervyn Ondaatje and Enid Doris Gratiaen, both relatively prominent members of the Burgher class, a well-to-do section of Ceylonese colonial society. The Burghers were for the most part descendants of European colonists from the sixteenth century onwards – the term 'burgher' derives from the Dutch word 'burger' meaning 'citizen' or 'resident' – and they were traditionally the most westernised ethnic grouping in colonial Ceylon. Ondaatje's European ancestor arrived in Ceylon in the early seventeenth century as 'a doctor who cured the residing governor's daughter with a strange herb and was rewarded with land, a foreign wife, and a new name which was a Dutch spelling of his own'. (RF, 64). From these beginnings the Ondaatjes gradually amassed a considerable fortune as the owners of a tea plantation; unfortunately much of this wealth was squandered by Ondaatje's father Mervyn. Their inherited income did, however, enable Ondaatje's parents to occupy a comfortable social position midway between the majority native population and the British colonial ruling class. Mervyn Ondaaje's fierce nostalgia for the manners and mores of this neo-colonial social caste was a continuing presence throughout Ondaatje's childhood years.

These childhood years were darkened by the spectre of Mervyn Ondaatje's chronic alcoholism. Ondaatje's autobiographical poem 'Letters and Other Worlds' captures the nightmare of his father's descent into alcoholism in the stark line

'He came to death with his mind drowning' (*RJ*, 44). Mervyn's increasingly erratic behaviour – in one infamous episode in the summer of 1943 he commandeered a railway train at gunpoint and forced it to shunt backwards and forwards across the Ceylonese countryside before divesting himself of his military uniform and hiding naked in the Kalugannawa tunnel – eventually proved too much for Ondaatje's mother and the couple was divorced in 1945, when Michael was just two years old.[2] Following their divorce, Doris Ondaatje took her children to Colombo, where Michael later attended St Thomas College for Boys. In 1948 Ceylon finally threw off the yoke of British imperial rule and was reborn as independent Sri Lanka. This momentous event had one unhappy entailment for the Ondaatje family: the Bank of England's refusal any longer to underwrite the Sri Lankan currency precipitated an economic crisis which greatly reduced the value of Doris's divorce settlement.[3] The loss of her income came as a severe blow to Ondaatje's mother, who decided in 1949 to move to London where she eventually opened a boarding house in Lancaster Gate. Considered too young to travel, Michael and his sister Gillian were left behind in Colombo with relatives. Bereft of a father and temporarily separated from his mother, young Michael was now thrown back upon his own emotional resources. This situation lasted until 1952 when, at the age of nine, he made the first big move of his life by following his mother and his older brother and sister to England.

Whatever the exigency of family circumstance, Ondaatje was now a part of the great south-east Asian diaspora. Certainly this was the way he perceived the situation: 'I was part of that colonial tradition', he later explained, 'of sending your kids off to school in England'.[4] He spent ten largely unhappy years in England, where he finished his schooling in the sedate surroundings of Dulwich College, a school populated mainly by the children of upper-class families. England appeared dull, cold and monochrome to his young Sri Lankan eyes and he longed to return home or begin his life again elsewhere. His hopes were realised in 1962 when he followed his older brother Christopher

to create an unforgettable image of a new kind of artist. His poetic rewriting of the legend of Buddy Bolden, first man of jazz, struck a chord with both the critics and the wider reading public and showed that he had successfully negotiated the transition between the roles of poet and novelist. Such were the artistic strengths of *Coming Through Slaughter* that the book was judged to be the co-winner of the 1976 Books in Canada First Novel Award.

Encouraged by the reception of *Coming Through Slaughter*, Ondaatje spent some time trying to develop a screenplay of the novel. In preparation for this venture he collaborated with the Canadian writer Robert Kroetsch upon a movie version of the latter's novel *Badlands*. This project absorbed a good deal of Ondaatje's imaginative energy during 1977 without ever entering production; a version of the screenplay entitled 'The William Dawe Badlands Expedition 1916' eventually surfaced in an academic journal six years later.[23] Although Ondaatje completed a treatment of *Coming Through Slaughter* shortly afterwards, he was no more successful in securing finance to bring it to the screen. Refusing to be discouraged by this reverse, in 1978 he published *Elimination Dance*, a light-hearted collection of satirical maxims intended to lampoon 'All those bad poets who claim me as an early influence'. Despite its satirical tone, this volume indirectly acknowledged a change in Ondaatje's circumstances; he was now seen as an influence upon a new generation of Canadian writers: an influence that would steadily increase in the ensuing years.

The period following the publication of *Coming Through Slaughter* was a turbulent one for Ondaatje. In January 1978 he returned to Sri Lanka for the first time in a quarter of a century and spent five months travelling across the country and reacquainting himself with his extended family. This was to be the first of two trips to Sri Lanka – the second took place in 1980 – which he later wrote 'were central in helping me recreate the era of my parents' in *Running in the Family* (*RF*, 205). The next year Ondaatje travelled extensively in China; a year later he abandoned his usually strict code of privacy to attend a writer's conference in Hawaii. One reason for his peripatetic itinerary was the fact that his marriage was coming under increasing strain; in 1980 it collapsed completely. While in Hawaii Ondaatje met and began a relationship with Linda Spalding, a woman in her thirties, who worked in the arts and as a social services administrator for low-income families.[24] As their affair developed, Ondaatje decided to extend his visit to Hawaii for a year by accepting a temporary Creative Writing post at the University of Hawaii at Manoa. His developing relationship with Linda led inevitably to a separation from Kim; upon his return from Hawaii, he and Linda settled quietly together in Toronto.

The break-up of his marriage was a traumatic event for Ondaatje. The grief and guilt he felt at his separation from Kim and his estrangement from his children makes itself felt in almost every line of 'Tin Roof', a poem dating from this period. One of Ondaatje's bleakest and most unsparing poems, 'Tin Roof' is haunted by images of death and imminent catastrophe. 'This last year', the poem begins, 'I was sure / I was going to die', and it proceeds to describe the gradual disintegration of an individual 'drowning / at the edge of sea' (SL, 105). Cast hopelessly adrift between two very different worlds, the speaker can only imagine a future for himself at the expense of an agonising break with his former life: 'It is impossible to enter the sea here / except in a violent way' (SL, 110). Yet his brave new world of reclaimed love will be forever haunted by the memory of all that it has cost: 'He is joyous and breaking down' at exactly the same time (SL, 108). With their echo of T. S. Eliot's 'The Love Song of J. Alfred Prufrock', the poem's final lines express the agony of an emotional state in which any prospective 'release' from pain demands the death of a vital part of the self: 'I wanted poetry to be walnuts / in their green cases / but now it is the sea / and we let it drown us / and we fly to it released / by giant catapults / of pain loneliness deceit and vanity' (SL, 123).

Critics were quick to notice the unusually sombre and confessional tone of 'Tin Roof' and many of the other poems in *Secular Love*. Reviewing *Secular Love*, Sam Solecki observed that 'The book is made up of four chronologically arranged drafts, proofs, publicity and reviews for *In the Skin of a Lion*. A number of Ondaatje's other materials, including the manuscript of *The English Patient*, are held in the Canadian Literature Research Service collection of the Canadian National Library.

INTERVIEWS

Barbour, Douglas and Stephen Scobie. 'A Conversation with Michael Ondaatje', *White Pelican* 1.2 (Spring 1971) 6–15.

Bush, Catherine. 'Michael Ondaatje: An Interview', *Essays on Canadian Writing*, 53 (1994) 238–49.

Fagan, Cary. 'Where the Personal and the Historical Meet: Michael Ondaatje', in *The Power to Bend Spoons: Interviews with Canadian Novelists* ed. Beverly Daurio (Toronto: Mercury, 1998) 115–21.

Hutcheon, Linda. 'Interview', in *Other Solitudes: Canadian Multicultural Fictions* ed Linda Hutcheon and Marion Redmond (Toronto: Oxford University Press, 1990) 196–202.

Jaggi, Maya. 'Michael Ondaatje in Conversation with Maya Jaggi', *Wasafiri: A Journal of Carribean, African, Asian and Annotated Literature and Film* 32 (Autumn 2000) 5–11.

Pearce, Jon. 'Moving to the Clear', *Twelve Voices* (Ottawa: Borealis, 1980) 131–43.

Presson, Rebekah. 'Fiction as Opposed to Fact: An Interview with Michael Ondaatje', *New Letters* 62 (1996) 81–90.

Solecki, Sam. 'Interview with Michael Ondaatje (1975)', in *Spider Blues: Essays on Michael Ondaatje* ed. Sam Solecki (Montréal: Véhicule Press, 1985) 39–54.

Solecki, Sam. 'Interview with Michael Ondaatje (1984)', in *Spider Blues: Essays on Michael Ondaatje* ed. Sam Solecki (Montréal: Véhicule Press, 1985) 321–32.

Watchtel, Eleanor, 'An Interview with Michael Ondaatje', *Essays on Canadian Writing* 54 (Summer 1994) 250–61.

Selected criticism

GENERAL ARTICLES AND ESSAYS ON ONDAATJE

Brady, Judith. 'Michael Ondaatje: An Annotated Bibliography', *The Annotated Bibliography of Canada's Major Authors* ed. Robert Lecker and Jack David (Toronto: ECW Press, 1985) 129–205.

Davey, Frank. 'Michael Ondaatje', *From There to Here: A Guide to English-Canadian Literature Since 1960* (Erin, Ontario: Porcepic, 1974) 222–7.

Gefen, Pearl Shelley. 'If I were 19 Now I'd Maybe Be a Filmmaker', *Globe and Mail*, 4 May 1990, D3.

Mandel, Ann. 'Michael Ondaatje', *Canadian Writers Since 1960: Second Series* ed. W. H. New (Detroit: Gale Research Company, 1987).

Waldman, Neil. 'Michael Ondaatje (1943–)', *ECW's Biographical Guide to Canadian Poets* eds. Robert Lecker, Jack David and Ellen Quigley (Toronto: ECW, 1992) 271–7.

Waldman, Neil. 'Michael Ondaatje and His Works', *Canadian Writers and Their Works* eds. Robert Lecker, Jack David and Ellen Quigley (Toronto: ECW, 1992) 359–412.

Criticism

BOOKS ON ONDAATJE

Barbour, Douglas. *Michael Ondaatje* (New York: Twayne Publishers, 1993).

Bolland, John. *Michael Ondaatje's The English Patient* (London: Continuum, 2002).

Jewinski, Ed. *Michael Ondaatje: Express Yourself Beautifully* (Toronto: ECW Press, 1994).

Kella, Elizabeth. *Beloved Communities: Solidarity and Difference in Fiction by Michael Ondaatje, Toni Morrison, and Joy Kiogawa* (Uppsala: Uppsala University Press, 2000).

Lacroix, Jean-Michel (ed.). *Reconstructing the Fragments of Michael Ondaatje's Works* (Paris: Presses de Sorbonne Nouvelle, 1999).

Mundwiler, Leslie. *Michael Ondaatje: Word, Image, Imagination* (Vancouver: Talonbooks, 1984).

Siemerling, Winfried. *Discoveries of the Other: Alterity in the Work of Leonard Cohen, Hubert Aquin, Michael Ondaatje and Nicole*

Brossard (Toronto: University of Toronto Press, 1994).

Solecki, Sam (ed.). *Spider Blues: Essays on Michael Ondaatje* (Montréal, Canada: Véhicule Press, 1985).

Solecki, Sam. *Ragas of Longing: The Poetry of Michael Ondaatje* (Toronto: University of Toronto Press, 2003).

Töstöy de Zepetnek, Steven (ed.). *Comparative Cultural Studies and Michael Ondaatje's Writing* (West Lafayette, IN: Purdue University Press, 2005.

York, Lorraine M. *The Other Side of Dailiness: Photography in the works of Alice Munro, Timothy Findley, Michael Ondaatje and Margaret Laurence* (Toronto: ECW Press, 1988).

ARTICLES AND ESSAYS ON THE EARLY POETRY

Chamberlin, J. E. 'Let There Be Commerce Between Us: The Poetry of Michael Ondaatje', *Descant* 43 (Fall 1983) 89–98.

Glickman, Susan. 'From "Philoctetes on the Island" to "Tin Roof": The Emerging Myth of Michael Ondaatje', *Spider Blues: Essays on Michael Ondaatje* ed. Sam Solecki (Montréal: Véhicule Press, 1985) 70–81.

Harding-Russell, Gillian. 'A Note on Ondaatje's "Peter"': A Creative Myth', *Canadian Literature* 112 (1987) 205–11.

Heighton, Steve. 'Approaching "That Perfect Edge": Kinetic Techniques in the Poetry and Fiction of Michael Ondaatje', *Studies in Canadian Literature* 13 (1988) 223–43.

Hunter, Lynette. 'Form and Energy in the Poetry of Michael Ondaatje', *Journal of Canadian Poetry* 1.1 (Winter 1978) 49–70.

Kahn, Sy. 'Michael Ondaatje, *The Dainty Monsters*', *The Far Point* 1 (Fall/Winter 1978) 70–6.

Lewis, Tanya. 'Myth-Manipulation through Dismemberment in Michael Ondaatje's *the man with seven toes*', *Studies in Canadian Literature* 24.2 (1999) 100–13.

Murkherjee, Arun. 'The Sri-Lankan Poets in Canada: An Alternative View', *Toronto South Asian Review* 3.2 (1984) 32–45.

Scobie, Stephen. 'His Legend a Jungle Sleep: Michael Ondaatje and Henri Rousseau', *Canadian Literature* 76 (Spring 1978) 5–23.

Solecki, Sam. 'Point Blank: Narrative in Michael Ondaatje's *the man with seven toes*', *Canadian Poetry* 6 (Spring/Summer 1980) 14–24.

Solecki, Sam. 'Nets and Chaos: The Poetry of Michael Ondaatje', *Studies in Canadian Literature* 2.1 (Winter 1977) 36–48.

Sugunasiri, Suwanda H. J. '"Sri Lankan" Canadian Poets: The Bourgeoisie that Fled the Revolution', *Canadian Literature* 132 (1992): 60–79.

Summer-Bremner, Eluned. 'Reading Ondaatje's Poetry', *Comparative Cultural Studies and Michael Ondaatje's Writing* ed. Stephen Töstöy de Zepetnek (West Lafayette, IN: Purdue University Press, 2005) 104–14.

Travis Lane, M. 'Dream as History: A Review of *the man with seven toes*', *Spider Blues Essays on Michael Ondaatje* ed. Sam Solecki (Montréal: Véhicule Press, 1985) 150–5.

ARTICLES, ESSAYS AND REVIEWS ON
THE COLLECTED WORKS OF BILLY THE KID

Bethell, Kathleen I. 'Reading Billy: Memory, Time and Subjectivity in *The Collected Works of Billy the Kid*', *Studies in Canadian Literature* 28.1 (2003) 71–89.

Cooley, Dennis. 'I am Here on the Edge: Modern Hero/Postmodern Poetics in *The Collected Works of Billy the Kid*', *Spider Blues: Essays on Michael Ondaatje*, ed. Sam Solecki (Montréal: Véhicule Press, 1985) 211–39.

Godard, Barbara. 'Stretching the Story: The Canadian Story Cycle', *Open Letter*, 7th series, no. 6 (Fall 1989) 27–71.

Harrison, Keith. 'Montage in *The Collected Works of Billy the Kid*', *Journal of Canadian Poetry* 3.1 (1980) 32–8.

Heble, Ajay. 'Michael Ondaatje and the Problem of History', *CLIO: Journal of Literature, History, and the Philosophy of History* 19.2 (1990) 97–110.

Jones, Manina. '*The Collected Works of Billy the Kid:* Scripting the Docudrama', *Canadian Literature* 122–23 (Autunm-Winter 1989) 26–38.

Kertzer, J.M. 'On Death and Dying: The Collected Works of Billy the Kid', *English Studies in Canada* 1 (Spring 1975) 86–96.

Lee, Dennis. 'Savage Fields: *The Collected Works of Billy the Kid*' in *Spider Blues: Essays on Michael Ondaatje*, ed. Sam Solecki (Montréal: Véhicule Press, 1985) 166–84.

Nodelman, Perry M. 'The Collected Photographs of Billy the Kid', *Canadian Literature* 87 (Winter 1980) 68–79.

Owens, Judith. 'I Send You a Picture: Ondaatje's Portrait of Billy the Kid', *Studies in Canadian Literature* 8.1 (1983) 117–39.

Scobie, Stephen. 'Two Authors in Search of a Character: bpNichol and Michael Ondaatje' in *Spider Blues: Essays on Michael Ondaatje*, ed. Sam Solecki (Montréal: Véhicule Press, 1985) 185–210.

Van Wart, Alice. 'The Evolution of Form in Michael Ondaatje's *The Collected Works of Billy the Kid* and *Coming Through Slaughter*', *Canadian Poetry* 17 (Fall/Winter 1985). 1–28.

Watson, Sheila. 'Michael Ondaatje: The Mechanization of Death', in *Spider Blues: Essays on Michael Ondaatje* ed. Sam Solecki (Montréal: Véhicule Press, 1985) 156–65.

ARTICLES, ESSAYS AND REVIEWS ON *COMING THROUGH SLAUGHTER*

Bjerring, Nancy E. 'Deconstructing the Desert of Facts: Detection and Antidetection in *Coming Through Slaughter*', *English Studies in Canada* 16.3 (September 1990) 325–38.

Kamboureli, Smaro. 'The Poetics of Geography in Michael Ondaatje's *Coming Through Slaughter*', *Descant* 14.4 (Fall 1983) 112–26.

Maxwell, Barry. 'Surrealistic Aspects of Michael Ondaatje's *Coming Through Slaughter*', *Mosaic* 18.3 (Summer 1985) 101–14.

Orr, Jeffrey. 'Coming Through Language: Intersemiotic Translation and Michael Ondaatje's *Coming Through Slaughter*', *Journal of Language and Literature* 2.1 (2003) 18–27.

Rooke, Constance. 'Dog in a Gray Room: The Happy Ending of *Coming Through Slaughter*' in *Spider Blues: Essays on Michael Ondaatje*, ed. Sam Solecki (Montréal: Véhicule Press, 1985) 268–92.

Scobie, Stephen. '*Coming Through Slaughter*: Fictional Magnets and Spider's Webbs', *Essays on Canadian Writing* 12 (Fall 1978) 5–23.

Solecki, Sam. 'Making and Destroying: *Coming Through Slaughter* and Extremist Art' in *Spider Blues: Essays on Michael Ondaatje* ed. Sam Solecki (Montréal: Véhicule Press, 1985) 246–67.

Wilson, Ann. '*Coming Through Slaughter*: Storyville Told Twice', *Descant* 14.4 (Fall 1983) 99–111.

ARTICLES, ESSAYS AND REVIEWS ON
RUNNING IN THE FAMILY

Carey, Cynthia. 'Reinventing (Auto)Biography: The (Im)possible Quest of Michael Ondaatje in *Running in the Family*', *Commonwealth Essays and Studies* 24.1 (2001) 41–51.

Heble, Ajay. 'Rumours of Topography': The Cultural Politics of Michael Ondaatje's *Running in the Family*', *Essays on Canadian Writing* 53 (1994) 186–203.

Huggan, Graham. 'Exoticism and Ethnicity in Michael Ondaatje's *Running in the Family*', *Essays on Canadian Writing* 57 (1995) 116–27.

Kamboureli, Smaro. 'The Alphabet of the Self: Generic and Other Slippages in Michael Ondaatje's *Running in the Family*', in *Reflections: Autobiography and Canadian Literature* ed. K. P. Stich (Ottawa: University of Ottawa Press, 1988) 79–91.

Kanaganyagam, Chelva. 'A Trick with a Glass: Michael Ondaatje's South Asian Connection', *Canadian Literature* 132 (Spring 1992) 33–42.

MacIntryre, Ernest. 'Outside of Time: *Running in the Family*' in *Spider Blues: Essays on Michael Ondaatje* ed. Sam Solecki (Montréal: Véhicule Press, 1985) 315–19.

Russell, John. 'Travel Memoir as Nonfiction Novel: Michael Ondaatje's *Running in the Family*', *Ariel* 22.2 (1991) 23–42.

Snelling, Sonia. '"A Human Pyramid: An (un)Balancing Act of Ancestry and History in Joy Kogawa's *Obasan* and Michael Ondaatje's *Running in the Family*"', *Journal of Commonwealth Literature* 32.1 (1997) 21–33.

ARTICLES, ESSAYS AND REVIEWS ON
IN THE SKIN OF A LION

Beddoes, Julie. 'Whose Side is It On? Form, Class and Politics in *In the Skin of a Lion*', *Essays on Canadian Writing* 53 (1994) 204–15.

Bölling, Gordon. 'Metafiction in Michael Ondaatje's Historical Novel *In the Skin of a Lion*', *Symbolism: An International Journal of Critical Aesthetics* 3 (2003) 215–53.

Duffy, Dennis. 'A Sub-Sub-Librarian Looks beneath the *Skin of a Lion*', *Essays on Canadian Writing* 53 (1994) 125–40.

Lowry, Glen. 'The Representation of "Race" in Ondaatje's *In the Skin of a Lion*', in *Comparative Cultural Studies and Michael Ondaatje's*

Writing ed. Steven Tötösy de Zepetnek (West Lafayette, IN: Purdue University Press, 2005) 62–72

Sarris, Fotios. '*In the Skin of a Lion:* Michael Ondaatje's Tenebristic Narrative', *Essays on Canadian Writing* 44 (1991) 183–201.

Siemerling, Winnfried. 'Oral History and the Writing of the Other in Michael Ondaatje's *In the Skin of a Lion*', *Comparative Cultural Studies and Michael Ondaatje's Writing* ed. Steven Tötösy de Zepetnek (West Lafayette, Indiana: Purdue University Press, 2005) 92–103.

Simmons, Rochelle. '*In the Skin of a Lion* as a Cubist Novel', *University of Toronto Quarterly: A Canadian Journal of the Humanities* 67.3 (1998) 699–714.

ARTICLES, ESSAYS AND REVIEWS ON *THE ENGLISH PATIENT.*

Cook, Rufus. '"Imploding Time and Geography": Narrative Compressions' in Michael Ondaatje's *The English Patient*', *Journal of Commonwealth Literature* 33.2 (1998) 108–25.

Dawson, Carrie. 'Calling People Names: Reading Imposture, Confession and Testimony in and after Michael Ondaatje's *The English Patient*', *Studies in Canadian Literature* 25.2 (2000) 50–73.

Ellis, Susan. 'Trade and Power, Money and War: Rethinking Masculinity in Michael Ondaatje's *The English Patient*', *Studies in Canadian Literature* 21.2 (1996) 22–36.

Forshey, Gerald E. '*The English Patient:* From Novel to Screenplay', *Creative Screenwriting* 4.2 (1997) 91–8.

Lowry, Glen. 'Between *The English Patients*: "Race" and the Cultural Politics of Adapting CanLit', *Essays on Canadian Writing* 76 (Spring 2002) 216–46.

Mantel, Hilary. 'Wraith's Progress', *New York Review of Books* 14 January 1993, 22–3.

Roberts, Gillian. 'Sins of Omission: *The English Patient* and the Critics', *Essays on Canadian Writing* 76 (2002) 195–215.

Scobie, Stephen. 'The Reading Lesson: Michael Ondaatje and the Patients of Desire', *Essays on Canadian Writing* 53 (1994) 92–106.

Seligman, Craig. 'Sentimental Wounds', *New Republic* 15 March 1993, 38–41.

Simpson, Mark D. 'Minefield Readings: The Postcolonial *English Patient*', *Essays on Canadian Writing* 53 (Summer 1994) 216–37.

Töstöy de Zepetnek, Steven. 'Michael Ondaatje's *The English Patient:*

"Truth is Stranger than Fiction"', *Essays on Canadian Writing* 53 (1994) 141–53.

ARTICLES, ESSAYS AND REVIEWS ON *ANIL'S GHOST*

Burton, Antoinette. 'Archive of Bones: *Anil's Ghost* and the Ends of History', *Journal of Commonwealth Literature* 38.1 (2003) 39–56.

Cook, Victoria. 'Exploring Transnational Identities in Ondaatje's *Anil's Ghost*', *Comparative Cultural Studies and Michael Ondaatje's Writing* ed. Steven Tötösy de Zepetnek (West Lafayette, IN: Purdue University Press, 2005) 6–15.

Goldman, Marlene. 'Representations of Buddhism in Ondaatje's *Anil's Ghost*' in *Comparative Cultural Studies and Michael Ondaatje's Writing* ed. Steven Töstöy de Zepetnek (West Lafayette, IN: Purdue University Press, 2005) 27–37.

Ismail, Qadri. 'A Flippant Gesture Towards Sri Lanka: Michael Ondaatje's *Anil's Ghost*', *Pravada* 6.9 (2000) 24–9.

Leclair, Tom. 'The Sri Lankan Patients', *The Nation*, 19 June 2000, 31–3.

Scanlan, Margaret. *Anil's Ghost* and Terrorism's Time', *Studies in the Novel* 36.3 (2004) 302–17.

General Works

Adorno, Theodor and Max Horkheimer. *Dialectic of Enlightenment* trans. John Cumming (London: Verso, 1979).

Agamben, Giorgio. *The Open: Man and Animal*, trans. Kevin Attell (Stanford: Stanford University Press, 2004).

Barthes, Roland. *S/Z* trans. Richard Miller (New York: Hill and Wang, 1975).

Berger John. *The Moment of Cubism and Other Essays* (London: Weidenfeld and Nicolson, 1969).

Berger, John. *G* (Harmondsworth: Penguin, 1973).

Bhabha, Homi. *The Location of Culture* (London: Routledge, 1994).

Bishop, Elizabeth. *Complete Poems* (London: Chatto and Windus, 1991).

Bonta, Mark and John Protevi. *Deleuze and Geophilosophy: A Guide and Glossary* (Edinburgh: Edinburgh University Press, 2004).

Burns, Walter Noble. *Billy the Kid* (London: Geoffrey Bles, 1926).

Caruth, Cathy. *Trauma: Explorations in Memory* (Baltimore: Johns Hopkins, 1995).

Caruth, Cathy. *Unclaimed Experience: Trauma, Narrative and History* (Baltimore: Johns Hopkins University Press, 1996).

Clark, Kenneth, Colin MacInnes and Bryan Robertson. *Sidney Nolan* (London: Thames and Hudson, 1961).

Colebrook, Claire. *Gilles Deleuze* (London: Routledge, 2002).

De Certeau, Michel. *The Practice of Everyday Life* trans. Steven Rendall (Berkeley: University of California Press, 1988).

Deleuze, Gilles and Félix Guattari. *Anti-Oedipus: Capitalism and Schizophrenia* trans Robert Hurley, Mark Seem and Helen R. Lane (Minneapolis: University of Minnesota Press, 1983).

Deleuze, Gilles and Félix Guattari. *A Thousand Plateaus: Capitalism and Schizophrenia* trans Brian Massumi (Minneapolis: University of Minnesota Press, 1987).

Deleuze, Gilles and Félix Guattari. *Kafka: Towards a Minor Literature* trans. Dana Polan (Minneapolis: University of Minnesota Press, 1986).

Derrida, Jacques. *Edmund Husserl's Origin of Geometry: An Introduction* trans. John P. Leavey Jr (Lincoln: University of Nebraska Press, 1989).

De Silva, K. M. *A History of Sri Lanka* (Berkeley: University of California Press, 1981).

Epic of Gilgamesh trans. N. K. Sanders (Harmondsworth: Penguin, 1972).

Felman, Shoshana and Dori Laub, *Testimony: Crises of Witnessing in Literature, Psychoanalysis and History* (London: Routledge, 1992).

Foucault, Michel. *The Archaeology of Knowledge and The Discourse on Language* trans. A. M. Sheridan Smith (New York: Pantheon, 1972).

Hallward, Peter. *Absolutely Postcolonial: Writing Between the Singular and the Specific* (Manchester: Manchester University Press, 2001).

Heaney, Seamus. *Opened Ground: Poems 1966–1996* (London: Faber and Faber, 1998).

Herodotus. *The Histories* trans. Aubrey de Sélincourt (London: Penguin, 2003).

Hutcheon, Linda. *The Canadian Postmodern: A Study of English-Canadian Fiction* (Toronto: Oxford University Press, 1988).

Hutcheon, Linda. *A Poetics of Postmodernism: History, Theory, Fiction* (London: Routledge, 1992).

Jackson, Rosemary. *Fantasy: The Limits of Subversion* (London: Methuen, 1981).

Jameson, Fredric. *The Political Unconscious: Narrative as a Socially Symbolic Act* (London: Routledge, 2003).

Jarvis, Simon. *Adorno: A Critical Introduction* (Cambridge: Polity Press, 1998).

Kemper, Steven. *The Presence of the Past: Chronicles, Politics and Culture in Sinhala Life* (Ithaca: Cornell University Press, 1991).

Kipling, Rudyard. *Kim* (London: Everyman Library, 1995).

Kroetsch, Robert. 'Unhiding the Hidden', *The Lovely Treachery of Words* (Oxford: Oxford University Press, 1989).

Lloyd, Genevieve. *The Man of Reason: Male and Female in Western Philosophy* (London: Routledge, 1993).

Marquis, Donald M. *In Search of Buddy Bolden: First Man of Jazz* (Baton Rouge: Louisiana State University Press, 1978).

McClement, Fred. *The Strange Case of Ambrose Small* (Toronto: McClelland and Stewart, 1974).

McNaught, Kenneth. *The Pelican History of Canada* (Harmondsworth: Penguin, 1983).

Metcalfe, William (ed.). *Understanding Canada: A Multidisciplinary Approach to Canadian Studies* (New York: New York University Press, 1982).

Nietzsche, Friedrich. *The Birth of Tragedy and Other Writings* trans. Ronald Speirs, ed. Raymond Guess and Ronald Speirs (Cambridge: Cambridge University Press, 1999).

Senaratne, Jagarth P. *Political Violence in Sri Lanka: Riots, Insurrections, Counterinsurgencies, Foreign Intervention.* Sri Lankan Studies in the Humanities and Social Sciences (Amsterdam: VU University Press, 1997).

Stitch, K. P. (ed.). *Reflections: Autobiography and Canadian Literature* (Ottawa: Ottawa University Press, 1988).

Wordsworth, William. *Complete Poetical Works* ed. Thomas Hutchinson (Oxford: Oxford University Press, 1996).

Yeats, W. B. *Selected Poems* ed. Timothy Webb (London: Penguin, 2000).

Young, Robert. *White Mythologies: Writing History and the West* (London: Routledge, 1990).

Index

Page numbers followed by n and a number (eg. 252n.9) indicate the page where a note can be located and the number of the note.

and place' (AG, 55). In some ways Anil's commitment to the language of 'human rights' demands this universalising perspective: it is impossible, after all, to speak in the name of human rights without recourse to an idea of 'rights' or the 'human' in general. Elsewhere, though, the presumptive universalism of Anil's language is repeatedly challenged by Sarath's quiet dedication to what he calls the 'archaeological surround of a fact' (AG, 44). Implicit in this oblique phrase is Sarath's commitment to the singularity of the event of experience before its meaning is determined by an already given system of truths. In this way his continuing fidelity to the 'archaeological surround' of facts on the ground reveals the singular genesis of every universal truth or value.

The dialectical relationship at the heart of the novel between the singular and the universal can be explicated in the following terms. For Anil the historical event that goes by the name of 'Sailor' is merely the extrinsic circumstance for the emergence of an already constituted truth: the widespread and continuing violation of human rights in a time of political emergency. But as she discovers during her tortuous forensic investigation of Sailor's remains, this event, like every event, has the potential to open us to an experience of the 'not yet', to the beyond of the here and now, to the singularity of an experience that we cannot imagine, anticipate or universalise. This discovery has profound implications for Anil's habitual mode of vision: if to speak in the name of 'human rights' is necessarily to invoke the support of a universal truth and a general concept of humanity, this truth remains vulnerable in turn to an event that would transform what counts as universal, as human, or as a way of thinking universally about the rights of 'man'. It is, she belatedly recognises, only by conceiving universal truth from the perspective of the singular event – by means of an encounter with *this* body and *this* death – that we can preserve the radical particularity and ethical promise of each 'historical' situation.

One advantage to considering the novel in these terms is that it illuminates the way Anil's relationship with Sarath transforms her ethical and political vision. By following Sarath's example and rethinking the collective figure of suffering humanity from the perspective of singular life, Anil accords the universal idea of justice to a local habitation and a name. Before returning to Sri Lanka, Anil 'never usually translated the time of a death into personal time'; afterwards she experiences personal and political time as elements of a common horizon (AG, 13). To reconstruct the fragments of a life from the scattered traces of the 'unhistorical dead' is for her much more than a simple act of forensic restitution: such solicitude enables her to establish an imaginative link between the ruined physical body and the ravaged body politic (AG, 56). It is during her struggle to restore Sailor's identity and history that Anil begins for the first time to develop a political perspective upon her native culture. Standing in the courtyard of the Wickramasinghe house, she realises that she could deduce 'two possible versions of a life' from the skeleton before her: the first suggests an existence spent in hard physical labour; the second indicates that the victim was 'a man static and sedentary' (AG, 177–8). But by taking responsibility for Sailor, Anil has also chosen between two possible versions of her own life: the woman who arrived in Colombo as a disaffected émigré has now become a politically engaged citizen. Like the epigraphist Palipana she has, almost unbeknown to herself, begun to 'study history as if it were a body'; by the end of her investigation she will have come to know her own country as if for the first time (AG, 193).[4]

Anil's belated recognition that there are at least two possible versions of a life is symptomatic of a novel which exposes each of its principal characters to the limits of their own mode of vision. Ondaatje offers an arresting image of the unsettling experience his protagonists undergo in the figure of the *makamkruka*, who is variously described as a 'churner', an 'agitator', someone 'who perhaps sees things more truly by turning everything upside down' (AG, 165). The pervasiveness of this experience in the novel suggests that far more than Anil's own revaluation of values is at stake in her discovery that she would 'always carry the ghost of Sarath Diyasena' (AG, 305). It is, after all, Sarath who begins the novel by informing Anil that the chaos of Sri

Lanka's 'unofficial war' means that there is 'no hope of affixing blame' in cases of political abduction and murder but who eventually sacrifices himself to expose the government's campaign of extra-juridical violence (*AG*, 17). While it may be true that for Sarath Sailor's remains 'offer knowledge(s) rather than truth *per se*, and that such knowledge(s) are vulnerable to use and abuse by anyone, including the archaeologist, the forensic scientist and, of course, the government-sponsored commission', his fastidious reconstruction of the burial scene confronts him with an ethico-political decision about the value and function of testimony.[5] Sarath's triumphant and tragic response to this demand is to speak by not speaking at all: instead his calculated subterfuge at the Armoury Auditorium enables Anil to consecrate the archaeological surround of Sailor's burial site as the ground of ethical and political witness.

Crucial though these moments of revelation and revaluation are to the novel's ethico-political drama, it is not just Ondaatje's characters that are exposed to the limits of their own mode of vision. Throughout the novel Ondaatje's writing periodically pierces its own narrative surface to render uncertain the relation between lived history as it is experienced by the perceiving subject and the collective representations that underlie cultural and national self-consciousness. This anxiety concerning the relationship between personal and impersonal time manifests itself in a series of seemingly random italicised passages – such as the fragmentary account of the murder of a government official aboard the train to Kurunegala – that seem to bear no discernible relation to the main sweep of the narrative (*AG*, 31–2). Typically these sections flicker between a dispassionate scene-setting narrative prose and moments of blank inexpressible horror in which the novel seems no longer able to come to terms with the experience it wants to communicate. Perhaps the most poignant illustration of this technique is the passage that elliptically recounts the disappearance of Sirissa, Ananda's wife, presumably at the hands of rebel insurgents. A sentence placed unobtrusively at the heart of this passage makes Sirissa's fate a metonym for a national tragedy: 'For when people leave our company in our time we are never certain of seeing them again, or seeing them unaltered' (*AG*, 174). Yet although this scene purports to tell the story of Sirissa's disappearance, her abduction is an event that cannot be narrated by the novel because it is of such a traumatic nature that it resists the composure and mastery that narrative would provide. Commenting upon the enigmatic structure of the traumatic experience, Cathy Caruth observes that the traumatised 'carry an impossible history within them, or they become themselves the symptom of a history that they cannot entirely possess'.[6] That what is true of the traumatised body is also true of the traumatic text becomes clear in Ondaatje's subtle modulation of tenses: a scene that begins with a retrospective image of the familiar and known world ('This is where Sirissa would start to see the teenagers, some with catapults hanging off their shoulders, some smoking') abruptly mutates into a terrifying present-tense encounter with unspeakable barbarism ('She sees two more heads on the far side of the bridge and can tell even from here that she recognises one of them') before arresting itself upon the brink of an unimaginable, because impossible, future ('She keeps running forward, and then she sees more' (*AG*, 171–4)).

The traumatic experience of inhabiting an 'impossible history' or a history that can be grasped 'only in the very inaccessibility of its occurrence' inflects almost every page of *Anil's Ghost*.[7] Indeed, the psychological and historical structure of the traumatic event – that overwhelming occurrence that cannot be grasped in the moment of its appearance but periodically returns to unhinge our sense of the relation between present and future time – provides a metaphor for the effect of the political emergency upon Sri Lanka's benighted citizens. Anil is struck by the pervasiveness of this sense of simultaneously lived and 'unfinished' time shortly after her return to Colombo:

> In a fearful nation, public sorrow was stamped down by the climate of uncertainty. If a father protested a son's death, it was feared another family member would be killed. If people you knew disappeared, there was every chance they might stay alive if you did not cause trouble. This was the

scarring psychosis in the country. Death, loss, was 'unfinished', so you could not walk through it. (*AG*, 56)

Death and loss are 'unfinished' in the immediately historical sense because the ravages of the civil war continue to this day. Yet the divided temporality of traumatic experience suggests that the effect of trauma persists long after its immediate cause is removed. To take one example, the phenomenon of so-called 'survivor guilt' reminds us that the passage 'beyond' trauma, as much as the experience itself, constitutes a key element of the traumatic effect. As Caruth explains:

> What is enigmatically suggested ... is that the trauma consists not only in having confronted death, but in *having survived, precisely, without knowing it*. What one returns to in the flashback is not the incomprehensibility of one's own near death, but the very incomprehensibility of one's own survival. Repetition, in other words, is not simply the attempt to grasp that one has almost died, but, more fundamentally and enigmatically, the very attempt to *claim one's own survival*. If history is to be understood as the history of a trauma, it is a history that is experienced as the endless attempt to assume one's survival as one's own.[8]

One of the ways this traumatic awakening to a history *that must, but which can't, continue* reveals itself in *Anil's Ghost* is in the dissociation of the individual from social relationships. Ondaatje has observed that 'one of the things I did almost subliminally, or subconsciously recognise, was that everything in the book becomes about one thing: separations'.[9] This insight is borne out by the fact that none of the novel's chief protagonists has living spouses, current lovers or children. Ondaatje fills in the place where these relationships should be with Gamini's tortured romantic history, Anil's divorce and subsequent break-up with Cullis, Sarath's estrangement from Gamini, Leaf's descent into the temporal chaos of Alzheimer's, Sirissa's last terrible moments, and Sarath's continuing inability to come to terms with the 'trauma' of his wife's death (*AG*, 279). 'My marriage disappeared', Gamini tells Sarath upon their reunion in Colombo. 'All that ceremony – and then it evaporated in a couple of months. I was too intense then. I'm probably another example of trauma, you see. That happens when there is no other life' (*AG*, 132). Socially isolated and emotionally paralysed, Gamini appears to have passed beyond death without knowing it. The imbrication of knowing with not knowing and death with life is, of course, fundamental to traumatic experience, a point subtly reinforced during Anil's anatomical training in London. Dissecting the stem of a brain at Guy's Hospital, she suddenly alights upon the 'amygdala', a small knot of fibres made up of nerve cells where the brain stores its traumatic and fearful memories (*AG*, 134). The function of this nerve bundle, she learns, is to control auto-nomic responses associated with fear and anger by preserving the memory trace of emotions engendered by a traumatic event or feeling. What Anil gleans from this anatomical revelation is how fear can come to dominate thinking and feeling; it is there-fore no surprise that to her ears the word 'amygdala' retains a decidedly Sri Lankan inflection (*AG*, 135).

It is perhaps no coincidence that this flashback to Anil's discovery of the amygdala – that shadowy region of the brain where fearful memories are housed – takes place shortly after her encounter with Palipana at the Grove of Ascetics. With their curious blend of Sinhala cultural history and Buddhist mysti-cism, the passages exploring Palipana's intellectual history and working environment are consistently tuned to a visionary pitch; unsurprisingly, given their often opaque symbolism and imagery, these sections of the novel have provoked a number of conflicting interpretations.[10] Whatever the relative merits of these readings may be, it is hard to demur from Qadri Ismail's contention that 'the most significant feature of Palipana is that he rejects Western knowing and does so from a nationalist posi-tion', although this assertion needs to be supplemented by an awareness that such 'nationalism' is partly a response to the trauma of Sri Lanka's colonial history. Ondaatje underscores this point in his brief biographical sketch of Palipana's intellectual career:

The epigraphist Palipana was for a number of years at the centre of a nationalistic group that eventually wrestled archaeological authority in Sri Lanka away from the Europeans ... The main force of a pragmatic Sinhala movement, Palipana wrote lucidly, basing his work on exhaustive research, deeply knowledgeable about the context of the ancient cultures. While the West saw Asian history as a faint horizon where Europe joined the East, Palipana saw his country in fathoms and colour, and Europe simply as a landmass on the end of the peninsula of Asia. (*AG*, 79)

This passage has proved controversial among some critics, not least because Palipana's 'nationalistic' perception of Europe as a mere 'landmass' upon the edge of Asia might be thought to take insufficient account of the political, economic and cultural forces that determine the imperial vision of history.[11] Rejecting the presuppositions of imperial cartography, Palipana developed his own idiosyncratic vision of cultural origins by presenting a radical new interpretation of sacred Buddhist texts that 'stunned archaeologists and historians' in the field (*AG*, 81). His project was underpinned by his discovery of a 'linguistic subtext' to a collection of ancient rock graffiti that 'explained the political tides and royal eddies of the island in the sixth century'. Initially Palipana's revisionist history swept everything before him: his findings were 'applauded in journals abroad and at home' and 'seemed at first to have ended arguments and debates' by historians of the subject. His intellectual state of grace was, however, brought to an abrupt conclusion when one of his protégés declared that there was 'no real evidence' for the existence of these texts upon which his conclusions were based. 'No one', it transpired, 'could find the sentences he had quoted and translated from dying warriors, or any of the fragments from the social manifestos handed down by kings, or even the erotic verses in Pali supposedly by lovers and confidants of the court mentioned by name but never quoted in the *Cŭlavamsa*'. In the wake of this revelation Palipana's work was dismissed as a 'betrayal of the principles on which he had built his reputation' and he was 'turned gracelessly out of the establishment' by his peers (*AG*, 81–2).

Palipana is, notwithstanding the enigma of his presentation, a pivotal figure in *Anil's Ghost*: he taught both Diyasena brothers in their youth; and he it is who instructs Anil and Sarath to seek out Ananda Udugama. But Palipana's influence upon the novel extends far beyond these local matters of plot and characterisation; the story of his academic apostasy is one of the devices by which Ondaatje addresses 'the complex relationship between religion, politics and violence in Sri Lanka'.[12] He establishes this relationship in a variety of ways. In its most simplified form it appears in Palipana's mystical assertion of the evanescence of secular authority before an idea of spiritual unity towards which all human actions should tend. 'Nothing lasts', Palipana informs Sarath and his fellow students. 'It is an old dream. Art burns, dissolves. And to be loved with the irony of history – that isn't much. He said this in his first class to his archaeology students. He had been talking about books and art, about the "ascendancy of the idea" being often the only survivor' (*AG*, 12). Such rhetorical commitment to the 'ascendancy of the idea' cannot obscure the fact that in Sri Lanka religion, far from being sequestered from political concerns, has too often been the site of political violence and division. Palipana implicitly concedes this point to Anil when he recounts to her the ancient story of the massacre of monks by King Udaya the Third. Tragically this historical anecdote is framed by another, more personal, tale of political violence and dispossession: Palipana's own brother Narada, a Buddhist monk, was murdered some years before in what may well have been a 'political killing' (*AG*, 48).

As Palipana's melancholy example from the ancient Buddhist chronicles suggests, the fraught relationship between religion and politics is much more than a tributary effect of the ongoing civil war. What is at stake in this dispute is nothing less than the meaning and ideological character of Sri Lankan history. Steven Kemper establishes the importance of Buddhist teaching to this struggle in a lapidary sentence: 'The early establishment of Buddhism in the island is the fundamental fact of Sri Lankan history'.[13] Beginning in the sixth century with the Buddhist monk Mahānāma, Sinhala monks 'have kept a chronicle of the island, its people, and their governance, celebrating the role of Buddhism in holding all these elements together'.[14] The *Mahăvamsa*, as this chronicle is known, is an amalgam of sacred teaching and historical commentary that provides a spiritual and moral framework within which to interpret the passage of worldly affairs. Crucially, the *Mahăvamsa* provides a continuous imaginative connection with the spiritual past: its history has been updated several times, sometimes to take account of moments of political upheaval and change. The spiritual and ideological centrality of the *Mahăvamsa* to elite strands of Sri Lankan culture continues to this day; as recently as 1977 the Sri Lankan prime minister, J. R. Jayewardene, extended the chronicle to include his own administration, although this manoeuvre was widely dismissed as 'the modern-day exploitation of a sublime tradition of historical writing'.[15]

From the sixth century until the present day the Buddhist historical chronicles collected in the *Mahăvamsa* underpinned one form of social identity and cultural community. Yet their heterogeneous blend of historical, spiritual and moral discourse presents an historiographical dilemma insofar as their account of events and practices is intertwined with elements that were 'clearly ideological when written and nowadays serve as a basis for Sinhala ethnic chauvinism'.[16] Such chauvinism entrenches and reproduces itself by insisting upon an unbroken connection between national and spiritual identity. 'Great emphasis has been placed throughout the history of Buddhism in Sri Lanka on the idea that the connection between past and present must be unbroken', Kemper explains, 'whether between a sacred place and the historical events that created its importance or between a group of monks and the historical origins that guarantee the authenticity of their teaching'.[17] The role of the monk or guide is to maintain this connection between the word and the world by making nature the spiritual ground of Sinhala Buddhist tradition.

Some knowledge of Sinhala Buddhist tradition is crucial to an understanding of Palipana's ideological function in *Anil's Ghost*. Reading Palipana in this context suggests that what in his

work appears at first as a subaltern rejection of Western ethno-
centrism seeks instead to assert the pre-eminence of a particular
indigenous cultural tradition. Initially it seems that his indifference to global theories of culture afforded him renewed insight
into the complex relationship between place, cultural inscription and historical consciousness. Certainly the juxtaposition
of the 'local' and the 'historical' in his best work promised to
extend the resonance of both terms: 'He approached runes not
with a historical text but with the pragmatic awareness of locally
inherited skills', the narrator relates. 'His eyes recognized how
a fault line in a rock wall might have insisted on the composure
of a painted shoulder' (AG, 82). Ultimately, however, Palipana's
'local' allegiance to Sinhala nationalism overcame the rigour of
his archaeological method: he 'began to see as truth things that
could only be guessed at', although this visionary intuition in
no way felt to him 'like forgery or falsification' (AG, 83). The
reason, of course, that it does not feel like forgery or falsification is that the continuing authority of the sacred texts depends
upon establishing precisely this visionary connection between
the past and the present moment. 'History was ever-present
around him', the novel declares in studiously neutral terms;
but this 'history', it is vital to recognise, is a Sinhala Buddhist
history that has its roots in one particular version of the broader
national story (AG, 80).

Palipana's nostalgic Sinhala nationalism should not, however,
be taken to be the novel's last word on the subject. His visionary
mode is counterbalanced by a number of passages, such as the
concluding narrative sequence, in which Ondaatje simultaneously marks and calls into question Palipana's identification
of Sinhala Buddhism as the Sri Lankan national chronicle. In
the novel's last pages Ananda arrives in a Buduruvagala field to
rebuild a giant statue of the Buddha whose image has been shattered into 'one hundred chips and splinters of stone' (AG, 303).
The symbolism of this scene has unmistakable overtones to a Sri
Lankan audience versed in Buddhist history and nomenclature:
according to custom Ananda was for many years the Buddha's
closest friend and companion; following the Buddha's death he

was able to safeguard Buddhist tradition by reciting the sacred texts from memory. Here, it seems, is the defining moment of the novel in which the restoration of the Buddha's formal integrity by a victim of communal violence offers 'a metaphor for restoring a pure Buddhism in war-torn Sri Lanka'.[18]

Surrounded by the evidence of civil carnage the artist is initially drawn to the timeless serenity of the Buddha's features: 'It had seen the wars and offered peace or irony to those dying under it' (*AG*, 304). But gazing at the icon Ananda finds himself unmoved by a devotional impulse: 'As an artificer now he did not celebrate the greatness of a faith. But he knew if he did not remain an artificer he would become a demon' (*AG*, 304). The implications of the second sentence should not be overlooked: refusing to commit himself to a transcendent spiritual principle, Ananda embraces instead an aesthetic mode of vision that cleaves to the singularity of perception before it is assimilated into an abstract system of values. This point is deftly made at the very end of the novel: looking into the Buddha's eyes Ananda is almost seduced by the divine perspective on human affairs ('Ananda briefly saw this angle of the world. There was a seduction for him here'); yet this impulse is immediately checked when the briefest pressure from his nephew's arm reminds him once more of the 'sweet touch' of the world (*AG*, 307).

Some critics remain unconvinced about Ondaatje's critical distance from the worldview of Sinhala nationalism. Noting the almost complete absence of Tamils from the text, Qadri Ismail questions the privilege the novel accords to the Sinhala Buddhist point-of-view:

> The cardinal actants of *Anil's Ghost* are: one forensic anthropologist (Sinhala, female); one epigraphist (Sinhala, male); one archaeologist (Sinhala, male); one doctor (Sinhala, male), and one 'eye-painter turned drunk gem-pit worker turned head restorer' (also Sinhala, also male). The last, the only cardinal actant who is not a full time professional, also happens to be the sole proletarian. All of these, as emphasized, are Sinhala; and all the men have names that resonate deeply within Buddhist iconography: Palipana (a recently

deceased mahanayake); Sarath Diyesena (Diyasena being
the name of the prince who was supposed to rejuvenate
Lanka in the Buddha Jayanthi); Gamini Diyasena (Gamini,
a synonym for Gemunu); Ananda Udugama (Ananda was
one of Siddhartha Guatama's closest disciples). The female
anthropologist is named Anil Tissera.[19]

Ismail's insistence upon the selectiveness of Ondaatje's use
of ethnic and religious example does not always acknowledge
those instances where the novel touches on the reality of Tamil
suffering; certainly the remark on its penultimate page that
the Buddha's restored eyes 'would always look north' offers 'a
haunting reminder of the outcome of the bloody conflicts in the
northern provinces'.[20] But notwithstanding the novel's presentation of a number of viewpoints irreducible to the culture of
Sinhala nationalism – such as those of the returning exile or
the recovered artisan – the elimination of any real Tamil presence from the text inevitably weakens its account of Sri Lanka's
emergency years. This account is not improved by Ondaatje's
curious decision to present the civil war as a symptom of a
broader political crisis. Interviewed soon after the novel's publication, Ondaatje observed that 'In many ways, the book isn't just
about Sri Lanka; it could be Guatemala or Bosnia or Ireland. The
stories are very familiar in other parts of the world'.[21] His belief
that the Sri Lankan situation is part of a broader international
political crisis probably explains his decision to frame the Sri
Lankan sections of the novel with an account of Anil's forensic
work in Guatemala in the 1980s. Unfortunately one effect of this
framing device is to deny the specificity of the political forces
that shaped the Sri Lankan civil war by envisaging it as merely
one episode in a universal – or certainly pan-national – conflict
between terrorism and civil society.

The full consequences of this mode of narrative presentation emerge in a key paragraph early in the novel:

There had been continual emergency from 1983 onwards,
racial attacks and political killings. The terrorism of the
separatist guerrilla groups, who were fighting for a homeland in the north. The insurrection of the insurgents in

the south, against the government. The counterterrorism
of the special forces against both of them. The disposal of
bodies by fire. The disposal of bodies in rivers or the sea.
The hiding and then reburial of corpses.

It was a Hundred Years' War with modern weaponry,
and backers on the sidelines in safe countries, a war spon-
sored by gun- and drug-runners. It became evident that
political enemies were secretly joined in financial arms
deals. '*The reason for war was war*'. (AG, 42–3)

Two points are worth considering here. The first is the political
utility of the distinction between 'terrorism' and 'insurrection' that now distinguishes the Northern and Southern antigovernment groupings – a distinction that significantly recasts
the more neutral description of 'the antigovernment insurgents in the south and the separatist guerrillas in the north'
proposed in the 'Author's Note' to the novel. The second is how
far Ondaatje's representation of the civil war as an expression
of atavistic violence – a view implied by the repetition of the
despairing phrase 'The reason for war was war' to characterise
the conflict – enables him to evade the fact that the Tamils were
fighting for a homeland. The reasons for the Tamil insurrection
– which are not to be confused with excuses for the violence
that accompanied it – are left wholly unexamined by the text;
so is the undistinguished record of Sinhala nationalist political
repression. And while 1983 is cited as the inaugural date of the
emergency, no mention is made of the preceding pogrom against
the Tamil population or the passing of the sixth amendment to
the Sri Lankan constitution in August of that year which effectively outlawed advocacy for the establishment of an independent Tamil state. It is difficult to avoid the conclusion that the
narrator's recasting of the civil war as a new 'Hundred Years'
War' serves to obfuscate the historical origins of the conflict and
to reduce the resonance of his meditation upon the contribution of his former homeland to the 'harsh political events of the
twentieth century' (*AG*, 300).

Looking back over the praise and controversy *Anil's Ghost*
has generated, there appears to have been a pervasive feeling that

here was Ondaatje's 'big' political book, his long-awaited settling of accounts with the country of his birth. Such a view does scant justice, of course, to the scope and ambition of a literary career in which he has consistently probed the relationship between culture and politics and sought imaginatively to reinvigorate our sense of what historical memory might be. It also takes too little account of those moments of quiet tenderness and intimacy, such as Anil and Leaf's gently comic forensic reconstruction of *Point Blank*, in which private attachments express themselves in the abeyance of political systems and demands. These moments may not seem much consolation to political cultures where the war on memory is one of the ways in which power reproduces itself in its various forms. Yet by weaving the stories of Sarath's sacrifice, Gamini's fortitude, Ananda's artistry and Anil's final victory into a dazzling and disconcerting narrative, Ondaatje has created abiding images of those human qualities that promise the possibility of redemption from this 'out-of-focus world' (*AG*, 59).

Critical overview and conclusion

This chapter provides a brief summary of some of the main strands of Ondaatje criticism. Despite Ondaatje's international celebrity and reputation, there are relatively few critical monographs dedicated to his work; fortunately some of those that do exist offer useful overviews of significant aspects of his writing. Three books in particular repay close attention. Douglas Barbour's 1993 study *Michael Ondaatje* provides a detailed examination of all of Ondaatje's work up to and including *In the Skin of a Lion* and contains illuminating reflections upon his literary styles and influences. Sam Solecki's *Ragas of Longing: The Poetry of Michael Ondaatje* presents the first full-length study of Ondaatje's poetry, while his collection of essays and reviews *Spider Blues: Essays on Michael Ondaatje* is a treasure trove of some of the best and most influential Ondaatje criticism. The remarks that follow draw substantially upon these main critical sources; they are supplemented throughout by reference to various key critical articles.

A number of themes crystallise in discussions of Ondaatje's early poetry. Critics were quick to notice his fascination with a perceived schism between nature and culture in modern technological society, the nature and modes of perception of animal and inhuman life, and the relationship between violence and creativity. Douglas Barbour, one of Ondaatje's most consistent champions, observed that his early poems 'are obsessed with animals and birds, often seen in some violent relation to humanity.'[1] 'Over and over again,' he continues, 'these early poems invoke a fantastic vision of the evolutionary theme of "survival of the fittest".[2] Continuing the same theme, Sam Solecki suggests that the surrealism and ambiguity of Ondaatje's poems are intended to extend our perception of reality beyond its usually given forms. 'The entire thrust of his vision is directed at compelling the reader to reperceive reality,' he argues, 'to assume an unusual angle of vision from which reality appears surreal, absurd, inchoate, dynamic, and, most importantly, ambiguous. His poetic world is filled with mad or suicidal herons, one eyed mythic dogs, tortured people, oneiric scenes, gorillas, dragons, creative spiders and imploding stars. These extraordinary images function as a kind of metaphoric shorthand to disorient the reader, to make him enter a psychological or material reality which has been revealed as almost overwhelmingly anarchic or chaotic.'[3]

For Lynette Hunter the crucial dynamic of Ondaatje's early poetry lies in the tension between chaos and form. The importance of art for Ondaatje, she argues in broadly Nietzschean terms, is that it enables us to feed off the chaotic and inhuman energies that exceed 'moral' or 'civilised' existence while sublimating them into new and potentially more expansive images of human experience. At the core of Ondaatje's work she identifies a 'conscious statement that poetry is a metaphor for all experience. While the poet uses metaphor to express yet control the energy within his own work, he also uses the poetry itself as a direct metaphor for how a man experiences reality.'[4] For this reason 'Peter' emerges as a crucial poem in Ondaatje's development because it is explicitly 'about the process of art, about learning to make metaphors so that we can find an equilibrium in life to control yet release energy.'[5] Sam Solecki echoes this sentiment by claiming that Ondaatje's concern in 'Peter' with the relationship between violence, creativity and form foreshadows the poetics of all his books.[6] He compounds this observation with the intriguing suggestion that 'the cause or causes of the fear of disorder, displacement, loss, exile or chaos' in Ondaatje's early poems 'are usually traceable to events in the writer's life that he won't be able to deal with directly in his writing for another decade.'[7] This insight illuminates later scenes in Ondaatje's work such as the phantasmagorical opening of *Running in the Family*, where the experience of displacement, exile and loss illuminates some of the text's key themes.

Reviewing other responses to Ondaatje's early poetry, many critics agreed that it presented a dualistic vision of life experienced as a struggle between 'a dark, instinctual and surreal world and one of reason and daylight.'[8] The more astute among them were quick to locate the roots of this dualistic vision in Ondaatje's experience of existing both within and between different cultural traditions. Beginning from the premise that Ondaatje as a writer is in possession of 'complex inheritances,'[9] J. E. Chamberlin noted that his position 'is close to that of other contemporary poets writing out of situations that define essentially colonial predicaments, where language or audience or the identity and role of the poet are indeterminate.'[10] Ondaatje's first extended response to this 'colonial predicament' in *the man with seven toes* excited and divided his critics in equal measure. Douglas Barbour read the poem as 'haunted by a 1960s spirit of revolutionary social and sexual idealism in which, to borrow a phrase from Marshall McLuhan and Wilfred Watson, psychological, social or cultural breakdown leads to breakthough.'[11] But not everyone shared the utopian view that the 'breakdown' of personality the poem dramatised lead necessarily to 'breakthough' in psychological and cultural terms. M. Travis Lane read the poem instead as a cautionary tale about the menace posed to civilised values by the forces of irrational and instinctive life. In his account Ondaatje's poem dramatises the 'loss of the conscious self and a descent into the female subconscious' in which 'the woman's own sexual fears (her bad, wild desires) become analogous to all that is uncivilised, hot, wounding, ugly.'[12] Occupying a position midway between the two, Sam Solecki argues for the central importance of the poem to Ondaatje's early work while reading it as a traumatic and deeply ambivalent account of the colonial encounter. In Ondaatje's hands the story of Eliza Fraser becomes

a mythic exploration, in the forms of related brief
and often imagistic poems, of how an unnamed white
woman perceives and experiences a primitive and anarchic world totally alien to her civilised assumptions and
mode of being. Like Margaret Atwood's Susanna Moodie
she is compelled into a confrontation in which she must
acknowledge violent and primitive aspects of life within
and outside herself which she had previously either not
known or ignored.[13]

A number of critics read *Billy the Kid* as a continuation of this
conflict between instinctive and rational life. In an influential
account Dennis Lee argued that '*Billy the Kid* makes most sense
as a picture of civilisation and instinct at war' before concluding
that the poem should be read in mythic and cosmological terms
as 'a struggle between the whole of planet constructed as instinctive force and the whole of planet constructed as the empire of
consciousness, driving to mastery.'[14] Stephen Scobie was more
circumspect in his discussion of the poem's notorious violence,
arguing that the poem in fact tries to 'maintain a balance (a
project which I think is typical of Ondaatje) between the two
aspects of artist and outlaw.'[15] *Billy the Kid*, he insists, is, after
all, 'a tightly controlled book: Ondaatje is a careful artist and
the images of violence are never allowed to get out of hand in
the book. The book is not chaos, the book is not manic. It is an
attempt to comprehend the legend of Billy the Kid, to see him
as one of the exemplary figures of modern consciousness, outlaw
as artist, artist as outlaw.'[16] This emphasis upon the interdependence of the figures of outlaw and artist dovetails neatly with
Susan Glickman's view that Ondaatje's work presents a gradually evolving myth of the Romantic artist who 'needs to hone
his edge' by preserving his distance from social obligations and
relations even though 'the *man* longs for affiliation and comfort
and family.'[17]

Taking his distance from the implied romanticism of these
accounts, Dennis Cooley suggests that we should read the poem
in terms of Ondaatje's transition from a modernist to a postmodernist poetics. Recasting literary 'modernism' as an imaginative

imperative to impose order and fixed form upon the motility of experience, Cooley argues that Ondaatje's fascination with Billy's fluid and amorphous style of existence 'invites us to see that the world is postmodern-fluid, unpredictable and ultimately uncontrollable (Livingstone is eaten by his twisted creations) or wrongly controlled (Garrett gains power by becoming the greatest human casualty in the entire book).'[18] While sympathetic to aspects of Cooley's 'postmodern' reading, Douglas Barbour sees in the textual complexity of *Billy the Kid* persuasive evidence of the limits of conventional thematic criticism. Beginning from the premise that *Billy the Kid* is 'one of the most interpreted texts in recent Canadian Literature,' he observes that most of the early interpretations of the poem attempted 'to explicate in mythic and philosophical terms the essential opposition between Billy the Kid and Pat Garrett.' This antagonism between the poem's two protagonists was subsequently formalised in thematic terms that came to dominate later accounts of Ondaatje's work which interpreted it a struggle between 'life vs death, energy vs statis, chaos vs order, creation vs destruction, affirmation vs negation, historical knowledge vs mental obliviousness, emotional connection and its denial.' Unwilling to accept the standard terms of this debate, Barbour argues that the poem's full resonance can only be gauged by a deconstructive, rather than merely thematic, style of criticism attentive to the way 'the formal energies of the work overwhelm, or at least scandalously supplement, any strict thematic reading, and engage us in a powerful, if enigmatic, reading experience, a rush of surging and contradictory rhythms that refuses finally to submit to a nice thematic outline.'[19] Reading *Billy the Kid* becomes, in his hands, a more general lesson about the nature of reading itself.

Billy the Kid established Ondaatje's reputation as a poet of originality and distinction. Perhaps with this reputation in mind, critics were initially unsure whether to read *Coming Through Slaughter's* allusive and symbolist prose in poetic or novelistic terms. Smaro Kamboureli spoke for many when she remarked that '[a]s Bolden's jazz is undefined, because it was by nature improvisational and because it was never recorded, so is the genre of the text hard to define.'[20] Douglas Barbour reads it as a vibrantly postmodern text that presents a subaltern counter-narrative of American modernity.[21] In a now classic account, Sam Solecki claims the novel as an example of 'extremist art' which he describes as 'a particular kind of art of creativity in which making and destroying, particularly self-destroying, are integrally related.'[22] Locating Ondaatje's version of the life of Buddy Bolden within a cultural tradition of doomed or self-destructive artists including Paul Celan, Sylvia Plath, Anne Sexton, Cesare Pavese and John Berryman, Solecki discovers in *Coming Through Slaughter* 'a compelling study of the compulsively destructive nature of the creative impulse.'[23] Bolden is, Solecki speculates, in many ways a negative image of Ondaatje's own personality and aesthetic: the imaginative embodiment of that part of him that is drawn to, but must finally renounce, a style of existence that 'rejects language and art' and wants to dissolve itself back into the singular flux of life.[24] *Coming Through Slaughter* therefore represents a turning point in Ondaatje's continuing reflection on art, creativity and violence; notwithstanding the charismatic intensity of Bolden's portrayal, the novel declares the ultimate 'bankruptcy of extremist art.'[25] This conclusion is disputed by Constance Rooke, who sees in Bolden's final creative ecstasy an affirmation, rather than a renunciation, of the transformative potential of such extremist art. 'Bolden the extremist artist knows what Ondaatje knows,' she maintains, 'that the need to break through "certainties", to find new ways of thinking and seeing and being, is the very essence of creativity. Extremist art is that which in its style and subject matter takes that "breaking through" somehow more literally than the normal artist may do.'[26] For Stephen Scobie, though, Bolden's ultimate end dramatises the fate awaiting all those whose unconditional surrender to being leaves them unable to maintain any relation to cultural memory or historical time.[27]

A recurrent concern of critical writing upon *Running in the Family* has been the text's interrogation of the historical constitution of cultural authority and the relationship between ideology, textuality and power. Citing the book as a key example of what she calls the 'Canadian postmodern,' Linda Hutcheon reads *Running in the Family* as a historiographic metafiction which exposes the ideological determination of representations of Ceylonese cultural history. Both the pleasure and the provocation of the book arise from its playful foregrounding of the 'fictionalising (as well as ordering and selecting) process involved in any attempt to reconstruct the past.'[28] So attuned is Ondaatje to the inherently textual nature of the past as it comes down to us 'through books, movies, records, even memories' that *Running in the Family* should really be seen as a product of 'the critical poststructuralist context as well as the literary postmodernist one.'[29] Concurring with this judgement, Smaro Kamboureli suggests that the text's eclectic mixture of sources and genres 'keeps its final intelligibility forever at bay by practicing a deferral of meaning and of generic definition related to the autobiographical elements of the book.'[30] Concentrating more narrowly upon Ondaatje's portrayal of his father's decline, Ernest Macintyre sees in Mervyn Ondaatje a metaphor for the self-divided colonial subject. By illuminating his father's cultural ambivalence, imperial nostalgia and latent self-destructiveness, Ondaatje 'shows the father carrying to extremes the same things that have been running in all the families of the times.'[31] Continuing this emphasis upon the hybridised nature of colonial culture, Ajay Heble's reading of *Running in the Family* explores the 'genuinely complex, if problematic, nature of the text's interplay between ethnicity, nationality and imperialized modes of self-understanding.'[32] In an appreciative, if occasionally sceptical, review of the book, Chelva Kanaganyagam struck a dissenting note by alluding to a 'problematic and controversial' aspect of Ondaatje's relation to his former homeland. While conceding that 'Ondaatje's choice of beginning his work in Jaffna and not in Colombo suggests at least a partial recognition of his father's claim to be a Jaffna Tamil,' Kanaganyagam points out that he then retreats from the implications of this identification and 'hardly draws attention to the ethnic conflict between the Tamils and the Sinhalese during the past four decades' (36).

Similar concerns about the limitations of Ondaatje's representation of recent Sri Lankan social and political history would
trouble many readers of *Anil's Ghost*.

In an aside that captures the dominant tone of critical
response to *In the Skin of a Lion*, Douglas Barbour remarked
that the novel's primary subject is the 'unacknowledged history'
of the modern immigrant experience.[33] Many critics were
impressed by the ethical dimension of Ondaatje's reclamation
of a lost stratum of Canadian cultural history for the purpose
of contemporary reflection. Linda Hutcheon, in particular, highlights the way Ondaatje's 'postmodern' reinvention of historical memory enables him to reinscribe the ex-centric cultural
subject (figured variously as woman, the proletarian worker
or the immigrant outsider) at the very centre of the Canadian
national narrative.[34] Considering the influence upon *In the Skin
of a Lion* of Cubism and the visual arts, Fortios Sarris identifies a
correspondence between the novel's collocation of multiple and
sometimes irreconcilable points of view into a single narrative
plane and Ondaatje's insistence that no single story or cultural
tradition can claim to speak for the entirety of modern Canadian
experience.[35] Writing from a Marxian perspective, Julie Beddoes
is less convinced of the political efficacy of the novel's subversion of the conventions of realist narrative, claiming that 'the
novel's self-subversions, its lacunae and ambivalences, make it
impossible to assign clear meanings to the political violence that
it describes. That is not to attribute ambivalence or any other
stance to Ondaatje himself but to point out the effects of the
text's formal operations on its thematic content.'[36] For Dennis
Duffy, however, the novel's success lies in the way Ondaatje's
imaginative reconstruction of archival material creates a dialectical tension between historical memory and the desire for
political change.

Much of the critical discussion generated by *The English
Patient* centred upon the novel's depiction of the trauma of
colonial history. In an important contribution to this debate,
Mark D. Simpson explores the way the novel's reinvention of
time and cultural memory provokes a series of 'epistemolog-

ical crises' that make us re-examine the relationship between history, identity and tradition.[37] Continuing this theme, Carrie Dawson considers Ondaatje's treatment of the relationship between historical trauma and narrative testimony before concluding that the patient's inability to organise his memories into coherence precipitates a wider 'crisis of truth' that compels each of his interlocutors to re-examine their own relation to their past.[38] Exploring the uses to which Ondaatje puts historiography in *The English Patient*, Stephanie M. Hilger helpfully situates the novel 'within the long-standing Western tradition of writing about the cultural 'Other' from Herodotus to Michel de Montaigne to Rudyard Kipling.'[39] Elsewhere Stephen Scobie provides an intriguing stylistic account of the novel's patterns of imagery, symbol and metaphor and an astute analysis of the novel's reworking of its intertextual sources.[40] Some critics were unnerved by Kip's angry denunciation of the Western powers following the atomic bombing of Japan and regretted what they saw as its conflation of anti-colonial and anti-war sentiment. Hilary Mantel articulated this strand of opinion in her review of the novel when she complained that Kip's proclaimed solidarity with the 'brown races of the world' is 'a crude polemic … exploding into the final pages of the book … It is fashionable not to know why certain wars were fought. Does this incomprehension now stretch to World War Two?'[41] Turning to Anthony Minghella's cinematic adaptation of *The English Patient*, Gillian Roberts provides a useful survey of the initial reception of both film and novel while pondering the broader implications of the film's relative indifference to the novel's colonial dimension.[42] In a trenchant analysis of the same subject, Glen Lowry commends Ondaatje's 'engagement with colonialism and the cultural politics of "race"' before claiming that Minghella's strategic revision of Ondaatje's colonial critique risks effacing the violent undertones of racism and exclusionary nationalism that continue to disfigure Western society.[43]

Doubtless because of its imaginative intervention into the continuing Sri Lankan civil war, *Anil's Ghost* has proved to be the most controversial and critically divisive of all of Ondaatje's works. Summarising the prevailing critical landscape Antoinette Burton notes that 'reviews of the book have consistently linked the novel to the ongoing story of the civil war there, juxtaposing its contemporaniety with the more obviously historical setting of Ondaatje's best-known novel, *The English Patient*.'[44] In a nuanced reading of *Anil's Ghost*, Burton explores the tension at the heart of the novel between Ondaatje's deeply political intervention into contemporary Sri Lankan history and his relatively 'apolitical' equation of 'Sri Lankan ethnic conflict with epic Greek tragedy' before concluding that the book's engagement with Sri Lankan history remains compelling '*precisely* because of the bourgeois political sensibilities and ultimately reactionary commitments it lays bare.'[45] Margaret Scanlan points to the contemporary urgency of the novel's subject matter by placing it in the broader context of fiction that tries to examine the changes wrought on political life and the historical sense by the culture of terrorism. For Victoria Cook the significance of *Anil's Ghost* lies in the way Ondaatje 'problematizes notions of either individual or national identity as being fixed and immutable, adopting instead a perspective that considers such boundaries as both flexible and permeable.'[46] Tom Leclair, however, takes a very different view, bemoaning what he sees as Ondaatje's failure to examine the political causes of the ethnic violence that consumed Sri Lanka. Ondaatje's failure to adopt a political position upon the civil war results, Leclair claims, in a bland and apolitical humanism:

> The reconstructed Buddha of the Sinhalese gazes across killing fields, sees what Ondaatje implies is the human condition anytime anywhere: senseless violence, pockets of love. Ondaatje and the Buddha could be right, but the author's apolitical gaze seems irresponsible when there's so much politics to see in Sri Lanka.[47]

In perhaps the most damning critique of *Anil's Ghost*, Qadri Ismail complains that far from adopting no clear position the novel displays a clear political bias in its presentation of the civil war. Observing that Ondaatje's excision of Tamil culture and history from the *Anil's Ghost* means that 'the only Lankan history it presents is Sinhalese history,' Ismail angrily concludes that the novel's sympathies clearly lie on the side of 'Sinhala nationalism.'[48] Marlene Goldman, however, forcibly challenges Ismail's view by arguing that the novel's imaginative rewriting of Buddhist history and tradition in fact 'calls into question the longstanding ties between Buddhism and Sinhala nationalism.'[49]

The passionate debate that Ondaatje's writing provokes is one measure of its lasting imaginative vitality. One of the abiding themes of this book has been that we miss the meaning of Ondaatje's work when we try to account for it within a 'postmodern' or 'postcolonial' framework. Throughout his career Ondaatje has steadfastly refused to envisage experience in merely ideological and political terms. His work is distinguished instead by a continuing tension between the singularity of perception and those larger narratives of modernity, decolonisation and postmodernity that shape so much of contemporary history. Much of the best of Ondaatje's writing is driven by his desire to step back from our everyday or represented world and to think the differences from which it is composed. At the same time, his commitment to provide a voice for those individuals and groups marginalised and displaced by cultural modernity demands substantial engagement with some of the defining events of the era in which we live. What gives a novel like *Anil's Ghost* its enduring fascination is Ondaatje's attempt to negotiate between the complexity, singularity and integrity of cultural life on the one hand and the global language and perspective of political rights on the other. It is hardly surprising, given everything that is at stake in Ondaatje's work, that there is as yet no critical consensus regarding his oeuvre. Such a consensus is neither possible nor desirable in relation to a writer whose work continues to open fresh perspectives upon many of the central issues of our time.

Notes

Chapter 1

1   Not Colombo, as is commonly reported. See Ed Jewinski, *Express Yourself Beautifully* (Toronto: ECW Press, 1994) 10.

2   Ibid., 13.

3   Ibid., 18.

4   Ibid., 23.

5   Kenneth McNaught, *The Pelican History of Canada* (Harmondsworth: Penguin, 1976) 289.

6   Ibid., 289.

7   William Metcalfe (ed.), *Understanding Canada: A Multidisciplinary Approach to Canadian Studies* (New York: New York University Press, 1982) 463.

8   Ibid., 33.

9   Ibid., 37.

10 Douglas Barbour, 'The Dainty Monsters', *Spider Blues: Essays on Michael Ondaatje*, ed. Sam Solecki (Montréal: Véhicule Press, 1985) 111.

11 Sam Solecki, *Ragas of Longing: The Poetry of Michael Ondaatje* (Toronto: Toronto University Press, 2003) 59.

12 Catherine Bush, 'Michael Ondaatje: An Interview', *Essays on Canadian Writing* 53 (Summer 94) 240.

13 Jewinski, *Express Yourself Beautifully* 60.

14 Ibid., 83.

15 Bush, 'Michael Ondaatje: An Interview', 240.

16 Sam Solecki, 'An Interview with Michael Ondaatje (1975)', *Spider Blues* 14.

17   Ed Jewinski, *Express Yourself Beautifully* 73.

18   The relationship between film and literature is a staple theme of Ondaatje's work. He explores it at greatest length in his recent book *The Conversations: Walter Murch and the Art of Editing Film* (London: Bloomsbury, 2003).

19   Ed Jewinski, *Express Yourself Beautifully* 90.

20   Linda Hutcheon, *A Poetics of Postmodernism* (London: Routledge, 1992) 123.

21   Pearl Shelley Gefen, 'If I were 19 Now I'd Maybe Be a Filmmaker', *Globe and Mail*, 4 May 1990, D3.

22   Ed Jewinski, *Express Yourself Beautifully* 98.

23   Michael Ondaatje, 'The William Dawe Badlands Expedition 1916', *Descant* 14 (Fall 1983) 51–73.

24   Ed Jewinski, *Express Yourself Beautifully* 108.

25   Sam Solecki, 'Coming Through: A Review of *Secular Love*', *Spider Blues* 127.

26   Ed Jewinski, *Express Yourself Beautifully* 125.

27   Eleanor Wachtel, 'An Interview with Michael Ondaatje', *Essays on Canadian Writing* 53 (Summer 1994) 260.

28   John Bolland, *Michael Ondaatje's The English Patient: A Reader's Guide* (London: Continuum Books, 2002) 86.

29   Ibid., 86.

30   Perhaps inevitably given the political divisions exacerbated by the civil war, the appearance of *Anil's Ghost* met with praise and censure in roughly equal measure. For a summary of some of the principal points of disagreement between readers of the novel see Marlene Goldman's Representations of Buddhism in Ondaatje's *Anil's Ghost*' in *Comparative Cultural Studies and Michael Ondaatje's Writing* ed. Steven Töstöy de Zepetnek (West Lafayette: Purdue, 2005) 27–37, Qadri Ismail's 'A Flippant Gesture Towards Sri Lanka: Michael Ondaatje's *Anil's Ghost*', *Pravada* 6.9 (2000) 24–9 and Tom Leclair's 'The Sri Lankan Patients', www.thenation. com/doc/20000619/leclair. Ondaatje's refusal to be cowed by criticism of his personal motives or political position was subsequently underlined by his decision to narrate Helene Klodawsky's searing 2004 documentary account of the human costs of Sri Lanka's ethnic turmoil, *No More Tears Sister: Anatomy of Hope and Betrayal*.

31   Linda Hutcheon. 'Interview', *Other Solitudes: Canadian Multicultural Fictions* ed Linda Hutcheon and Marion Redmond (Toronto: Oxford University Press, 1990) 199.

32 Homi K. Bhabha. *The Location of Culture* (London: Routledge, 1994) 25.

33 Ibid.,

34 Peter Hallward, *Absolutely Postcolonial: Writing between the Singular and the Specific* (Manchester: Manchester University Press, 2001) xii. I will be using the concept of the singular in several senses throughout this book. In its first sense, as defined by Hallward, the singular provides a way of thinking cultural experience beyond its circumscription by a dominant power. Elsewhere, I will explore the ways Ondaatje not only articulates his own cultural experience in singular terms, but confronts perceived singularities: aspects of our experience that are not yet defined, generalised or conceptualised. Finally, the singular can be understood not just as an autonomous experience of one's culture or a phenomenon we experience beyond our existing categories of thought but as an *event* that disrupts the categories of time and space through which we live the world.

35 Ibid., xi.

36 Ibid., 3.

37 Affect, in Ondaatje's work, is a received impulse or perception that is experienced in its singularity before it forms the basis of a concept, judgement or value.

38 Hallward, *Absolutely Postcolonial* 173.

Chapter 2

1 The poem also displays an affinity with Deleuze and Guattari's notion of a "line of flight." Thus while for them "nature" describes a tendency towards order and self-integration, there is always the possibility of a "line of flight" in which mutations and differences destroy the existing order of the world. Indeed, the capacity to see nature at once as an image of order and a web of life beyond our own control is itself a line of flight: a way of thinking beyond the limits of our own organism.

2 Friedrich Nietzsche, "On Truth and Lying in a Non-Moral Sense," *The Birth of Tragedy and Other Writings* trans. Ronald Speirs, ed. Raymond Guess and Ronald Speirs (Cambridge: Cambridge University Press, 1999) 146.

3 Giorgio Agamben, *The Open: Man and Animal* trans. Kevin Attell (Stanford: Stanford University Press, 2004) 12.

4 Ibid., 26.

5 Ibid., 37.

6 Ibid., 38.

7 It is revealing that Ondaatje uses "man" as the generic term for humanity in general. Man is indeed the subject who has insisted upon a distinction between subjectivity and the world as manipulable matter because the very structure of his rationality is defined by this division. See Genevieve Lloyd, *The Man of Reason: Male and Female in Western Philosophy* (London: Routledge, 1993).

8 W. B. Yeats, "The Circus Animals' Desertion," *Selected Poems* ed. Timothy Webb (London: Penguin, 2000) 224.

9 See Roland Barthes, *S/Z* trans. Richard Miller (New York: Hill and Wang, 1975) 5–6.

10 Theodor Adorno and Max Horkheimer, *Dialectic of Enlightenment* trans. John Cumming (London: Verso, 1979) 25.

11 Douglas Barbour, *Michael Ondaatje* (New York: Twayne, 1993) 26.

12 Adorno and Horkheimer, *Dialectic of Enlightenment* 5.

13 Ibid., 6.

14 Ibid., 4.

15 Ibid., 7.

16 Ibid., 12.

17 William Wordsworth, *Complete Poetical Works* ed. Thomas Hutchinson (Oxford: Oxford University Press, 1996) 377.

18 Simon Jarvis, *Adorno: A Critical Introduction* (Cambridge: Polity Press, 1998) 27.

19 Adorno and Horkheimer, *Dialectic of Enlightenment* 54.

20 Ondaatje adapted this slightly from Colin MacInnes, 'The Search for an Australian Myth in Painting', in Kenneth Clark, Colin MacInnes and Bryan Robertson (eds) *Sydney Nolan* (London: Thames and Hudson, 1961) 11–35.

21 Michael Ondaatje, "O'Hagan's Rough-Edged Chronicle," *Canadian Literature* 61 (1974) 24.

22 Clark, MacInnes and Robertson, *Sidney* 74.

23 Sam Solecki, 'Point Blank Narrative in *the man with seven toes*', *Spider Blues: Essays on Michael Ondaatje* ed. Sam Solecki (Montréal: Véhicule Press, 1985) 140.

24 Sam Solecki, 'Interview with Michael Ondaatje (1975)' *Spider*

Blues 24.

25   Claire Colebrook, *Gilles Deleuze* (London: Routledge, 2002) 111.

26   Solecki, 'Point Blank Narrative in *the man with seven toes*' 145.

27   Barbour, *Michael Ondaatje* 35.

Chapter 3

1   Walter Noble Burns, *Billy the Kid* (London: Geoffrey Bles, 1926) 178.

2   Ann Mandel, 'Michael Ondaatje', *Canadian Writers Since 1960: Second Series* ed. W. H. New (Detroit: Gale Research Company, 1987) 276.

3   Douglas Barbour, *Michael Ondaatje* (New York: Twayne, 1993) 36.

4   Ibid., 36.

5   Barbara Godard, 'Stretching the Story: The Canadian Story Cycle', *Open Letter*, 7th series, no. 6 (Fall 1989) 37.

6   Stephen Scobie has noted the different ways in which Billy the Kid has been represented from early tales of villainy to his reincarnation as a 'folk hero of the Robin Hood variety'. Stephen Scobie, 'Two Authors in Search of a Character: bpNicol and Michael Ondaatje', *Spider Blues: Essays on Michael Ondaatje* ed. Sam Solecki (Montréal: Véhicule Press, 1985) 186.

7   Sam Solecki, 'Interview with Michael Ondaatje (1984)', *Spider Blues* 20.

8   Linda Hutcheon, *A Poetics of Postmodernism: History, Theory, Fiction* (London: Routledge, 1992) 116. I take the distinction between historicity and history from Jacques Derrida. Historicity is the process or proliferation of events which *history* writes into the form of a meaningful linear narrative. See Derrida's *Edmund Husserl's Origin of Geometry: An Introduction* trans. John P. Leavey Jr (Lincoln: University of Nebraska Press, 1989).

9   Ibid., 122–3.

10   Burns, *Billy the Kid* 227.

11   Ibid., 47.

12   Steven Scobie, 'Two Authors in Search of a Character', *Spider Blues* 203.

13 I draw the term 'micropolitical' from Gilles Deleuze and Félix Guattari's *Anti-Oedipus: Capitalism and Schizophrenia* trans. Robert Hurley, Mark Seem and Helen R. Lane (Minneapolis: University of Minnesota Press, 1983). Micropolitical forces are those forces that *compose* characters and persons; they name the singular images, investments and desires from which general identities such as 'man' are extrapolated.

14 Gilles Deleuze and Félix Guattari, *A Thousand Plateaus: Capitalism and Schizophrenia* trans. Brian Massumi (Minneapolis: University of Minnesota Press, 1987) 238.

15 Billy's metamorphosis in this passage chimes with the strange process of 'becoming-rat' Deleuze and Guattari detect at work in Daniel Mann's 1972 film *Willard*: 'It is all there: there is a becoming-animal not content to proceed by resemblance and for which resemblance, on the contrary, would represent an obstacle or stoppage: the proliferation of rats, the pack, brings a becoming-molecular that undermines the great molar powers of family, career and conjugality . . . there is a circulation of impersonal affects, an alternate current that disrupts signifying projects as well as subjective feelings and constitutes a nonhuman sexuality; and there is an irresistible deterritorialisation that forestalls attempts at professional, conjugal or Oedipal reterritorialisation', Delueze and Guattari, *A Thousand Plateaus* 233.

16 Deleuze and Guattari's distinction between molecular and molar life is different from the liberal humanist conception of a private individual who then enters into a public and political sphere. The 'private', they argue, is already a political space that is formed when *molar* representations of 'man' (as rational, competitive, acquisitive, violent and dominant life) are used to code and organise feelings, affects and perceptions that are *not yet* coded into regular and stable images.

17 Seamus Heaney, 'Oysters', *Opened Ground: Poems 1966–1996* (London: Faber and Faber, 1998) 146.

18 Gilles Deleuze and Félix Guattari, *Kafka: Towards a Minor Literature* trans. Dana Polan (Minneapolis: University of Minnesota Press, 1986) 37.

Chapter 4

1   The phrase is Sam Solecki's. See his essay , 'Making and Destoying: *Coming Through Slaughter* and Extremist Art', *Spider Blues: Essays on Michael Ondaatje* ed. Sam Solecki (Montréal: Véhicule Press, 1985) 246–67.

2   Clifton Whiten, 'PCR Interview with Michael Ondaatje', *Poetry Canada Review* 2.2 (Winter 1980–1) 9.

3   Ibid., 10.

4   Peter Hallward, *Absolutely Postcolonial: Writing Between the Singular and the Specific* (Manchester: Manchester University Press, 2001) xii.

5   Friedrich Nietzsche, *The Birth of Tragedy Out of the Spirit of Music* trans Shaun Whiteside (Harmondsworth: Penguin, 1993) 76.

6   Ibid., 17.

7   Ibid., 16,

8   This double movement perhaps accounts for the profoundly uncertain status of historical reference in *Coming Through Slaughter*. Recourse to Donald M. Marquis's study *In Search of Buddy Bolden: First Man of Jazz* (Baton Rouge: Louisiana State University Press, 1978), the most authoritative examination of Bolden's legend, casts doubt upon the integrity of a number of historical incidents central to Ondaatje's narrative. There is, Marquis maintains, no reliable evidence that *The Cricket* ever existed, nor that Bolden's fateful fight with Tom Pickett ever took place (Marquis, 7 and 88). Bolden was never a licensed barber, Marquis continues, nor was he the proprietor of a barbershop. Marquis also questions the veracity of the sole remaining photograph of Bolden's band, an image faithfully reproduced within Ondaatje's pages (Marquis, 76–7). Little mention, indeed, is made in Marquis's account of Bolden's presence at the climactic Labor Day parade, a reticence wholly congruent with the contemporary report of the event presented in the New Orleans *Item*: 'No mention, however, was made of Buddy Bolden, who at some point dropped out of the parade, either from exhaustion, or, perhaps more likely, from some conduct that caused concerned musicians or friends to take him home' (Marquis, 117).

9   Hallward, *Absolutely Postcolonial* 143.

10 Ondaatje's idiosyncratic portrait of Bolden's performance is, it should be noted, written at some distance from those historical

accounts like Marquis's which offer a far less radical view of Bolden's stylistic innovation. Seeking to explain Bolden's difference from his predecessors, Marquis explicitly repudiates the notion that his originality lay in the improvisational character of his approach: 'What was it that sounded so different to Baquet and brought about the changes Dominguez mentions? It was not so much an improvised quality, since the terms 'jazzing' or 'ragging' as applied to Bolden's music did not mean the same as the improvisation that was later to be identified with jazz. It was more a matter of adding extra touches to the music' (Marquis, *In Search of Buddy Bolden* 100).

11   Douglas Barbour, *Michael Ondaatje* (New York: Twayne, 1993) 100.

12   Winfried Siemerling, *Discoveries of the Other: Alterity in the Work of Leonard Cohen, Hubert Aquin, Michael Ondaatje and Nicole Brossard* (Toronto: Toronto University Press, 1994) 129.

13   Barbour, *Michael Ondaatje* 129–30.

14   Hallward, *Absolutely Postcolonial* 172.

15   My reading of *Coming Through Slaughter* therefore stands at some distance from those accounts, such as Constance Rooke's, which take the novel to be an unconditional affirmation of Bolden's singular vision. Commenting upon what she understands to be the novel's 'happy ending', Rooke argues that if we 'go far enough with Ondaatje, follow through the immensely complex and proliferating images, his yearnings, as Ondaatje followed Bolden's', then we will discover the 'affirmation' that 'lies on the other side' of Bolden's breakdown and asylum experience (Constance Rooke, 'Dog in a Gray Room: The Happy Ending of *Coming Through Slaughter*', *Spider Blues* 268). While Rooke's reading of Ondaatje's fascination with the singular transcendence of worldly relations is often acute, her elision of Bolden's and Ondaatje's points-of-view encourages her to disregard the latter's concern with the cost of singularisation. Such disregard proves particularly expensive in her analysis of Bolden's experience in the State Hospital. It is one thing, after all, to say that Bolden's chaotic perception of his prison rape suggests that this 'violence' is 'unreal'; it is quite another to imply that Ondaatje's novel *colludes* with this deranged perception (Rooke, 290).

Chapter 5

1 Homi Bhabha, *The Location of Culture* (London: Routledge, 1994) 153.

2 Ibid., 153.

3 Ibid., 144.

4 Kanaganyagam, 'A Trick with a Glass', *Canadian Literature* 132 (Spring 1992) 38.

5 John Russell, 'Travel Memoir as Nonfiction Novel: Michael Ondaatje's *Running in the Family*', *Ariel* 22.2 (1992) 23.

6 Kanaganyagam, 'A Trick with a Glass', 35.

7 Ibid.

8 Bhabha, *The Location of Culture* 114.

9 A contrary and cautionary view of the political character of 'Jaffna Afternoons' has been propounded by Chelva Kanaganyagam. Observing that Ondaatje's choice of Jaffna, not Colombo, as his first Sri Lankan location 'suggests at least a partial recognition of his father's claim to be a Jaffna Tamil', Kanaganyagam thinks it strange that he then 'isolates himself in the Fort and hardly draws attention to the ethnic conflict between the Tamils and the Sinhalese during the last few decades'. Although the ethnic violence in Sri Lanka 'did not escalate until 1983', he continues, 'the growing tension between the communities was too obvious to be missed. Presumably, the author's intention was to distance himself from ideological issues that he did not feel strongly about' (Kanaganyagam, 'A Trick with a Glass', 36).

10 Rosemary Jackson, *Fantasy: The Limits of Subversion* (London: Methuen, 1981) 4.

11 Bhabha, *The Location of Culture* 63.

12 Peter Hallward, *Absolutely Postcolonial: Writing Between the Singular and the Specific* (Manchester: Manchester University Press, 2001) 333.

13 Robert Kroetsch, 'Unhiding the Hidden', *The Lovely Treachery of Words* (Oxford: Oxford University Press, 1989) 58.

14 Homi Bhabha, 'Of Mimicry and Man', *The Location of Culture* 86.

15 K. M. De Silva, *A History of Sri Lanka* (Berkeley: University of California Press, 1981) 540.

16 Ibid., 541.

17   Ibid., 541–2.

18   Ernest MacIntryre, 'Outside of Time: *Running in the Family*', *Spider Blues: Essays on Michael Ondaatje* ed. Sam Solecki (Montréal: Véhicule Press, 1985) 315.

19   Kanaganyagam, 'A Trick with a Glass' 37.

20   Ibid., 40–1.

21   Douglas Barbour, *Michael Ondaatje* (New York: Twayne, 1993) 146.

22   Ibid., 158.

Chapter 6

1   Michel de Certeau, *The Practice of Everyday Life* trans. Steven Rendall (Berkeley: University of California Press, 1988) 92.

2   Ibid., 103.

3   *The Epic of Gilgamesh* trans. N. K. Sanders (Harmondsworth: Penguin, 1972) 63.

4   See John Berger's *G* (Harmondsworth: Penguin, 1973) 149.

5   John Berger, *The Moment of Cubism and Other Essays* (London: Weidenfeld and Nicolson, 1969) 25.

6   Ibid., 24.

7   John Bolland, *Michael Ondaatje's The English Patient* (London: Continuum, 2002) 25.

8   Douglas Barbour, *Michael Ondaatje* (New York: Twayne, 1993) 183.

9   Gilles Deleuze and Félix Guattari, *A Thousand Plateaus: Capitalism and Schizophrenia* trans. Brian Massumi (Minneapolis: University of Minnesota Press, 1987) 478.

10 Mark Bonta and John Protevi, *Deleuze and Geophilosophy: A Guide and Glossary* (Edinburgh: Edinburgh University Press) 154.

11 Deleuze and Guattari, *A Thousand Plateaus* 490.

12 Ibid., 474.

13 Fred McClement, *The Strange Case of Ambrose Small* (Toronto: McClelland and Stewart, 1974) 42.

14 Ibid., 139.

15 Glen Lowry, 'The Representation of "Race" in Ondaatje's *In*

the Skin of a Lion', *Comparative Cultural Studies and Michael Ondaatje's Writing* ed. Steven Tötösy de Zepetnek (West Lafayette, IN: Purdue University Press, 2005) 66–7.

16 Fredric Jameson, *The Political Unconscious: Narrative as a Socially Symbolic Act* (London: Routledge, 2003) 1.

17 Barbour, *Michael Ondaatje* 198.

18 See Deleuze and Guattari, *A Thousand Plateaus* 282.

Chapter 7

1 Throughout this chapter I will refer to the 'English patient' as 'the patient'. Although the preponderance of textual evidence suggests that the 'English' patient is not, in fact, 'English' at all, but the Hungarian-born Count Ladislaus de Almásy, the exact nature of his provenance – whether English, Hungarian or otherwise – is the very ambiguity upon which much of the novel's meaning depends.

2 Eleanor Watchtel, 'An Interview with Michael Ondaatje', *Essays on Canadian Writing*, 54 (Summer 1994) 25–56.

3 Ibid., 252.

4 John Bolland, *The English Patient: A Reader's Guide* (London: Continuum, 2002) 30.

5 Michael Ondaatje with Stephen Smith, 'In the Skin of a Patient: Michael Ondaatje on the Structure, Intimacy and Politics of his New Novel', *Quill and Quire* (September, 1992) 69.

6 Wachtel, 'An Interview with Michael Ondaatje', 253–4.

7 Stephen Scobie, 'The Reading Lesson: Michael Ondaatje and the Patients of Desire', *Essays on Canadian Writing* 53 (1994) 99.

8 As Michel Foucault famously declared, 'The frontiers of a book are never clear-cut: beyond the title, the first lines, and the last full-stop, beyond its internal configuration and its autonomous form, it is caught up in a system of references to other books, other texts, other sentences: it is a node within a network ... The book is not simply the object that one holds in one's hands; and it cannot remain within the little parallelepiped that contains it: its unity is variable and relative. As soon as one questions that unity, it loses its self-evidence; it indicates itself, constructs itself, only on the basis of a complex field of discourse' (Michel Foucault, *The*

Archaeology of Knowledge and The Discourse on Language trans.
A. M. Sheridan Smith (New York: Pantheon, 1972) 23).

9   For background information on Herodotus's biography and
historical reputation I am indebted to Aubrey de Sélincourt's introduction to the Penguin Classics edition of *The Histories* (London:
Penguin, 2003) lx–xlv.

10   Ibid., xxi.

11   Rudyard Kipling, *Kim* (London: Everyman Library, 1995) 12.

12   Ibid., 4.

13   Ibid., 88.

14   Ibid., 11.

15   Ibid., 15.

16   Ibid., 238.

17   Cathy Caruth, *Unclaimed Experience: Trauma, Narrative and
History* (Baltimore: Johns Hopkins University Press, 1996) 91.

18   Carrie Dawson, 'Calling People Names: Reading Imposture,
Confession and Testimony in and after Michael Ondaatje's *The
English Patient*', *Studies in Canadian Literature* 25.2 (2000) 51.

19   Shoshana Felman and Dori Laub, *Testimony: Crises of Witnessing
in Literature, Psychoanalysis and History* (London: Routledge,
1992) 6.

20   Ibid., 5.

21   Ibid., 15–16.

22   Ibid., 9.

23   Elizabeth Bishop, *Complete Poems* (London: Chatto and Windus,
1991) 3, italics mine.

24   For the historian Arnold Toynbee, this phase of decolonisation, and
the challenge it posed to European culture's sense of its own world-
historical importance, had been underway since the last decades of
the nineteenth century. See Robert Young, *White Mythologies:
Writing History and the West* (London: Routledge, 1990) 19.

25   Morton A. Kaplan, 'The English Patient', *The World and I* (1993)
16–17.

26   Mark D. Simpson, 'Minefield Readings: The Postcolonial *English
Patient*', *Essays on Canadian Writing* 53 (Summer 1994) 232.

27   Glen Lowry, 'Between *The English Patients*: "Race" and the Cultural Politics of Adapting CanLit', *Essays on Canadian Writing* 76
(Spring 2002) 230.

Chapter 8

1   Amnesty International Report, quoted in Jagarth P. Senaratne, *Political Violence in Sri Lanka: Riots, Insurrections, Counterinsurgencies, Foreign Intervention*. Sri Lankan Studies in the Humanities and Social Sciences (Amsterdam: VU University Press, 1997) 146.

2   Maya Jaggi, 'Michael Ondaatje in Conversation with Maya Jaggi', *Wasafiri* 32 (Autumn 2000) 7.

3   Antoinette Burton, 'Archive of Bones: *Anil's Ghost* and the Ends of History', *Journal of Commonwealth Literature* 38.1 (2003) 49.

4   This is an aspect of the novel that Ondaatje has highlighted in interview: 'Anil's return is ironic, because she doesn't really know the country very well; she has to re-learn it' (Jaggi, 'Michael Ondaatje in Conversation with Maya Jaggi' 6).

5   Burton, 'Archive of Bones' 43.

6   Cathy Caruth, *Trauma: Explorations in Memory* (Baltimore: Johns Hopkins University Press, 1995) 231.

7   Ibid., 8.

8   Cathy Caruth, *Unclaimed Experience: Trauma, Narrative, and History* (Baltimore: Johns Hopkins University Press, 1996) 64.

9   Jaggi, 'Michael Ondaatje in Conversation with Maya Jaggi' 7.

10 In the remarks that follow I have drawn upon two very different readings of religion and politics in *Anil's Ghost*: Qadri Ismail's 'A Flippant Gesture Towards Sri Lanka: Michael Ondaatje's *Anil's Ghost*', *Pravada* 6.9 (2000) 24–9 and Marlene Goldman's 'Representations of Buddhism in Ondaatje's *Anil's Ghost*' in *Comparative Cultural Studies and Michael Ondaatje's Writing* ed. Steven Töstöy de Zepetnek (West Lafayette, IN: Purdue University Press, 2005) 27–37.

11 See Ismail, 'A Flippant Gesture Towards Sri Lanka' 27.

12 Goldman, 'Representations of Buddhism in Ondaatje's *Anil's Ghost*' 30.

13 Steven Kemper, *The Presence of the Past: Chronicles, Politics and Culture in Sinhala Life* (Ithaca: Cornell University Press, 1991) 26.

14 Ibid., 26.

15 Ibid., 29.

16 Ibid., 28.

17   Ibid., 33.

18   Ismail, 'A Flippant Gesture Towards Sri Lanka' 29.

19   Ibid., 24.

20   Goldman, 'Representations of Buddhism in Ondaatje's *Anil's Ghost*' 36.

21   Jaggi, 'Michael Ondaatje in Conversation with Maya Jaggi' 7.

Chapter 9

1   Douglas Barbour, *Michael Ondaatje* (New York: Twayne, 1993) 11.

2   Ibid., 17.

3   Sam Solecki, 'Nets and Chaos: The Poetry of Michael Ondaatje,' *Spider Blues: Essays on Michael Ondaatje* ed. Sam Solecki (Montréal: Véhicule Press, 1985) 93.

4   Lynette Hunter, 'Form and Energy in the Poetry of Michael Ondaatje,' *Journal of Canadian Poetry* 1.1 (1978) 50.

5   Ibid., 51.

6   Sam Solecki, *Ragas of Longing* 59.

7   Ibid., 40.

8   Ibid., 26.

9   J. E. Chamberlin, 'Let There Be Commerce Between Us: The Poetry of Michael Ondaatje,' *Spider Blues* 32.

10   Ibid., 41.

11   Barbour, *Michael Ondaatje* 35.

12   M. Travis Lane, 'Dream as History: A Review of *the man with seven toes*,' *Spider Blues* 154.

13   Sam Solecki, *Spider Blues* 137.

14   Dennis Lee, 'Savage Fields: *The Collected Works of Billy the Kid*,' *Spider Blues* 177.

15   Stephen Scobie, 'Two Authors in Search of a Character: bp Nicol and Michael Ondaatje,' *Spider Blues* 207.

16   Ibid., 204.

17   Susan Glickman, 'From "Philoctetes on the Island" to "Tin Roof": The Emerging Myth of Michael Ondaatje', *Spider Blues* 80.

18   Dennis Cooley, 'I am Here on the Edge: Modern Hero/Postmodern Poetics in *The Collected Works of Billy the Kid*', *Spider Blues* 232.

19   Barbour, *Michael Ondaatje* 36–7.

20   Smaro Kamboureli, 'The Poetics of Geography in Michael Ondaatje's *Coming Through Slaughter*,' *Descant* 14.4 (Fall 1983) 17.

21   Barbour, *Michael Ondaatje* 100–1.

22   Sam Solecki, 'Making and Destroying: *Coming Through Slaughter* and Extremist Art', *Spider Blues* 246.

23   Ibid., 247.

24   Ibid., 264.

25   Ibid.

26   Constance Rooke, 'Dog in a Gray Room: The Happy Ending of *Coming Through Slaughter*', *Spider Blues* 269.

27   Stephen Scobie, '*Coming Through Slaughter*: Fictional Magnets and Spider's Webbs', *Essays on Canadian Writing* 12 (Fall 1978) 20.

28   Linda Hutcheon, *The Canadian Postmodern: A Study of English-Canadian Fiction* (Toronto: Oxford University Press, 1988) 82.

29   Ibid., 83.

30   Smaro Kamboureli, 'The Alphabet of the Self: Generic and Other Slippages in Michael Ondaatje's *Running in the Family*,' *Reflections: Autobiography and Canadian Literature* ed. K. P. Stich (Ottawa: Ottawa University Press, 1988) 80.

31   Ernest Macintyre, 'Outside of Time: *Running in the Family*', *Spider Blues* 318.

32   Ajay Heble, '"Rumours of Topography": The Cultural Politics of Michael Ondaatje's *Running in the Family*', *Essays on Canadian Writing* 53 (1994) 188.

33   Barbour, *Michael Ondaatje* 197.

34   Hutcheon, *The Canadian Postmodern* 93.

35   Fortios Sarris, '*In the Skin of a Lion*: Michael Ondaatje's Tenebristic Narrative.' *Essays on Canadian Writing* 44 (1991) 190.

36   Julie Beddoes, 'Whose Side is It On? Form, Class and Politics in *In the Skin of a Lion*', *Essays on Canadian Writing* 53 (1994) 207.

37   Mark D. Simpson, 'Minefield Readings: The Postcolonial *English Patient*', *Essays on Canadian Writing* 53 (Summer 1994) 217.

38 Carrie Dawson, 'Calling People Names: Reading Imposture, Confession and Testimony in and after Michael Ondaatje's *The English Patient*', *Studies in Canadian Literature* 25.2 (2000) 57.

39 Ibid., 2.

40 Stephen Scobie, 'The Reading Lesson: Michael Ondaatje and the Patients of Desire', *Essays on Canadian Writing* 53 (1994) 92.

41 Hilary Mantel, 'Wraith's Progress,' *New York Review of Books* 14 January 1993, 23.

42 Gillian Roberts, 'Sins of Omission: *The English Patient* and the Critics', *Essays on Canadian Writing* 76 (2002) 211.

43 Glen Lowry, 'Between *The English Patients*: "Race" and the Cultural Politics of Adapting CanLit,' *Essays on Canadian Writing* 76 (Spring 2002) 217.

44 Antoinette Burton, 'Archive of Bones: *Anil's Ghost* and the Ends of History,' *Journal of Commonwealth Literature* 38.1 (2003) 40.

45 Ibid., 51.

46 Victoria Cook, 'Exploring Transnational Identities in Ondaatje's *Anil's Ghost*', in Stephen Töstöy de Zepetnek (ed.), *Comparative Cultural Studies and Michael Ondaatje's Writing* (West Lafayette, IN: Purdue University Press, 2005) 13.

47 Tom Leclair, 'The Sri Lankan Patients,' *The Nation*, 19 June 2000, 32.

48 Qadri Ismail, 'A Flippant Gesture Towards Sri Lanka: Michael Ondaatje's *Anil's Ghost*', *Pravada* 6.9 (2000) 28.

49 Marlene Goldman, 'Representations of Buddhism in Ondaatje's *Anil's Ghost*' in Töstöy de Zepetnek (ed.), *Comparative Cultural Studies and Michael Ondaatje's Writing* 28.

Select bibliography

The primary bibliography lists Ondaatje's novels, his collections of verse and a selection of his essays and published interviews. The secondary bibliography, while necessarily highly selective, seeks to highlight key themes in Ondaatje criticism. See the Chronology for details of the first screenings of Ondaatje's films.

Works by Michael Ondaatje

FICTION

Coming Through Slaughter (Toronto: House of Anansi, 1976; London: Marion Boyars, 1979; London: Picador, 1984).

Running in the Family (Toronto: McClelland and Stewart, 1982; London: Picador, 1984).

In the Skin of a Lion (Toronto: McClelland and Stewart, 1987; London: Picador, 1988).

The English Patient (Toronto: McClelland and Stewart, 1992; London: Picador, 1993).

Anil's Ghost (Toronto: McClelland and Stewart, 2000; London: Picador, 1993; New York: Alfred A. Knopf, 2000; London: Picador, 2001).

Divisadero (Toronto: McClelland and Stewart, 2007; London: Bloomsbury, 2007).

POETRY

The Dainty Monsters (Toronto: Coach House Press, 1967).

the man with seven toes (Toronto: Coach House Press, 1969; 3rd edn 1975).

The Collected Works of Billy the Kid: Left Handed Poems (Toronto: Anansi, 1970; London: Marion Boyars, 1981).

The Broken Ark: A Book of Beasts (Ottawa: Oberon Press, 1971).

Rat Jelly (Toronto: Coach House Press, 1973).

Elimination Dance (Ontario: Nairn Coldstream, 1978).

Claude Glass (Toronto: Coach House Press, 1979).

There's a Trick with a Knife I'm Learning to Do: Poems 1963–1978 (Toronto: McClelland and Stewart, 1979).

Rat Jelly and Other Poems 1963–1978 (London: Marion Boyars, 1980).

Tin Roof (British Columbia: Island Writing Series, 1982).

Secular Love (Toronto: Coach House Press, 1984; New York: W. W. Norton, 1985).

Two Poems (Milwaukee, WI: Woodland Pattern, 1986).

The Cinnamon Peeler (London: Picador, 1989).

Handwriting (Toronto: McClelland and Stewart, 1998; London: Picador, 2000).

The Story (Toronto: Anansi, 2005).

NON-FICTION

Leonard Cohen (Toronto: McClelland and Stewart, 1970).

The Broken Ark: A Book of Beasts (Ottawa: Oberon Press, 1971).

Personal Fiction: Stories by Munro, Wieve, Thomas and Blaise, selected by Michael Ondaatje (Oxford: Oxford University Press, 1977).

The Long Poem Anthology, ed. Michael Ondaatje (Toronto: Coach House Press, 1979).

Brushes with Greatness: An Anthology of Chance Encounters with Greatness, ed. Russell Banks, Michael Ondaatje and David Young (Toronto: Coach House Press, 1989).

From Ink Lake: An Anthology of Canadian Short Stories, ed. Michael Ondaatje (New York: Viking, 1990).

The Faber Book of Contemporary Canadian Short Stories, ed. Michael Ondaatje (London: Faber and Faber, 1990).

The Brick Reader, eited by Linda Spalding and Michael Ondaatje. (Toronto: Coach House Press, 1991).

An H in the Heart: A Reader, selected by George Bowering and Michael Ondaatje (Toronto: McClelland and Stewart, 1994).

The English Patient: A Screenplay, by Anthony Minghella; based on the novel by Michael Ondaatje.; introduction by Michael Ondaatje (New York: Hyperion Miramax Books, 1996).

Lost Classics: Writers on Books Loved and Lost, Overlooked, Under-Read, Unavailable, Stolen, Extinct, or Otherwise Out of Commission, ed. Michael Ondaatje, Michael Redhill, Esta and Linda Spalding (New York: Anchor Books, 2001).

The Conversations: Walter Murch and the Art of Editing Film (London: Bloomsbury, 2003).

CRITICAL ARTICLES

'O'Hagan's Rough-Edged Chronicle', *Canadian Literature* 61 (1974) 24–31.

'García Marquez and the Bus to Aracataca', in *Figures in a Ground: Canadian Essays Collected in Honor of Sheila Watson* ed. Diane Besai and David Jackel (Saskatoon, Sask.: Western Producer Prairie Books, 1978), 19–31.

FILMS AND SCREENPLAYS

Sons of Captain Poetry. Mongrel Films/Canadian Film-Makers Distribution Centre (1970) 35 min.

Carry on Crime and Punishment. Mongrel Films/Canadian Film-Makers Distribution Centre (1972) 5 min.

The Clinton Special. Mongrel Films/Canadian Film-Makers Distribution Centre (1972) 71 min.

'The William Dawe Badlands Expedition 1916', *Descant* 14 (Fall 1983) 51–73.

Love Clinic. Border Crossings 9.4 (October 1990) 14–19.

AUDIO

Previous Canoes (Toronto: Coach House Press, 1994).

MANUSCRIPTS

Library and Archives Canada holds research notes, manuscripts and typescripts for *Dainty Monsters, the man with seven toes, The Collected Works of Billy the Kid, Rat Jelly, Coming Through Slaughter, There's a Trick with a Knife I'm Learning to Do* and *Running in the Family*; and research notes, manuscripts, typescripts, to Montreal, Canada, where he enrolled as a major in English and History at Bishops University, Lennoxville, in Quebec. If Ondaatje was looking for change he had come to the right place; the Canada to which he migrated was undergoing a period of sustained social and political transformation. This upheaval was initially economic and demographic in origin: in the late 1950s and early 1960s a 'renewed stream of immigration' poured into the country accompanied by 'an immense flow of direct capital investment' from America.[5] Between 1941 and 1976 Canada's population virtually doubled (rising from 11.5 million to 22 million); almost 2 million of this increase were immigrants.[6] This demographic transformation had a number of social and cultural effects. Foremost among them was the emergence of a 'new kind of nationalism' which sought to replace the conventional image of Canada as a national 'melting-pot' in order to assert the continuing multicultural diversity of its immigrant inheritance.[7] Almost inevitably these social and cultural changes brought other tensions to the surface: the liberal beginnings of Jean Lesage's 'Quiet Revolution' in Quebec soon metamorphosed into a more strident francophone nationalism, a reaction only partly assuaged by the passing of the Official Language Act in 1969 that officially defined Canada as a bilingual nation. Many of the tensions bequeathed by Canada's history as a bilingual nation colonised by Britain and France persist to this day, but they emerged with particular force in the years after Ondaatje's arrival in the country, giving an added urgency to debates about the role of culture in the formation of regional and national identity.

The rapid changes Canadian society experienced at the beginning of the 1960s were accompanied by the emergence of an exciting new literary scene. The decade witnessed important new work by young writers like Daphne Marlatt, bpNichol, Raymond Souster, Dennis Lee, Al Purdy, Margaret Avison and Nicole Brossard; in the years that followed the appearance of writers like Margaret Atwood, Alice Munro, Margaret Laurence and Robert Kroetsch would give Canadian literature an international profile. Encouraged by the vibrancy of the local literary culture, Ondaatje became serious about writing poetry; he formed a close attachment to the poet in residence Ralph Gustafson at Bishops University and began to show him drafts of his earliest work. Meanwhile his burgeoning academic talents were rewarded by his receipt of the President's Prize for English. For the first time in many years Ondaatje felt himself to be happily settled in Quebec; but his life was about to change for ever. While studying at Bishops he met and fell in love with the artist Kim Jones, wife of his friend and mentor Doug Jones. Ondaatje had been very close to Doug Jones, one of his English professors at Bishops. Jones had quickly sensed the literary ability of his unassuming young protégé, invited him to summer poetry workshops at the Joneses' cottage in Keewaydin, and introduced him to the work of important figures in the Canadian literary world like A. J. M. Smith and Louis Dudek.[8] His marriage was, however, already upon the point of collapse; when he saw Ondaatje and Kim together he knew that it was finished. But although Jones agreed to divorce his wife, even travelling with the couple to Mexico to expedite the process, his position as a professor made Ondaatje's continuing presence at the university untenable. Thus soon after their marriage in 1964 Ondaatje and his new wife moved to Toronto, where he finished his BA in 1965. At the University of Toronto his literary talent continued to attract attention and he was awarded the Ralf Gustafson Award for poetry later that year. He subsequently completed his MA at Queens University, Kingston, Ontario, in 1967, by which time he was the father of a daughter Quintin and a son Griffin.

Ondaatje's time at Queens was a period of considerable creative significance. In 1966 his first poems were published in a major anthology of new Canadian writing, *New Wave Canada*. Around this time Ondaatje also began his abiding involvement with the small but increasingly prestigious Coach House Press, where he met a number of writers – such as bpNichol, Frank Davey, Bob Fones and Roy Kiyooka – who would have a profound influence upon his work. The next year, following his move to take up a teaching position at the University of Western Ontario, his first collection of poems, *The Dainty Monsters*, appeared in

Toronto. His handwritten dedication to Kim in her copy of the book revealed that the collection was 'begun in Lennoxville in 1962 [where he had first met Kim] and was finished [while he was living with her] in Kingston in 1967 and shown to her in its various stages'.[9] With their apocalyptic undertone and appalled fascination with violence, these poems offer an oblique commentary upon their historical moment: the expanding conflagration of the Vietnam War and the domestic resistance it spawned upon the streets of North America. Reviewing the volume, Douglas Barbour noted the pervasiveness in these poems of 'images of violence and terror' before concluding that *The Dainty Monsters* is 'the finest first book of poems to appear since Margaret Avison's *Winter Sun'*.[10] Ondaatje's modernist inheritance was already clearly evident in his first volume; his rewriting of Greek myth in the short sequence 'Paris' won him the President's Medal at West Ontario. The final poems in *The Dainty Monsters* exhibit what would become some of Ondaatje's most enduring themes: the borderline between 'form and formlessness, civilization and nature, the human and the natural, reason and instinct, and the relationship between violence and creativity'.[11] Each of these themes resonates throughout his extended poetic sequence *the man with seven toes*, which he published two years later in 1969. Pondering his decision to adopt a mythic and archetypal narrative in this sequence, Ondaatje remarked that these poems reveal 'a jump from the self to a mask of some kind'.[12] In *the man with seven toes* this 'jump' enabled him to 'escape the confines of the lyric voice' by recasting poetic narrative as a dramatic encounter between a polyphony of voices. Exactly the same technique would lie behind the success of his breakthrough third book *The Collected Works of Billy the Kid*.

Throughout the period between the publications of Ondaatje's first two books he was a full-time instructor in English. During this time he was commissioned to write a study of the novelist Leonard Cohen for McClelland and Stewart's Canadian Writers Series. The volume duly appeared in 1970. Although the book was in places little more than a gentle paraphrase of Cohen's principal themes and motifs, Ondaatje's preoccupation with Cohen's use of American pop-cultural figures 'reflects his own interest in such characters as Billy the Kid and Pat Garrett'.[13] Ondaatje's interest in this aspect of Cohen's work was more than coincidental; he was by now fully absorbed in writing the book that would seal his early literary reputation. *The Collected Works of Billy the Kid* was an overnight sensation when it appeared in 1970 and won the Governor General's Award the following year. Critics were fulsome in their praise of its thrilling distillation of modernist avant-garde technique, although John Diefenbacker, a former prime minister of Canada, articulated the view of a vocal minority when he lamented the bestowal of a major Canadian prize upon a writer preoccupied with American cultural history.[14] Ondaatje was supremely indifferent to the public repercussions of this local *succès de scandale*: the life of Billy the Kid, he explained, was merely the frame by which he brought his poetic vision into focus. '*Billy* is a personal book', he reflected some years later, 'very much about my world then, even though it's set in a different country and it's about an absolute stranger to me. I found I could both reveal and discover myself more through being given a costume. I could be more honest about the things I wanted to talk about or witness'.[15]

The critical reception of *Billy the Kid* was a signal moment in Ondaatje's developing literary career. But before he could savour his success he experienced a set-back on another front. After three years as an assistant professor at Western Ontario, his lack of either a doctorate or a record of significant academic publication meant that he was refused a permanent teaching position in the Department of English. The loss of a regular income came as a considerable shock to him, but his situation was quickly eased when he accepted another teaching position at Glendon College, York University in Toronto. In retrospect, this change of scenery may have come at a fortuitous time for Ondaatje; conscious of having exhausted a particular style with *Billy the Kid*, he was already casting around for a new artistic direction:

> I'd just finished the actual writing of *Billy the Kid*, and there was a real sense of words meaning nothing to me anymore, and I was going around interpreting things

into words. If I saw a tree I just found myself saying tree:
translating everything into words and metaphors. It was
a dangerous thing for me mentally and I didn't want to
carry on in that way. I just felt I had to go into another
field, something totally unusual.[16]

Ondaatje's response to this sense of creative exhaustion was to
make a documentary film about his friend and fellow poet b. p.
Nichol entitled *Sons of Captain Poetry*. He had long admired
Nichol's exuberantly avant-garde concrete poetry while feeling
himself temperamentally unsuited to the form. Not wishing to
pay Nichol tribute in his own coin, Ondaatje chose instead to
offer his friend this affectionate visual celebration of his art and
literary career. *Sons of Captain Poetry* was not Ondaatje's first
foray into film – as a student in Toronto he had performed a
small role in David Secter's *The Offering* in 1965 – but it gave
him his first experience of the editing process by which film
achieves its final form. *Sons of Captain Poetry* was in several
respects something of a failure: the film did not really cohere
as a narrative, it received little publicity or recognition, and it
was considered unsuitable as an entry for the Canadian Film
Awards.[17] However, the experience of making and editing the film
broadened his sense of the formal possibilities of literary narrative.[18] The effects of his immersion in film are clearly evident
in a novel like *Coming Through Slaughter*, which systemati-
cally dissolves its formal structure into a series of short 'takes' in
order to accentuate the tension between biographical narrative
and the experience of lived history.

Ondaatje reprised his interest in film when he became a
member of the team that made *The Clinton Special*. The film
was a cinematic version of Theater Passe Muraille's *The Farm
Show*, a variety of 'living theatre' in which actors mingled with
a local rural audience and encouraged them to collaborate in
a collective performance of their everyday lives.[19] In 1972 *The
Farm Show*'s director, Paul Thompson, decided to take the show
back to the farming communities in Clinton County, Ontario in
which it had originated and make a film involving some of the
principal characters upon which the play was based. Ondaatje

contributed to the production as a cameraman and editor and he learned a good deal from the experience. Like *The Clinton Special*, *Coming Through Slaughter* and *Running in the Family* both interweave history and fiction in order to 'inscribe and undermine the authority and objectivity of historical sources and explanations'.[20] The film's subtle modulation between long-shot and close-up and its delicate interplay between still shots and narrative action also anticipates the rhythmic unfolding of each of these prose texts. 'Making the documentaries influenced my writing, just as my writing influenced the way I made documentaries', Ondaatje later reflected. 'I don't want to make films that are part of a genre someone else has invented. I want to make movies related to what I am writing'.[21]

The period following the completion of *The Clinton Special* was a busy time for Ondaatje as he completed his poetic collection *Rat Jelly* and began to work on his first novel, *Coming Through Slaughter*. Back in 1970 his eye had been caught by a small newspaper article about the legendary jazz pioneer Buddy Bolden, who had gone insane while playing in a parade. The story of Bolden's brief tragic career and his radically innovative improvisatory style offered Ondaatje an opportunity to reflect upon both the relationship between art and life and the social and political forces that determined the emergence of the New South. To research the novel he travelled extensively throughout Louisiana in 1973, spending considerable stretches of time in New Orleans and Baton Rouge, where he read widely upon the history of New Orleans jazz, studied period newspapers and photographs, delved through masses of archive material, listen to taped interviews with turn-of-the-century jazz musicians and interviewed anyone remotely connected with the descendants of the Bolden circle.[22] Eventually Ondaatje's research took him to Slaughter, the hamlet through which Bolden passed on his final journey to Calvary, and the East Louisiana State Hospital in Jackson where the musician finally died. For all his efforts Ondaatje was able to discover very little reliable biographical information about Bolden's life and circumstances; but these lacunae in the historical narrative afforded him the freedom

poem. The poetic 'I' that designates Billy's historical identity, we might say, is always also the 'we' of a collective historical judgement that recomposes Billy's identity from the scant textual traces he left behind. Ondaatje's Billy the Kid is, in this sense, alive and dead, singular and plural, speaker and spoken, visible symbol of the American frontier and metaphorically suggestive of the residue of contemporary sensibility within every act of historical evaluation.

The poem's continual oscillation between first- and third-person perspectives becomes the subject of one of its most important early fragments:

> Not a story about me through their eyes then. Find the beginning, the slight silver key to unlock it, to dig it out. Here then is a maze to begin, be in.
>
> Two years ago Charlie Bowdre and I criss-crossed the Canadian border. Ten miles north of it ten miles south. Our horses stepped from country to country, across low rivers, through different colours of tree green. The two of us, our criss-cross like a whip in slow motion, the ridge of action rising and falling, getting narrower in radius till it ended and we drifted down to Mexico and old heat. That there is nothing of depth, of significant accuracy, of wealth in the image, I know. It is there for a beginning. (*BTK*, 20)

Here the reader's broader problems of attribution and context are concentrated within a passage that counsels us, ironically enough, upon the ways in which to read Billy's story. Its first sentence, apparently spoken by Billy, bespeaks his determination to preserve the integrity of his biography from the interference of external forces, although it is not immediately clear whether the phrase 'through their eyes' refers to Garrett and his cohorts or the ranks of commentators who span the hundred years from Billy's time to Ondaatje's own. The two subsequent sentences, however, narrow the distance between Billy and Ondaatje to a point of imperceptibility; while both restate Billy's desire for control of his own narrative, the lexical play between 'begin' and 'be in' betrays the presence of the poetic intelligence that devised

the 'maze' of these 'collected works'. The remainder of the fragment plays off Billy's concern to find a 'way in' or productive point of departure for the story of his own life against Ondaatje's ironic awareness that any 'beginning' will inevitably return us to the labyrinth of existing historical accounts of the outlaw's life and times. There is, these sentences imply, no interpretative position exterior to these narratives: they have already flattened Billy's image upon the plane of 'frontier history', draining it in the process of substantial 'depth' and leaving it devoid of any 'significant accuracy' to his own lived experience. That Billy's quest for a new beginning is destined to be outflanked by Ondaatje's poetic irony is already apparent to us; the entire sequence begins, after all, by reinscribing the force of the narrative frames that produce and mediate Billy's historical image. Billy's story will, in this sense, always be a story 'through their eyes'; this dissident fragment, which articulates momentarily 'Billy's' resistance to such discursive enclosure, is merely one further confirmation of his unavoidable defeat.

Billy's nervousness about the selective rewriting of his own biography would be compounded, rather than allayed, by the 'maze' of Ondaatje's poetics. Ondaatje initially discovered a 'key' to 'dig out' the buried details of Billy the Kid's life in Walter Noble Burns's biography *Billy the Kid*. However, this summary acknowledgement of Ondaatje's literary indebtedness provides few clues to the extent of his radical rewriting of his source material, which fundamentally reshapes the historical context within which the climatic events of Billy's life unfold. The impression that Ondaatje maintained only the slenderest interest in historical verisimilitude is reinforced by his selection of Burns's book as his narrative template; conceived for an audience brought up on the mythical 'Outlaw West' of dime novels, Burns's biography cheerfully transforms narrative history into the stuff of popular historical drama. The vignette in which Burns describes Billy's escape from Lincoln Gaol gives a flavour of the whole:

> The Kid gathered up his bridle reins, gripped the pommel, and swung into the saddle. Burdened with his two six-

shooters, rifle and cartridge belts, he was immediately kicked off. He struck the ground on his hands and knees, still holding the bridle. He leaped to his feet; for a moment he stood there in the middle of the sun-drenched road, legs braced, rifle cocked and ready for instant use, a tense, thrilling figure of a fighting man at bay. The watchers on the porch made no move, but on their minds this quick picture of Billy the Kid remained indelibly engraved for all their lives.[10]

Although cleaving to Burns's account for a number of its key narrative details, Ondaatje's version substantially revises the historical context that informs the earlier work. Perhaps Ondaatje's most important revision lies in his suppression of significant reference to the Lincoln County War. This brutal local conflict, in which, as Billy points out in his apocryphal jailhouse interview near the end of the poem, 'EVERYBODY' was shooting at everyone else, forms one of the main narrative strands of Burns's biography; but the only allusions Ondaatje includes to these events are a few stray hints unlikely to be recognised by a reader unfamiliar with the local history of the New Mexico frontier (*BTK*, 82). The deletion of this episode has a crucial bearing upon the story: by excising this history from his poetic narrative Ondaatje is able to relegate to the background numerous examples of Billy's own murderous exploits. Besides dispensing with the determining context of the Lincoln County War, Ondaatje also diminishes the force of one of Burns's central historical themes: the escalating struggle in 1880s New Mexico between the expansionary economic force of large landed interests and the essentially nomadic and lawless existence of social outsiders like Billy the Kid and his band of followers. Both the landowners' realisation that Billy's erratic activities now posed a significant threat to their economic and social authority and their decision to hire Pat Garrett to hunt him down constitute, for Burns, defining moments in Billy's story; the fight to the death between Billy and Garrett becomes for him emblematic of the climactic struggle between the 'Old' and the 'New' West during which the nature of frontier law and society underwent

a rapid and irreversible transformation. Despite permitting himself a cursory glance towards 'cattle politicians like Chisum', Ondaatje almost completely effaces from his poem the decisive role of the new mercantile forces represented by these expansionist landowners (*BTK*, 7). His indifference to the social and economic factors behind Garrett's remorseless pursuit of Billy may be gauged by an aside made halfway through the sequence. In response to the question whether there might have been 'A motive, some reasoning we can give to explain all this violence' comes the laconic reply 'yup' followed by a slab of Burns's narrative recounting the murder of the outlaw Tunstall (*BTK*, 54).

The killing of Tunstall was a brutal, but hardly untypical, incident within the increasingly ferocious clan warfare between the Murphy and McSween factions for control of Lincoln County. Burns locates this event near the beginning of his narrative to suggest that Billy's subsequent actions may be cast in the benevolent light of a revenge motive: 'With the murder of the Englishman, the Kid threw himself into the feud to avenge his friend's death'.[11] Where Burns's account of Tunstall's murder has an exclusively exculpatory function, Ondaatje's decision simply to quote Burns's narrative in the absence of an explanatory context that might illuminate its significance effectively pushes the poem further away from comprehension, rendering the violence it relates both atavistic and inexplicable. This assault on historical context is compounded by a number of poems, like the early description of Boot Hill, in which arbitrary violence is presented almost as the metaphysical condition of frontier culture. Viewed in the context of the three hundred violent deaths recorded in Boot Hill cemetery, Billy's orgy of killing becomes part of the texture of common experience rather than a constant threat to social order in New Mexico.

Not content with reinventing key aspects of Billy the Kid's story, Ondaatje's selective reworking of Burns's partial and exculpatory narrative also crucially redefines the role of Pat Garrett. The redefinition of Garrett's image is partly the consequence of Ondaatje's blithe disregard of the preceding years of Billy's outlaw career; by choosing to begin his poem *in media res*

and devoting the main burden of his narrative to Billy's doomed and desperate flight from his pursuers, Ondaatje inevitably casts Billy in a sympathetic light. From the moment that the poem begins, Garrett is portrayed as an assassin, an opportunist and a turncoat; Billy, by contrast, is presented in the romantic light of a man already marked by death. Three of the most graphic acts of violence in the entire poem – the killings of Tom O'Folliard, Charlie Bowdre and Billy himself – are performed by Garrett; Billy, meanwhile, stands curiously apart from the general mayhem, simultaneously fascinated and appalled by the damage that men do ('Jesus I never knew that did you / the nerves shot out / the liver running around there / like a headless hen jerking / brown all over the yard / seen that too at my aunt's / never eaten hen since then' (*BTK*, 12)).

Ondaatje's skewed vision of Billy as a commentator upon, rather than a proponent of, violence has inevitable implications for our judgement of each of the principals. By representing Billy throughout the poem as a hunted man, Ondaatje, Steven Scobie argues, significantly 'stacks the deck' in the gunslinger's favour; if the reader recoils in shock from the poem's scenes of graphic violence, she is 'reacting mainly *against* Garrett'.[12] The intermittent identification of the poem's perspective with Billy's point-of-view enables him to justify and excuse the violence employed in his execution of his rivals and present himself as a man fundamentally unlike his cold-hearted antagonist (*BTK*, 15).

Ondaatje's strategic revision of the biography of Billy the Kid, then, establishes his poem as both a critique and an example of the historical constitution of cultural memory. But the recognition of Ondaatje's historical self-consciousness cannot account for the full aesthetic force of *Billy the Kid* because the poem repeatedly retreats from the historical horizon of experience to meditate upon the phenomenological plane of life and consciousness. The persistent tension at the core of *Billy the Kid* between phenomenological and historical levels of experience offers a clue to the profound originality of Ondaatje's version of the story: where the struggle between Billy and Garrett has historically

been represented as a conflict between the forces of law and social disorder, Ondaatje's poem also portrays it as a struggle between two styles of being and two modes of perception. This emphasis upon the phenomenology of perception leads Ondaatje to couple his representation of character with an examination of the way subjects come to conceive of their worlds. The literary exploration of consciousness, sensation and intuition provides the ground for many of Ondaatje's most striking poetic effects; it is also the aspect of the poem that most stubbornly frustrates our conventional habits of reading.

It is immediately clear from the poem's first pages that to speak of different interpretations of the 'character' of Billy the Kid is already to impose a particular style of thought upon a text that persistently questions how we come to conceive of life in terms of characters, interests and ideologies. The difficulty we often feel in understanding the various images of Billy that the poem circulates arises because Ondaatje frequently presents a micropolitical, rather than 'historical' or 'ideological', vision of the outlaw's life and times.[13] Instead of portraying Billy as a particular type of personality who represents a particular set of beliefs and values, Ondaatje focuses upon the way Billy's subjectivity is composed from a series of investments, desires and affects. This poetic vision of Billy the Kid embodies what Deleuze and Guattari have called a 'molecular' perception of life: a vision, that is, that remains resolutely at the level of singularities and pre-personal attachments before they are organised and extended into collective or 'molar' formations such as law, ideology, history and subjectivity. To begin from the perspective of molecular experience is to think of life in terms of the singular and partial investments from which individual ways of being are composed. Certainly conceiving of Ondaatje's poem in this way helps to illuminate otherwise impenetrable aspects of Billy's world, which, created as it is from a network of partial and incomplete memories, unfocused perceptions and seemingly random affections, is apt to appear simply chaotic and inexplicable when discussed in conventional terms.

The importance of reading Billy's image in molecular rather

than molar terms is underscored in a number of early scenes. It is glimpsed first in the curious lyric that relates the death of Charlie Bowdre, one of Billy's outlaw companions ('When I caught Charlie Bowdre dying ... while the eyes grew all over his body' (*BTK*, 12)).

The inadequacy of conventional notions of 'subject' and 'character' to the style of life Billy embodies is immediately apparent in this lyric. In the poem's first explicit act of violence, a man is ripped apart before Billy's eyes; but what is striking about his response is the absence of shock or emotional empathy with the victim. His response, such as it is, is unsympathetic in the fullest sense because sympathy involves an imaginative relation to another quality or condition of being. But Billy is unable to maintain the distinction between subject and object or self and world upon which such sympathy depends; instead he projects himself *into* the bodies and objects he perceives all around him. At no point in this scene can Billy be said to occupy a position 'outside' the event of Bowdre's killing, from which he might supply an emotional or moral context for the action he witnesses; his perspective is, in fact, already immanent to the event itself, an 'eye' that grows all over Bowdre's body and becomes inseparable from the man that is dying. Ondaatje's syntax and diction underline the affective, rather than emotional or moral, quality of Billy's reaction by preserving the shock of this murderous experience before it can be ordered into sense: the shuttling passage between the phrases 'giggling / at me' and 'face tossed in a gaggle' deletes the temporal delay between event and consequence within which empathy might be engendered, capturing instead the raw force of the shooting in a blank instant of perception.

Some sense of Billy's attentiveness to the singularity and intensity of affects rather than the broader system of social values and judgements that they come to constitute is required to illuminate passages of writing that otherwise appear almost wholly unfocused. One such passage is the description of Billy's earlier behaviour at Bowdre's place (*BTK*, 39). The unsettling aspect of the style of the sequence at this point is once more its dissolution

of subjectivity into singular, partial and affective experience. This mode of dissolution is reflected in the gradual disintegration of poetic syntax, which collapses from the grammatical propriety of 'she is boiling us black coffee' to the aphasic conjunction 'and with a bit the edge of my eye'. The point of this syntactical disarray is to express an impersonal flow of desire and affect that moves across and between bodies before it is recomposed into fixed images of subjectivity and sexuality. What appears in the second stanza is the obliteration of relations between discrete subjectivities and the reassertion of the singular and affective force of life. Billy does not feel people close to him ('Strange that how I feel people / not close to me') because proximity is still a mode of *relation* between individuated and autonomous bodies. His perception of this scene remains instead at the molecular level: the singularities of texture ('as if their dress were against my shoulder'), smell ('the strange smell of their breath / moving against my face') and light ('or my eyes / magnifying the bones across a room / shifting in a wrist'). This rupture with the logic of representation and the return to a deterritorialised flow of desire and affect becomes unavoidable for Billy whenever he passes from the codified spaces of frontier culture to the empty and unwritten Western landscape ('To be near flowers in the rain … nothing thick sugar death' (*BTK*, 55)).

This short lyric begins in a mood almost of bucolic reverie ('To be near flowers in the rain'), but quickly charts the same movement from relation and contemplation to an immersion in singularities and intensities. The passage from representation to singularity occurs once more at an affective level: the 'smell of things dying flamboyant' casts us adrift in the stream of pre-personal singularities before they are subsumed into the symbolic order of concepts, identities and values. By gradually opening these words up to the intensities they conceal, Ondaatje pushes language beyond representation towards its extremities or limits. Lyric rhetoric is brought here to the pitch of an asignifying intensity by several stylistic features: the recoil from narrative sense into the internal discordance of consonant and vowel ('All that pollen stink buds / bloated split'), the calculated

indistinction between adjective and noun ('bursting the white drop of spend') and the multiplication of these figures beyond the local demands of reference ('pollen stink buds / bloated split / leaves'). Through the affective intensity of this language, Ondaatje describes how Billy becomes a part of what he perceives; what we experience by the poem's climax is the disintegration of subjectivity into the singularities that compose it, culminating in a symbolic death of the self ('can hardly breathe nothing / nothing thick sugar death') and a transformed relation between human and inhuman life.

The remarkable feature of Ondaatje's molecular style is that it no longer conceives of the subject as the ground or truth of experience, but rather as a form through which life *passes*. Ondaatje develops this molecular conception of the self through Billy's relationship with animal and inhuman life. This relationship is first explored in an extended prose section recounting Billy's week-long retreat to a barn in order to burn out a fever. Completely isolated from the human world and surrounded only by birds and animals ('I saw no human and heard no human voice'), Billy undergoes a strange metamorphosis that leads by stages to the attenuation of self-consciousness ('I began to block my mind of all thought') and the reconstitution of life as a flow of inhuman affects:

> For that week then I made a bed of the table there and lay out my fever, whatever it was. I began to block my mind of all thought … The fly who sat on my arm, after his inquiry, just went away, ate his disease and kept it in him. When I walked I avoided the cobwebs who had places to grow to, who had stories to finish. The flies caught in those acrobat nets were the only murder I saw. (*BTK*, 17)

This putative metamorphosis ends, on one level, in fear and trembling. Poised for a terrifying moment at the very limit of the human world, Billy resists the dissolution of his identity by recoiling violently from animal life and massacring a horde of rats. But the impression that an internal division has already been made in his persona becomes clear in the passage's haunting final sentence where Billy, looking back upon the

epiphany visited upon him, can no longer recognise his former self ('the boy') as the subject of his own narration: 'Till my hand was black and the gun was hot and no other animal of any kind remained in that room but for the boy in the blue short sitting there coughing at the dust, rubbing the sweat of his upper lip with his left forearm' (*BTK*, 18).

The full implications of this scene are not lived out for another twenty pages. There the change that has been wrought in Billy's nature is explored in a frenzied lyric that details the deconstitution of a recognisably human personality:

> (To come) to where eyes will
> move in head like a rat
> mad since locked in a biscuit tin all day
> stampeding mad as a mad rats legs
> bang it went was hot
> under my eye
> was hot small bank did it
> almost a pop
> I didnt hear till I was red
> had a rat fyt in my head
> sad billys body glancing out
> body going as sweating white horses go
> reeling off me wet
> scuffing down my arms
> wet horse white
> screaming wet sweat round the house
> sad billys out
> floating barracuda in the brain. (*BTK*, 38)

Whatever we make of writing like this, little is to be gained by interpreting it as the expression of a form of subjectivity that has effectively been evacuated from the poem or as a metaphor for a crisis of historical modes of knowledge. A potentially more profitable, although initially hazardous, approach is to read Billy's metamorphosis as an example of that experience of intensity Deleuze and Guattari have described as a 'becoming-animal': a line of flight from the autonomous and located human body towards a wholly new and inhuman style of perception.[14] Conceived in these terms, Billy combines here his own mode of

becoming with that of animal life ('had a rat fyt in my head') and transforms himself in the act of perceiving the difference between the two.

The poem's breathless, fractured syntax and its stuttering opening parenthesis mime this movement towards a futural becoming. In the first half of the lyric, Ondaatje charts the passage beyond subject and object distinctions towards a third position that surpasses them by incorporating them both within itself ('had a rat fyt in my head / sad billy's body glancing out'). In perceiving the furious and unthinking energy of rat life, Billy suddenly experiences a becoming-rat; in so doing, he momentarily becomes one with the differential force through which all life emerges.[15] Because Billy may no longer be imagined simply as 'human', Ondaatje once again deterritorialises poetic language, opening his medium up to the flow of intensities that precede and exceed its structures. This phase of deterritorialisation is disclosed in the poem's fluid transposition of pronouns, its reversion from a world of sense into the thick materiality of assonance, alliteration and internal rhyme ('wet horse white / screaming wet sweat round the house'), the forcible tearing-away of one state of being towards a new point of vision ('(To come)'), and the apprehension of a metamorphosis so profound and unstable it can only be evoked by a random scattering of nouns ('was hot small bang did it / almost a pop'). By wrenching Billy's point-of-view from its anthropocentric perspective, Ondaatje recasts it upon the plane of inhuman and impersonal perceptions: in the midst of this poetic sequence Billy is variously hunter and hunted, man, rat and horse. To think the becoming of life from a position beyond the ground of the human subject is an ambitious undertaking that requires a revolution in the logic of sense; at points in this process Billy's image becomes almost literally unreadable as he is delivered over into the pure flow of singularities. Whatever implications this style of writing might hold for Ondaatje's potential readership – and it is noticeable that most commentators have chosen to focus their readings of the poem in other directions – these lyrics represent the culmination of his attempt to present a molecular view of life as an inhuman

world of difference and becoming. Nowhere else, not even in *Coming Through Slaughter*, would he go as far again in this direction, although the conflict between molecular and molar life would remain a persistent theme of his work. Certainly these lyrics are not utopian in their emphases: Billy rebels furiously against the transformation visited upon him and tries to reassert his autonomous sense of self by imposing his will violently upon others.

The conflict between molecular and molar life in *Billy the Kid* is also represented at a thematic level by the struggle between Billy and Pat Garrett.[16] As well as a battle of roles and personalities, this struggle also involves a conflict of ideas about life: where Billy expresses a commitment to molecular experience, Garrett stands for the imaginative transcendence of corporeal life and the molar structures of law and social order. Garrett's character is introduced in two long passages that establish his conformity to an idealised self-image:

> Pat Garrett, ideal assassin. Public figure, the mind of a doctor, his hands hairy, scarred, burned by rope, on his wrist there was a purple stain there all his life. Ideal assassin for his mind was unwarped ... (*BTK*, 28)

Garrett is an 'ideal assassin', the sardonic narrative voice implies, because he can turn killing into a pure idea: his mind is 'unwarped', precisely because his gaze never deflects itself from the social forces that legitimate public acts of violence. His remorseless subordination of private feeling to public action makes a social virtue out of the most pathological behaviour: the behaviour of the 'genial' man who had 'the ability to kill someone on the street walk back and finish a joke'. In one of the pivotal scenes describing the emergence of Garrett's 'ideal' public self, he wakes up in a hotel room and sets himself the task of breaking down his body's dependence upon instinct and reflex. Steadily drinking himself into a stupor for two years, Garrett transforms his body into a machine whose response he can programme and predict. His obsessive need to transcend molecular modes of becoming is tellingly illuminated halfway though his ordeal when he begins to evince a strange terror of

flowers. Garrett is terrified by natural organisms because they simply are what they do; they make no distinction between the primal force of life and its idea or representation:

> He would wake up in the mornings, his sheets soaked in urine 40% alcohol. He became frightened of flowers because they grew so slowly that he couldn't tell what they planned to do. His mind learned to be superior because of the excessive mistakes of those around him. Flowers watched him. (*BTK*, 28)

After two years, Garrett is able finally to subordinate his volatile nature to an abstract idea of law. Unlike Billy, whose life is increasingly suffused with a chaotic and inhuman vitality, Garrett comes to embody the social function he represents. However, the suspicion that the poem's anonymous and impersonal narrative voice maintains a certain ironic distance from Garrett's supreme act of self-constitution is wittily suggested at the conclusion of this process ('He had come to Sumner then, mind full of French he never used, everything equipped to be that rare thing – a sane assassin sane assassin sane assassin sane assassin sane assassin sane') where the manic repetition of the phrase denoting the lawman's heroic façade ('sane assassin') leads it to blur imperceptibly into its opposite ('insane assassin'), thereby exposing the violent origins of Garrett's absolute vision of justice (*BTK*, 29).

The crucial difference between Billy's and Garrett's perceptions of the world is rendered vividly in a key early lyric ('MMMMMMMM mm thinking / moving across the world on horses ... / that is why I can watch the stomach of clocks / shift their wheels and pins into each other / and emerge living, for hours (*BTK*, 11)). Much of Billy's personality is captured in the curious opening line, which enforces a momentary disjunction between a pre-personal mode of bodily plenitude ('mmm') and the mental representations ('thinking') that we use to organise these singular flows. The impression that the poem is narrated primarily from Billy's point-of-view is bolstered by its repeated use of verb-phrases and participles: Billy, after all, is always in transit, continually being changed by the landscape that he

changes; and it is Billy who decomposes forms and functions into their vital 'living' forces. However, Ondaatje's elliptical syntax and his unsettling of pronominal reference challenge the assumption that the poem is wholly focalised by Billy's consciousness; the poem resembles a field of force within which competing expressions of human responsiveness share a common space. Only when the poem's angle of vision is widened beyond Billy's immediate point-of-view does its rhetorical structure become clear. As the break between the first and second lines implies, the crucial dichotomy in the poem is between 'thinking' (a facility usually associated with Garrett) and 'moving' (a participle attuned to the erratic and unstable figure of Billy). These opening lines momentarily superimpose the image of each protagonist upon his rival; both men, like their horses, have their bodies 'split at the edge of their necks'. This insistent doubling of perspective reaches its apotheosis in the poem's middle section: both outlaw and lawman are prepared to 'eliminate much' in order to secure their reputations in the world of men, while the more general observation that 'one must eliminate much / that is one turns when the bullet leaves you / walk off see none of the thrashing' anticipates the later image of Garrett who '[h]ad the ability to kill someone on the street walk back and finish a joke' (*BTK*, 28). These lines also possess a stark premonitory quality: here Billy imaginatively projects himself into Garrett's consciousness and confronts for the first time the retributive force that will kill him. This act of projection is suggested by the poem's sudden shift into the conditional mode: if Billy, like Garrett, possessed the blithe moral certainty of a 'newsman's brain', he would be able to discern a transparent design at the heart of human 'morals' and reconcile his fundamental beliefs with the imperatives of the social machine. Only someone who perceives no connection between the mind that judges and the body that suffers could believe so absolutely in the 'morals of newspaper or gun' and perceive no ethical distinction between the two.

The complex interdependence between outlaw and lawman is a recurring theme of the poem. Perpetually enslaved to his

own chaotic drives, Billy is driven, like Garrett, to make his own vision the standard by which the world is judged (*BTK*, 74). Implicit in this stance is a longing for an obliteration of personality ('I am here on the edge of sun / that would ignite me'). Billy both desires and fears a return to inhuman and pre-reflective life and this ambivalence becomes more pronounced as the poem progresses. At points Billy wants to become 'pure verb', in Seamus Heaney's exacting phrase: a pure principle of movement and perception irresistibly attuned to a world of becoming and change.[17] Yet in other places Billy harbours a dreadful fear of change ('My eyes are burning from the pain of change'): his violence seems motivated by a terror of losing control over his image and identity (*BTK*, 68). Poignantly aware that his subjectivity is continually upon the brink of dissolution, Billy finds himself immersed within and terrified by a world of changing appearances that reflects back to him the image of his own mortality.

Some of the most remarkable poems in the sequence register the diffuse play of feeling characteristic of those moments when Billy perceives his world dissolving into flows of affect and desire ('The acute nerves spark / on the periphery of our bodies ... / The mind's invisible blackout the intricate never / The body's waiting rut' (*BTK*, 72)). Fascinated and appalled by the intuition of a mode of feeling that propels him towards the 'periphery' of his own body, Billy strives to arrest the dispersal of the self by becoming the director of his own biography: the creative 'eye' that confers shape and coherence upon the scattered details of his own experience. His vision attempts to become the define perspective of the poem: 'I am very still / I take in all the angles of the room' (*BTK*, 21). Gazing at the reclining body of Angela D, Billy's point of view begins to mimic the abrupt and inhuman movement of the cinematic camera (*BTK*, 16).

The threat posed to Billy's fragile self-image by flows of affect that push him to the periphery of his own body is intensified by his perception of sexual difference. Because sexual passion involves the coupling and merging of bodies, it places Billy's already perilous sense of self under sustained pressure.

This pressure leads by degrees to the emergence of sexual fear, which is expressed in his images of the alluring, but implicitly deathly, force of femininity. The images dominate Billy's two memories of lovemaking with Angela D ('Tilts back to fall / black hair swivelling off her ... / later my hands cracked in love juice / fingers paralysed by it arthritic / these beautiful fingers I couldn't move / faster than a crippled witch now' (*BTK*, 16)).

Far from confirming Billy's sense of virile masculinity, his encounter with Angela D brings his self-image to a point of crisis. The perceived castrating power of female subjectivity dominates this scene: Angela D's gaunt body spits 'electric' off the sheets onto his arm; the 'bright bush' of her sex jumps startlingly into the centre of his field of vision; while the ecstatic force of her body almost breaks off his fingers. The symbolic significance of this last detail is heavily underscored: his hands 'cracked in love juice', the 'beautiful fingers' that express Billy's expansive outlaw nature become 'paralysed' and useless. Momentarily deprived of a relation to the source of his vitality, Billy's image is insistently feminised: 'I couldn't move / faster than a crippled witch now'. This unexpected reversal of roles and identities reaches its apotheosis in the moment when Angela D 'hooks in two' and 'covers' him. Here lovemaking and gunslinging become inextricably entwined: but Billy is unmanned, his hand 'locked', his prone and helpless profile an eerie premonition of the figure Garrett will gun down in the climatic episode at Maxwell's ranch.

Billy finds sanctuary from his turbulent relationship with Angela D at the Chisum Ranch. The ranch represents an idyllic space in Billy's imagination: it is the still centre of his turning world, an environment in which he may briefly escape Garrett's remorseless pursuit and the 'flashy hawk' of the noontime sun that threatens to burn him back to bare and elemental nature (*BTK*, 26). The allure of the Chisum Ranch for Billy is indistinguishable from the ministering maternal figure of Sallie Chisum; Sallie shelters him from the inhuman ferocity of the western sun by leading him into cool enclosed spaces where he might regain his strength and hold his demons at bay. Ondaatje's prose

description of these scenes reflects the restorative calm of Sallie's presence; its rangy, unemphatic style is a world away from the delirious frenzy of the poem's early lyrics:

> She would get up and after a breakfast that she would eat wandering around the house slowly, she would begin the work ... She left the paraffin in the lamps; instead had had John build shutters for every door and window, every hole in the wall. So that at eleven in the morning all she did was close and lock them all until the house was silent and dark blue with sunless quiet. (*BTK*, 33)

But Billy will be spared neither Garrett's relentless attentions nor the sun's despoliation. The two forces come together in the surreal passage recounting Garrett's transportation of Billy and the remains of his outlaw band across New Mexico towards the nearest legal authority. Strapped and handcuffed to his horse, Billy is exposed to the midday sun; now the dissolution of his personality into the inhuman flux of life is finally visited upon him:

> The brain juice began to swell up. You could see the bones and grey now. The sun sat back and watched while the juice evaporated. By now the bone was dull white, all dry ... lobules gyres notches arcs tracts fissures roots' white insulation of dead seven years cells clinging things rubbing them off on the tracts of spine down the cool precise fingers went into the cistern of bladder down the last hundred miles in a jerk breaking through my sacs of sperm got my cock in the cool fingers pulled it back up and carried it pulling pulling flabby as smoke up the path his arm had rested in and widened. (*BTK*, 76–7)

In contrast with the way in which Billy's life will subsequently be reconstructed from its scant empirical details into a full-blown Western mythos, he is gradually stripped of his subjectivity and returned to pure elemental being. Billy's delirious account of his sunstroke represents the experience as a bizarre solar sexual assault during which his body is invaded, broken apart and reduced to a series of singular flows. His ordeal recalls what Deleuze and Guattari call a becoming-molecular:

Billy's image is deconstituted into a pure flow of intensities and libidinal energies.[18] What we see in this symbolically suggestive scene is a vision of life as what one part of Billy would like it to be: a life of deterritorialised desire and proliferating connections between intensities. By the conclusion of this passage Billy has metamorphosed beyond the human to become a continuum of pure sensation: 'I was drowned, locked inside my skin sensitive as an hour old animal, could feel everything, I could hear everything on my skin, as I sat, like a great opaque ostrich egg on the barebacked horse' (*BTK*, 77).

Billy's ecstatic decomposition in the sun's glare can be read as a symbolic death of the self; his vision of life as pure intensity brings the image of the 'human' to a point of absolute crisis. Certainly Billy's poetic image now becomes even more unstable; from this point he will be pushed to the margins of the poem as events speed towards the climactic shoot-out. One reason why Billy's experience on the plains is curiously *beyond* interpretation is that Ondaatje's writing progressively breaks down the distinction between signifier and signified or event and meaning. What makes this passage difficult to read is that Ondaatje no longer conceives of language as if it expresses the point-of-view of a particular subject or consciousness; instead his writing retreats from the logic of representation to immerse itself in the flow of singularities and affect from which all conceptual distinctions emerge. To 'interpret' this section is to try to make sense of Billy's perception of the western landscape when the text's real interest is in the multiplicity of flows from which perception is organised. Hence Ondaatje's prose-poetry gestures simultaneously to the birth and the limit of subjectivity and sense, as Billy is released into the proliferation of intensities from which these ideas come into being.

Ondaatje's reference beyond representation to the forces that compose it also inflects the poem's critique of historiography. One of the primary functions of historiography is to establish points of connection between different modes of historical emergence by organising them according to the logic of particular conceptual formations. *Billy the Kid*, on the other

hand, continually dissolves historiography into the various styles of perception that constitute it in the first place. The pages immediately before and after the scene of Billy's death present a shifting mosaic of textual sources, all of which have contributed to the meaning of Billy's history as it has accrued during the intervening years, none of which has the authority to bring a definitive image of the outlaw into focus. This ironic, and occasionally parodic, collection of 'historical' documents incorporates several different styles of historical inscription. It includes Billy's apocryphal jailhouse interview with the *Texas Star* which, in its playful allusion to the contemporary film-maker 'Mr Cassavetes', emphasises once more the ongoing cinematic rewriting of American frontier history; Sallie Chisum's generous, albeit unfocused, anecdotal recollections of her former friend; and a fantasy romance entitled 'Billy the Kid and The Princess' that transforms Billy into the dashing gentleman hero of sentimental fiction ('Once more Chivoto, you have saved my life, this time from that cougar. You have won my love!' (*BTK*, 102)). Ondaatje comically illustrates the ceaseless reconstruction of Billy's historical image in the ballad that brings his story to a tentative conclusion. With its stuttering rhythm and bathetic rhyme pattern, this song represents a first faltering attempt to reconstitute the outlaw as an historical object; such reinvention, as the ponderous pairing of 'Texas Star' and 'camera' attests, is already ineluctably marked by the commercial forces soon to remake Billy's identity in the popular imagination:

> I got the bullets, cleaned him up
> sold them to the Texas Star
> They weighted them, put them in a pile
> took pictures with a camera.

One of the principal ironies generated by Ondaatje's emphasis upon the cinematic and historiographical reconstruction of Billy's image is that Billy's final moments are marked by his despairing attempt to become once more the director of his own life story. His extended death scene even borrows from the format of a movie script: 'Sound up' (*BTK*, 90). Yet

as if in anticipation of the historical fate that will befall him, Bully is pushed throughout this sequence to the margins of his own narrative. Now it is Garrett who occupies the centre of the stage ('NOW dead centre in the square is Garrett with Poe'), while Billy is relegated to a shadowy background presence (*BTK*, 94). The establishing shot depicting Pete Maxwell's Ranch is accompanied by a voiceover inflected by the tone of one of Billy's early lyrics ('Mmmm'); but the need for Billy to project himself into Garrett's consciousness is long past: the lawman is about to bring the curtain down on Billy's entire existence (*BTK*, 92). Crucially, Billy's murder is presented as an existential limit and a symbolic metamorphosis. Made 'manic' by Garrett's intervention, Billy breaks through the frame of the window, symbolically shattering the mode of mimesis that underpins historiographical narrative. At this point Billy becomes precisely what can no longer be represented within the historical horizon of Ondaatje's poem:

> NOW dead centre in the square is Garrett with Poe –
> hands in back pockets – argues, nodding his head and then
> ALL TURNING as the naked arm, the arm from the body,
> breaks through the window. The window – what remains
> between the splits – reflecting all the moving too.
>
>   Guitterrez goes to hold the arm but it is manic, breaks
> her second finger. His veins that controlled triggers – now
> tearing all they touch. (*BTK*, 94)

Billy's image disintegrates, in his final moments, into the intensities that compose it. What we see through Billy's eyes is a vision of pure singularity as the room dissolves into the heat and light of 'thousands / of perfect sun balls' and perception splinters into waves of colour and affect:

> Garrett's voice going Billy Billy
> and the other two dancing circles
> saying we got him we got him the little shrunk bugger
> …
> it is my brain coming out like red grass
> this breaking where red things wade (*BTK*, 95)

Even as the poem narrates the 'breaking' of Billy's image it slips away from its historical moment to assume the vantage point of Ondaatje's own time. What would we find, Ondaatje ponders, if we exhumed Billy's leavings and exposed them to our contemporary gaze: buck teeth, Garrett's solitary bullet, a pair of handcuffs 'holding ridiculously the fine ankles bones' (*BTK*, 97)? All that remains of Billy the Kid is a scattering of historical traces bereft of a narrative that might establish their value and significance. Yet if the abrupt juxtaposition of historical epochs serves to underline the radical incommensurability of different forms of historical consciousness, the sequence also identifies an implicit connection between past and present in the mode of perception common to outlaw and poet. The superimposition of Ondaatje's image onto Billy's own recurs at several points in the sequence; one of its most suggestive instances appears when a figure we assume to be Billy reflects upon a landscape of 'slow moving animals' and the 'acute nerves' that stretch between different kinds of life ('The street of the slow moving animals / while the sun drops in perfect verticals / no wider than boots … / mapping my thinking going its own way / like light wet glasses drifting on polished wood' (*BTK*, 72)).

The figure of the outlaw alone 'with the range for everything' is displaced almost imperceptibly into the image of the writer tracing a pencil across a 'soft blue paper notebook' (*BTK*, 72). This conflation of images is repeated in the passage that concludes the poem where an ambiguous reference to 'smoke' – is this cigarette or gunsmoke? – elides the two figures once again:

> It is now early morning, was a bad night. The hotel room seems large. The morning sun has concentrated all the cigarette smoke so no one can see it hanging in pillars or sliding along the roof like amoeba. In the bathroom, I wash the loose nicotine out of my mouth. I smell the smoke still in my shirt. (*BTK*, 105)

The insistent rhyming of Ondaatje and Billy the Kid expresses, at one level, the writer's wry insight into the status of all our historical knowledge: the meaning of an historical event

arrives from the future and the contexts in which it is read and interpreted. The connection between the two figures is further reinforced by the implicit punning correspondence between 'corpse' and 'corpus' that underlies the sequence. Although some commentators have taken Ondaatje's coupling of poet and outlaw as evidence of his desire to establish a romantic portrait of the artist as a social outsider, his real interest in Billy the Kid lay in the evocation of a molecular vision unconstrained by social norms or a moral image of life. In his recreation of outlaw consciousness, Ondaatje developed for the first time a singular conception of the aesthetic as a force with the potential to free us from the habitual in order that we might rethink the genesis of the real. This singular idea of the aesthetic, and the conflict it charts between molecular life and molar authority, was to become the central motif of his first novel, *Coming Through Slaughter*.

Coming Through Slaughter

Although it has yet to attract the degree of critical attention paid to Ondaatje's most recent work, *Coming Through Slaughter* (1976), Ondaatje's first novel, marks a key stage in his literary development. Drawing once more upon the conflict between molecular and molar life explored in *Billy the Kid*, and anticipating the imaginative recreation of civic cultural history in *In the Skin of a Lion*, *Coming Through Slaughter* represents Ondaatje's most far-reaching examination of both the claims and the limits of art and the relationship between art and life. Nowhere else in Ondaatje's oeuvre is the power of art imaginatively to transcend historical consciousness depicted with more force or originality; and nowhere else does this power lead to greater pain or despair. Whether Ondaatje identifies with or disavows Buddy Bolden's 'extremist art' will be a matter for each reader to judge: the continuous verb form of the novel's title suspends the experience it describes perilously between redemption and catastrophe.[1] While not universally shared by other critics, my own view that *Coming Through Slaughter* bids an agonised farewell to the emancipatory promise of a purely singular vision has in one sense the weight of history on its side: the shift of interest in Ondaatje's subsequent fiction from the nature of molecular perception towards the (re)construction of public history underscores this shift in perspective. According to this itinerary the novel represents the bridge between two distinct literary modes: the transition from one to the other became crucial to the type of artist Ondaatje wanted himself to

be. Much more was at stake for Ondaatje in the story of Buddy Bolden, then, than the redemption of a creative talent now almost entirely lost from historical view; *Coming Through Slaughter* represents instead his final rupture with an entire vision of life.

Coming Through Slaughter takes for its subject the legend of Buddy Bolden, the *fin-de-siècle* musician and band-leader whose collapse into insanity in 1905 made him a resonant romantic symbol of the first Jazz Age. Ondaatje conceived the novel, he later recounted in an interview, 'when he came across the cryptic newspaper reference: "Buddy Bolden, who became a legend when he went berserk in a parade"'.[2] He was attracted to Bolden's 'legend' precisely because of its 'unfinished' or dubiously historical quality: 'I knew very little about Bolden. I'm really drawn to unfinished stories. There's all those empty spaces you can put stuff in'.[3] What drew Ondaatje to the various 'empty spaces' in Bolden's story is the opportunity they afford him simultaneously to consecrate and recreate a lost cultural experience. The tension between these two impulses helps to account for the double register upon which his novel plays. For if *Coming Through Slaughter* is, in one of its aspects, a marvellously intimate reconstruction of the everyday culture of black American life at the turn of the last century, it also seeks to evoke, in its portrait of Bolden's nomadic existence within and beyond the borders of that culture, a mode of being that transcends social and cultural relations and refuses to conform to a fixed image of life.

These preliminary remarks are intended to retain a slight polemical inflection: my claim will be that *Coming Through Slaughter* is, despite its relative critical neglect, in many ways an exemplary post-colonial work. This view derives a degree of support from recent developments in literary and post-colonial criticism. In his innovative analysis of contemporary post-colonial discourse, Peter Hallward argues that far from presenting what he calls a 'specific' vision of individuality and difference – a vision of life or subjectivity mediated by historical consciousness or representation – much post-colonial writing moves instead towards a 'singular' or wholly immanent conception of

reality. Whereas a 'specific' mode or poetics operates through the 'active negotiation of relations and the deliberate taking of sides, choices and risks, in a domain and under constraints that are external to these takings', Hallward continues, the term 'singular' describes

> configurations or procedures that are exceptional or solitary in the strictest sense – configurations or procedures that are truly one of a kind, that must ultimately be thought as self-constituent, as self-conditioning and self-regulating. As in every singular configuration, logics defined here as postcolonial will eventually defy modulation or mediation. As in every singular configuration, a distinctly postcolonial procedure will operate without criteria external to its operation. And ultimately, it will act even in the absence of *others* as such. Singular configurations replace the interpretation *of* reality with an immanent participation in its production or creation: in the end, at the limit of 'absolute postcoloniality', there will be nothing left, nothing outside itself, to which it could be specific.[4]

Hallward's notion of a singular vision of experience nicely encapsulates key aspects of Buddy Bolden's art and personality. The concept of singularity allows us to approach Bolden's diremption of his own mode of feeling from collective social life while anticipating key elements of the new jazz lexicon that he created. In passage after passage Ondaatje returns to the idea that Bolden's inauguration of a new jazz syntax expresses both his need actively to create the medium of his own expression and his intuition that the power of life appears most potently in the dissolution of self-consciousness and the liberation of desire from its habitual and normative representation. The fact that Bolden's singular aesthetic trajectory ends calamitously in madness and silence provides a crucial corrective to some of the novel's more utopian readings. It also offers a clue to Ondaatje's genuinely ambivalent attitude towards the relationship between art and social and historical experience. On the one hand, *Coming Through Slaughter* underscores once more Ondaatje's conviction that the creative power of being is expressed most powerfully

in those deterritorialised movements of perception that dissolve the 'real' by returning us to the impersonal and non-organic life of things. Art that is able to suspend worldly relations and imagine life as an experience of singularity and non-relation is uniquely well placed to express this creative power; it is therefore no coincidence that Ondaatje's most developed vision of singular being takes an artist as its subject. Yet on the other hand, Ondaatje's work is haunted by the danger posed to life by the renunciation of social and historical consciousness. It is this ambivalence that determines *Coming Through Slaughter* as Ondaatje's key transitional work. The novel's thoroughgoing subtraction of the aesthetic from social and historical experience enables us momentarily to conceive of life beyond the conventional representations we impose upon it. But its depiction of the calamitous existential losses precipitated by the dissolution of subjective into singular life suggests that the singular provides no coherent position from which to *intervene* within the specific field of forces that determine the limits of subjectivity in a particular time and place.

Read in these terms, *Coming Through Slaughter* reveals itself to be a highly nuanced critique of any simple post-colonial claim to autonomy. Its awareness of the political problem of seeking recognition within an already established discourse also draws upon a tradition of thought critical of the Western logos. Thus the conflict inherent to the novel between singular aesthetic vision and historical consciousness is central to a Western philosophical debate concerning the proper relationship between art and life. This debate finds its *locus classicus* in Nietzsche's *The Birth of Tragedy out of the Spirit of Music*. It is here Nietzsche isolates two mutually antagonistic creative tendencies, which he names the 'Apollonian' and the 'Dionysiac', that embody two wholly different expressions of life. As we recall from Chapter 1, the Dionysiac spirit embodies a state of chaotic and ecstatic energy which destroys the cultivated individuation of the human subject and reunites us with the 'innermost core' of nature.[5] The cult of Dionysius celebrates sexuality, unconscious desires and the amorality of natural forces; amidst

its orgiastic rites the individual experiences the complete break-down of its autonomous subjectivity as its 'self' is dispersed into a series of libidinal flows and investments. Crucially for Nietz-sche this Dionysiac spirit finds its most powerful expression in the narcotic and atavistic rhythms of music, which reawaken the Dionysiac impulse at the core of natural being by seducing the listener into a 'complete forgetting of the self'.[6] Apollonian art, by contrast, provides concepts and representations by which we can structure these anarchic and pre-reflective forces into ideas and images; yet the identification of being with representation threatens to hold us apart from the creative power of nature and petrify life within dead forms. Consequently, Nietzsche argues, it is only by developing Apollonian aesthetic forms capable simultaneously of *evoking* and *structuring* Dionysiac energies that we can apprehend the creative power of life. A truly Apol-lonian art enables us to think the force, possibility and limits of the human while establishing a 'restraining boundary' that prevents our 'wilder impulses' from 'becoming pathological' and collapsing identity into the flux of Dionysiac becoming.[7]

Nietzsche's remarks have a creative afterlife in the pages of *Coming Through Slaughter*. Ondaatje takes seriously Nietz-sche's belief that Dionysiac art – an art that demands we become one with the flow of difference and becoming that constitutes life – enables us to expand our perception beyond the human through a confrontation with the forces that compose us. Bold-en's music effects a Dionysiac liberation from subjectivity by transforming the point-of-view from which we judge and order life. His art suspends self-consciousness and unhinges time by dissolving experience into its virtual image or flow of becoming-life. But Bolden's openness to the pure event of difference comes at far too high a price: his commitment to molecular perception destroys his sense of himself as a social being and culminates in a psychotic break with the human world. This is Ondaatje's Nietz-schean lesson: without the interposition of an aesthetic form within which being can reflect upon its own self-differentiation, the power of Dionysic revelation destroys the very life it seeks to preserve. In Ondaatje's allegory of the creative process his

novel *is* this aesthetic form. By moving fluidly between imaginative positions within and beyond Bolden's angle of vision, *Coming Through Slaughter* manages simultaneously to expand perception beyond its human home while critically examining what this process involves.

The creative tension Nietzsche identifies between becoming and being resonates throughout *Coming Through Slaughter*. It first appears in Ondaatje's artful arrangement of textual material during the novel's earliest moments. The book begins, in effect, before a word is written with the reproduction of a grainy photograph of Bolden's band taken in 1905: six young men stare out impassively through and beyond us towards the history that will define them. The unscripted appearance of an image bereft of an establishing narrative or frame hints at the broader antagonism between historicity and context that the novel explores. The photograph tentatively evokes a cultural milieu which might pull the fragmentary details of Bolden's life into focus; but the style of Ondaatje's narrative renders progressively more elliptical Bolden's relation to the world this image describes. This equivocal relationship between image and discourse is accentuated by the novel's epigraph, which presents graphic representations of three sonographs or 'pictures of dolphin sounds made by a machine that is more sensitive than the human ear'. What interests Ondaatje in these sonographs is their potentially dual function: the images simultaneously *identify* each dolphin and transmit details of its *location*. The implicit correspondence these images maintain between a mode of expression, a type of nature and an experience of space crystallises Ondaatje's concern with the relationship between singular being and historical experience. Each of these images symbolises a possible approach to the question of representation; each approach will produce a completely different image of Bolden's art and culture. The top right sonograph records a 'whistle': a 'pure' sound that promises to 'identify each dolphin as well as its location'. This image presents one of the novel's main temptations: the belief that by identifying aspects of Bolden's history, character and art we will be able to see *through* him – in both senses of the word – in

order to reconstruct the world from which he came. The top left sonograph depicts a 'squawk': one of those 'common emotional expressions' whose 'many frequencies or pitches' are 'vocalized simultaneously'. This sound, which will come to evoke the pitch of Bolden's trumpet, represents a very different style of being: a singular style which becomes what it is through the process of its own self-differentiation from the world around it (*CTS*, 137). There is not, according to this singular style, an identity that *then* expresses itself in sound; the style of expression produces the mode of identity it describes. The middle sonograph shows a dolphin making both kinds of signal simultaneously in a wave of sound combining 'echolocation clicks' or 'sharp, multi-frequency sounds' and signature whistles. A phenomenon reproduced as a mere natural curiosity ('No one knows how a dolphin makes both whistles and echolocation clicks simultaneously') is, in fact, central to Ondaatje's narrative method: it describes the double register upon which representations of culture and place encounter a mode of becoming irreducible to historical consciousness. Jazz improvisation is for Ondaatje the very image of this double register: Bolden's music has no form or being prior to its performance; but once performed it can be repeated, identified and turned into a cultural commodity. But although the fluid dynamic of jazz may have solidified into a metaphor for one version of the modern black experience, it still retains its power to expose form to the multiple modes of its emergence. Jazz therefore embodies a power to think life differently: a singular style that steadfastly resists incorporation into a merely collective or historical point-of-view.

The double register upon which the novel plays announces itself in its opening sentences, which simultaneously introduce and suspend the worldly relations of Bolden's time and place.[8] It is also registered in the novel's initial phrase 'His geography', which plays off the broader cultural context of Bolden's biography against his own imaginative relation to his history and location (*CTS*, 2). The paragraph accompanying this phrase refuses to establish a relationship between these unsynchronised modes of perception: the coordinates of each

andscape are erased before they can be mapped. Our attention is deflected instead from turn-of-the-century New Orleans to its contemporary rebranding as a tourist experience: the streets of Bolden's city have since been 'obliterated by brand names' (*CTS*, 2). This commodification of cultural space is synonymous with the commodification of cultural history: 'This district, the homes and stores, are a mile or so from the streets made marble by jazz' (*CTS*, 2). The marginal position of Bolden's Storyville within the cultural iconography of New Orleans is represented as a form of historical dispossession; there is now 'little recorded history' to reveal its image to our gaze. Unattuned to the culture of the printed text, history was 'slow' in Storyville: the little that is known of Bolden's life drifts down to us in 'fragments' (*CTS*, 2). To enter this lost world and encounter the art that it made possible, we need to disrupt our conventional notion of time by opening ourselves to the flow of singularities that generates the historical sense.

The novel's style and structure rework our historical sense by returning to particular moments of perception. The dissolution of historical narrative into the flow of affects and percepts that make it possible is dramatised by the sheer difficulty of writing the life of a character that appears unable to maintain any relation to historical consciousness. From its earliest pages *Coming Through Slaughter* suggests that Bolden can never be represented within a narrative history; his nature unfolds itself upon an entirely different plane of becoming. Bolden's resistance to being read as a symbol of his cultural moment and location is implied by the sheer volatility of his image; as a 'character' he is nomadic, atopic, always out of his proper place. He is quickly distinguished by his inability to organise spatial relations or accommodate himself to social roles and conventions: 'Bolden could not put things in their place' (*CTS*, 9). His subjectivity is presented instead as a movement of singularity or non-relation that dissolves the world into pure creative intensity:

> But his own mind was helpless against every moment's headline. He did nothing but leap into the mass of changes and explore them and all the tiny facets so that eventually

he was almost completely governed by fears of certainty. He distrusted it in anyone but Nora for there it went to the spine, and yet he attacked it again and again in her, cruelly, hating it, the sure lanes of the probable. Breaking chairs and windows glass doors in fury at her certain answers. (*CTS*, 9–10)

Like Billy the Kid in those moments when he indulges his deathly fantasy of inhabiting a 'newsman's brain', Bolden's vitality is attenuated whenever his life is estranged from the mode of its becoming. Consequently his 'fears of certainty' hold him at a crucial distance from self-consciousness, which, far from guaranteeing his identity in all its subjective difference, is experienced by him as the repressive limit of instinct and creativity. In these lines Bolden embodies the process of singularisation itself: a process of 'becoming-unrelated' and 'unlimited' in which the subject immerses itself in the flow of perception from which all actual experience is derived.[9] A mind that is 'helpless against every moment's headline' has no sympathy with the historical imagination; it dissolves time into the molecular differences that constitute life before it is extended into an organised system of relations. The radical incommensurability of Bolden's nature with time, representation and history is prefigured by his resistance to the specular image upon which all representation depends (*CTS*, 10).

The emancipation of Bolden's nature from normal worldly relations is symbolised by the central conceit of jazz improvisation. The process of improvisation is crucial to the novel because it takes us to the very *limit* of representation by breaking musical form down into the play of singularities – such as breath, notation, phrasing, rhythm and tone – from which it is composed. Improvisation discloses the *virtual* image of music: the interplay between difference and actualisation that brings every musical 'world' into being. Improvisation only exists as the manifestation of a virtual condition – the modes and progressions that it is possible to vary – but this virtual condition is at the same time the precondition of representation in general. Bolden's style of performance embraces improvisation to expose what is at stake

in representation itself by creating affects that transform our perception of what form and narrative can be. The connection between improvisation and the opening of perception beyond itself is established by the first image of Bolden at play:

> He was the best and the loudest and most loved jazzman of his time, but never professional in the brain. Unconcerned with the crack of the lip he threw out and held immense notes, could reach a force on the first note that attacked the ear. He was obsessed with the magic of air, those smells that turned neuter as they revolved in his lung then spat out in the chosen key. The way the side of his mouth would drag a net of air in and dress it in notes and make it last and last, yearning to leave it up there in the sky like air transformed into cloud. He could see the air, could tell where it was freshest in a room by the colour. (*CTS*, 8)

In scenes like these we witness an aesthetic becoming that offers us neither a fixed image of art nor a new artistic subjectivity. Instead we see the 'becoming-imperceptible' of the actual world: the decomposition of the perceived present into the virtual flow of affect. Form is broken down here into the 'force' of particular notes that play upon the edge of form before they are organised into a coherent and ordered narrative. This singular trajectory connects Bolden once more with the image of Billy the Kid: his mode is spontaneous, nomadic and pre-reflective ('but never professional in the brain'); his style of perception, like Billy's, is immediate to and constitutive of whatever it perceives; while his point-of-view repeatedly widens to embrace the impersonal perspective of inhuman experience ('And so arrived amateur and accidental with the band on the stage of Masonic Hall, bursting into jazz, hurdle after hurdle … as he could see them, their bursts of air were animals fighting in the room' (*CTS*, 8)).

The jazz sections of the novel do not describe a character who simply abides in the world; they show a figure that imperceptibly *becomes* the world by taking it into himself and remaking it in his own singular image. Notes burn in the air but are then

swallowed by Bolden's body; his perception expands by becoming one with what it encompasses. Eventually Bolden's performance effaces the distinction between the subject who perceives and the objective world: 'The music was coarse and tough, immediate, dated in half an hour, was about bodies in the river, knives, lovepains, cockiness. Up there on stage he was showing all the possibilities in the middle of the story' (*CTS*, 41).

Bolden's art is tormented by the singularity of the aesthetic; it liberates affections and perceptions from their conventional representation. Through his 'coarse' and 'immediate' style the 'whole plot of song' dissolves into the play of its virtual possibility: 'Up there on the stage he was showing us all the possibilities in the middle of the story'. Yet what might be apprehended as mere anarchy is, in fact, a disciplined reinvention of form; a quest for the 'right accidental notes' that might open experience up to the multiple modes of its becoming ('But there was a discipline, it was just that we didn't understand … He would be describing something in 27 ways. There was pain and gentleness everything jammed into each number' (*CTS*, 35)).

Bolden's music is not 'about' his experience in any conventional sense; it transcends representation to occupy an unqualified level 'immediately on top of his own life' (*CTS*, 27). Ondaatje's highly stylised portrait of Bolden's jazz presents the becoming-singular of a subject increasingly liberated from external frames of reference; the power of Bolden's performances reconfigures the known world by remodelling time upon its own internal sequence of phrases.[10] Unlike the 'clear forms' of Bolden's musician rival John Robichaux, which 'dominated' their audience by putting their musical emotions 'into patterns which a listening crowd had to follow' (*CTS*, 97), Bolden's improvisations substitute intensities and affects for narrative structure in order to disclose the raw force of sensation itself:

> When I played parades we would be going down Canal Street and at each intersection people would hear just the fragment I happened to be playing and it would fade as I went further down Canal. They would not be there to hear the end of phrases, Robichaux's arches. I wanted them to

be able to come in where they pleased and leave when they pleased and somehow hear the germs of the start and all the possible endings at whatever point in the music that I had reached *then*. Like your radio without the beginnings or endings. The right ending is an open door you can't see too far out of. It can mean exactly the opposite of what you are thinking. (*CTS*, 98)

Bolden's molecular mode is, however, challenged in *Coming Through Slaughter* by molar formations that seek to regulate its force and ascribe it a specific place within the broader social economy. This challenge first manifests itself in the relationship between Bolden and his policeman friend Webb. By the time Webb appears upon Nora's doorstep at the beginning of the novel, Bolden's nomadic nature has already asserted itself: he has managed to 'get lost' for '5 or 6 months' without excuse or explanation (*CTS*, 13). Webb's role is to track Bolden down, establish the reasons for his disappearance and resituate him within the 'web' of a narrative history. To allow Bolden to wander free of his place, his past and his sense of social relationships is, Webb argues, to connive in the destruction of his entire personality: 'He won't last by himself Nora, he'll fall apart. He's not safe by himself' (*CTS*, 14). Webb sees what no one else perceives: Bolden's abandonment of his home place represents a profound gesture of self-erasure, a deterritorialising movement beyond relation that removes any trace of subjective coherence (*CTS*, 17).

Like Pat Garrett in *Billy the Kid*, Webb represents the molar principles of law, history and social consciousness. He controls social situations by defining the power relations interior to them: in their youth together 'it was Webb who was the public figure, Bolden the side-kick, the friend who stayed around' (*CTS*, 33). Despite his initial subjection to Webb, Bolden labours to develop a creative self unconstrained by social relations. The difference in perception between the two men is figured as a difference between *discourse* and *singularity*. This distinction emerges most strikingly in a scene where Webb's relentless interrogation of Bolden's history and circumstances is intercut with Bolden's molecular mode of vision:

While Webb is talking to Crawley, this is what Bolden sees:

> The woman is cutting carrots. Each carrot is split into 6 or 7 pieces. The knife slides through and hits the wood table that they will eat off later. He is watching the coincidence of her fingers and the carrots. It began with the colour of the fingers and then the slight veins on the carrot magnified themselves to his eyes. In this area of sight the fingers have separated themselves from her body and move in a unity of their own that stops at the sleeve and bangle. As with all skills he watches for it to fail. If she thinks what she is doing she will lose control. He knows that the only way to catch a fly for instance is to move the hand without the brain telling it to move fast, interfering. (*CTS*, 28)

In this scene Bolden does not envisage the actions of an independent subject; he sees a series of actions that express a world in the process of being formed. Far from perceiving the self as a discrete and autonomous identity, Bolden encourages us to see the body as most authentically itself when it is liberated from self-consciousness. Because self-expression can be synonymous with the *suspension* of consciousness, the earlier narrative suggestion that 'perhaps the only clue to Bolden's body was in Webb's brain' should be treated with a degree of circumspection (*CTS*, 17). The essence of Bolden's nature does not disclose itself in an idea, memory or image; it lies in his capacity to transcend the limits of the autonomous self and accept the ceaseless self-differentiation of the world as its immediate element. Bolden reveals this potential for creative self-transcendence in his wanderings across the liminal space of Shell Beach where he 'collected and was filled by every noise as if luscious poison entering the ear like a lady's tongue thickening it and blocking it until he couldn't be entered anymore' (*CTS*, 38–9). Bolden *becomes* what he *is* through the dissolution of the given; in his wanderings and musical performances he is reborn, like Dionysius, as a 'fat full king' (*CTS*, 39).

Where Bolden desires to become what he is though the dissolution of the given, Webb tries to account for him through

the relations he maintains with his environment and his cultural milieu. In this sense, Webb's attempts to recreate Bolden's place within a shifting network of social allegiances and affiliations casts him in the traditional role of an omniscient narrator: 'As it was he was trying to place himself casually in a mental position that was so high and irrelevant he hoped to stumble on the clues that were left by Bolden's disappearance' (*CTS*, 17). *Coming Through Slaughter* is therefore also a novel about the politics of representation that fluctuates between Bolden's unfolding story and Webb's fixation with narrative closure. The incompatibility between Webb's narrative perspective and Bolden's singular mode of becoming is heavily underscored: 'He came here', Bolden later complains of Webb, 'and placed my past and future on this table like a road' (*CTS*, 88). Bolden's hostility to the linear imperative of Webb's narrative account might be inferred from his jazz aesthetic; elsewhere Webb's inability to perceive the truth of Bolden's experience becomes one of the novel's staple themes. Perhaps because all biographical writing contains elements of detective fiction, the recapitulative form of *Coming Through Slaughter* seems often to collude with Webb's point-of-view; nevertheless the style of Ondaatje's narrative also registers Bolden's resistance to such discursive enclosure. This resistance emerges in those moments – such as the juxta-position of pages of contextual narrative prose with moments of charged lyric intensity or the novel's persistent fluctuation between first- and third-person point-of-view – when a singular mode of perception confronts a principle of mediation inimical to its own self-expression. For a novel so concerned with recon-stituting the 'subhistory' of Bolden's life and times, *Coming Through Slaughter* in fact 'consistently refuses to foreground psychological or sociological conditions'.[11] Instead, Ondaatje undertakes a far more ambitious project: to explore a style of subjectivity indifferent to any socially marked morality or collective order of truth which can only express itself through the destitution of the historical imagination.

One way in which Ondaatje brings out Bolden's singular mode of individuation is by insisting upon the power of the

death drive at the core of his personality. Ondaatje's fascination with this aspect of Bolden's character explains his decision to invent an apocryphal role for him as the editor of the local scandal sheet *The Cricket*. 'Looked at objectively', the narrator remarks of this mythical magazine, '*The Cricket* contained excessive reference to death' (*CTS*, 19). The presence of death in the midst of life terrifies and exhilarates Bolden: 'Whenever a celebrated murder occurred Bolden was there at the scene drawing amateur maps' (*CTS*, 19). What might be dismissed as a morbid amateur passion actually conceals a commitment to a particular vision of life: Bolden's obsession with mortality expresses his desire to become other than what he is by maintaining a purely singular inherence. From this position he no longer recognises an autonomous self within a field of social relations; instead he continually expands our idea of subjectivity to confront the very becoming and dynamism of life. One of Ondaatje's major stylistic achievements in *Coming Through Slaughter* is to create a style of being that no longer perceives life in terms of a distinction between self and world but as particular points upon a single plane of becoming. This singular vision expresses itself in a series of elliptical and uncanny sentences in which the subject *becomes* the very thing it *perceives*: 'He could step on the train or go back to the Brewitts. He was frozen. He woke to see the train disappearing away from his body like a vein' (*CTS*, 37). Listening to the stream of gossip and innuendo in the barbershop, Bolden's consciousness suddenly expands to incorporate every mode of utterance and point-of-view: 'Five minutes later Bolden would be back shaving a neck and listening to other problems. He loved it. His mind became the street' (*CTS*, 40). This singular movement beyond the subjective limits of perception characterises Bolden's collapse into insanity after his assault upon Tom Pickett (*CTS*, 77).

The drama of Bolden's becoming-imperceptible, elliptically evoked in Part One of the novel, becomes the explicit burden of Part Two. The first part concludes with Bolden's fevered appearance upon Robin Brewitt's lawn at the symbolic limit of his known world: 'For a moment he looked right through her, almost forgot

to recognize her' (*CTS*, 43). The second part presents us for the first time with Bolden's own narrative voice, which expresses his contempt for his subservient role within the local economy. The drudgery of barely professional work in the barbershop denies him the reality of who he is ('The layers of soap all day long have made another skin over me'); consequently he rebels against the 'slavery' of his socially defined image (*CTS*, 47). Scorning his barbershop customers who 'hate to see themselves change', Bolden exults in his power to 'manipulate their looks'. His memories of life in the barbershop culminate in a horrifying scene in which he slashes at flesh with the edge of his 'cold razor', violently imposing upon others his vision of a world of becoming and change (*CTS*, 47). The full force of this fantasmic image is realised later in Bolden's fight with Tom Pickett, where his flight through the 'empty frame' of the window hints at his singular transcendence of social relations (*CTS*, 76).

In the same way that music transports Bolden beyond the given world towards the impersonal – a perception of life that is no longer restricted to any one consciousness or point-of-view – the intensity of sexual passion transforms his sense of who he is. Bolden's brief affair with Robin Brewitt disorganises his perception of space and temporality; his first night under her roof 'made him lose the order of time' (*CTS*, 32). During their lovemaking Bolden experiences an inhuman becoming ('We are animals meeting an unknown breed') that folds all life onto a single plane; this experience of a univocal flow of desire represents for him a definitive 'step past the territory' of subjective consciousness (*CTS*, 63). At this point Webb tries once more to check Bolden's passage towards singular being by reinscribing his image within the linear form of a narrative history. Webb's pursuit takes him to the room of the photographer E. J. Bellocq, Bolden's onetime associate and custodian of the sole surviving photograph of Bolden with his band. Bellocq is, as his profession dictates, identified with the regime of representation and the economy of the image. His art, however, is presented as a mode of subjection that fixes the flow of experience into abstract and lifeless forms. The correspondence here between particular

modes of vision and forms of dispossession is established by Bellocq's idiosyncratic photographs of New Orleans prostitutes, which inscribe the objectification of their subjects at the heart of aesthetic disclosure:

> She now offering grotesque poses for an extra dollar and Bellocq grim and quiet saying No, just stand there against the wall there that one, no keep the petticoat on this time. One snap to quickly catch her scorning him and then waiting, waiting for minutes so she would become self-conscious towards him and the camera and her status, embarrassed at just her naked arms and neck and remembers for the first time in a long while the roads she imagined she could take as a child. And he photographed that. (*CTS*, 54)

Bolden's friendship with Bellocq affords him respite from the intensity of his public performances. But despite his indifference to Bolden's art and growing reputation, Bellocq remains a pivotal character in *Coming Through Slaughter*. Indeed, Bolden's exchanges with the photographer precipitate his definitive break with his known world. What makes the intimacy between the two men both unlikely and compelling is that their enthusiasms embody antithetical perspectives upon the relationship of art to life. While Ondaatje's lingering attention to Bellocq's hydrocephalic body highlights his lack of physical vitality ('Bellocq with his stoop, and his clothy hump, bent over the sprawled legs of his tripod'), the photographer's deformity is not represented solely in physical terms (*CTS*, 56). Bellocq's physical deformity also symbolises a distortion of aesthetic vision that expresses itself in his insistence upon self-consciousness as the primary ground of being ('The connection between Bellocq and Buddy was strange … What could Buddy have to do with him?' (*CTS*, 56)).

Bellocq's art is consistently viewed as a mode of corruption: he 'defiles' beauty by turning the flux of life into a representative image (*CTS*, 55). Bellocq later acknowledges the latent violence of his aesthetic by defacing his own photographs: 'Some of the pictures have knife slashes across the bodies', after he

tears at them in his studio, while others 'neatly decapitate the head of the naked body with scratches' (*CTS*, 55). Significantly, Bellocq's elevation of self-consciousness over pre-reflective life is expressed in machinic terms. The photographer does not just turn becoming into an image; he becomes part of the machinery of reproduction. In one of the novel's bleaker ironies, Bellocq's need to subject desire to the demand of representation is indicated by his grotesque metamorphosis into a perception-machine. Webb glimpses aspects of this mutation in his first encounter with Bellocq: 'There was something wrong with his legs and the tripod was now his cane' (*CTS*, 51). Bolden, who knows Bellocq much more intimately, begins to apprehend the true nature of his friend's condition:

> He pulled Bellocq up the steps, the camera strapped across his back like a bow. He had seen it so often on his friend that whenever he thought of him his body took on an outline which included the camera and the tripod. It was part of his bone structure. A metal animal grown into his back. He pulled him up the steps, through the doors. (*CTS*, 131)

Bellocq's reification of his affective capacities has tragic consequences for his own life; the change he undergoes also provokes a crisis in Bolden's relation to his own experience. Ondaatje hints at Bellocq's complicity in Bolden's subsequent collapse by casting him in the role of tempter ('Aware it was him who had tempted Buddy on'); during their conversations the two men move 'gradually off the edge of the social world' (*CTS*, 65). This fateful transition reaches its apotheosis in the moment when Bellocq 'pushed his imagination' – his occult knowledge of everything he has killed in himself – into Bolden's 'brain'. Up to this point, Bolden has at least retained some capacity to function in the public world ('Buddy who had once been enviably public'); but his immersion in Bellocq's 'joyless and private' existence inducts him into the 'mystic privacy' of a world where life can maintain no relation to anything beyond itself (*CTS*, 65). The self-denying character of a life devoid of *any* relation to exteriority is figured explicitly in Bellocq's suicide, which anticipates the beginning of Bolden's tragic death-in-life.

Now Bolden is 'full of the white privacy' as he slips inexorably off the map of shared experience (*CTS*, 69). Certainly Nora is unequivocal that Bellocq exerted a catastrophic influence upon her husband: 'Look at you', she screams at her husband. 'Look at what he did to you. Look at you. Look at you. Goddamit. Look at you' (*CTS*, 135). Bolden's inexorable passage beyond social consciousness is figured as a form of mental collapse: although he still briefly disports himself with Robin Brewitt, he is 'swimming towards the sound of madness' (*CTS*, 70). Increasingly Ondaatje begins to express the dissociation of Bolden's sensibility in formal and syntactic terms; the short passage 'Train Song' works powerfully to this end. In a proleptic gesture towards Bolden's final journey to East Louisiana State Hospital, 'Train Song' momentarily inhabits Bolden's consciousness in order to dramatise his profound alienation from the world around him. The section begins by reproducing Bolden's singular vision of the landscape flowing past the train window ('Passing wet sky chicory that lies in the fields like the sky') before dissolving this vision into the play of lexical possibilities ('like the sky like the sky like the sky', 'passing wet sky chicory', 'passing wet sky chicory lies') that makes it possible (*CTS*, 87). The dissolution of sense into the associative play of the signifying chain mimics Bolden's collapse into pure non-relation at the same time as it evokes a mode of being that can *never* be wholly accounted for in narrative terms (*CTS*, 87). For the 'meaning' of Bolden's experience, to employ a noun already rendered equivocal by the novel, lies in his oscillation or 'passing' *between* subjectivity and singularity: representation 'lies', in this sense, in the very act of providing images to encapsulate a flow of pure difference.

Ondaatje's ability to portray Bolden's radical refusal of subjective coherence without reconstituting such coherence in narrative terms is one measure of the novel's stylistic strength. Bolden's insistence that his singular orientation is crucial to full creative expression returns in one of his most powerful memories of the Brewitts:

> Here. Where I am anonymous and alone in a white room
> with no history and no parading. So I can make some-

thing unknown in the shape of this room. Where I am
King of Corners. And Robin who drained my body of its
fame when I wanted to find that fear of certainties I had
when I first began to play, back when I was unaware that
reputation made the room narrower and narrower, till you
were crawling on your own back, full of your own echoes,
till you were drinking in only your own recycled air. And
Robin and Jaelin brought me back to that open fright with
the unimportant objects. (*CTS*, 88)

The pathos of this scene lies in its subtle superimposition
of Bolden's memory of his brief sojourn at Shell Beach upon
the scene of his asylum incarceration. Here we glimpse Bolden's
tragic paradox: life with Robin reawakens in him the 'fear of
certainties' that generates his strongest art; but the decomposition of his subjectivity into pure becoming destroys his relationship to the public world. As 'King of Corners' Bolden is a
curiously subjectless subject: anonymous, isolated and stripped
of the expressive context of a living tradition. What he lacks is
any sense of the 'right audience' whose response to innovation
might provide a social dimension to aesthetic experience (*CTS*,
92). At the same time, Bolden's intuition of the limitations of
his singular vision is forcefully, if intermittently, conveyed: 'All
the time I hate what I am doing and want the other' (*CTS*, 91).
But once Bellocq tempted Bolden 'out of the world of audiences'
he could find no way to restore this broken covenant (*CTS*, 95).
Trapped between his fear of certainties and his terror of his
singular vision, Bolden tries desperately to create an audience
from Ondaatje's prospective community of readers. His appeal is
conveyed by Ondaatje's artful handling of the second-personal
plural: 'Come with me Webb I want to show you something, no
come with me I want to *show* you something. You come too.
Put your hand through this window' (*CTS*, 95). *You* come too,
Bolden entreats the reader: follow me through the window, and
reconfigure your own life upon a singular plane of becoming.

Bolden's relentless incorporation of the world into the
force of his own becoming reaches its climax during the Labor
Day parade. Here Bolden enters into his dream of Dionysius

by dissolving what is left of his autonomous subjectivity into streams of pure libidinal energy that reunites him with the innermost core of nature. His metamorphosis is recounted in ecstatic terms: 'I had wanted to be the reservoir where engines and people drank, blood sperm music pouring out and getting hooked in someone's ear', he reflects on the eve of the parade, 'The way flowers were still and fed bees' (*CTS*, 118). The parade records precisely this disintegration of the self into a 'reservoir' of creative energy. As the parade begins Bolden 'struts' before the crowd, indulging himself in a 'parade of ego' that sets him apart from the watching throng (*CTS*, 137). The creative self-consciousness demanded by Bolden's egotistical sublime momentarily stabilises his field of vision, enabling him to observe the 'boundary' between himself and the mass of bodies around him. This boundary between self and other cannot, however, survive the beginnings of Bolden's Dionysian performance; a shift in tone and perspective takes place when he prepares his cornet 'for the note sharp as a rat's mouth under Allen's soft march tune'. With its sly allusion to the process of Billy the Kid's inhuman metamorphosis, this simile hints at the transformation Bolden is about to experience: his parade of ego will, in fact, *dissolve* the ego by presenting the death of the self as the precondition for genuinely creative expression.

Bolden's metamorphosis begins as soon as the 'squawk' of his cornet is heard. As his opening notes float upon the air, a woman and her male companion separate themselves from the crowd and dance ecstatically to the music. Their frenzied gestures inspire in Bolden a new flood of creative energy ('Watch them through the sun balancing off the horn till they see what is happening and I speed Henry Allen's number till most of them drop off and just march behind') which is only arrested by the first premonition of his imminent collapse: 'Eyes going dark in the hot bleached street' (*CTS*, 137). The impression that Bolden sees the incipient disintegration *of* the self as a release *from* the self is supported by Ondaatje's pun upon the street name Liberty: 'Get there before it ends, but it's nearly over nearly over, approach Liberty' (*CTS*, 137). And as the historical scene of the

parade dissolves into the intensity of Bolden's creative present tense, the integrity of the visible image breaks down into waves of affective becoming: the woman dancing in the crowd becomes variously 'Robin, Nora, Crawley's girl's tongue' (*CTS*, 138).

In a vertiginous paragraph describing Bolden's collapse we experience 'the breakdown of the boundary between the musician's improvising voice and the pattern against which it finds its definition'.[12] This 'breakdown' is signalled, as so often in Ondaatje, by the shattering of the 'mirror' which the subject employs to give definite form to its own various aspects. As the parade winds down to its conclusion, Bolden suddenly begins to improvise a new riff while watching the woman 'mirroring my throat in her lonely tired dance' (*CTS*, 138). From this moment the expressive power of Bolden's art abolishes any distinction between self and other: the woman who initially stood *outside* Bolden's performance, anticipating in her movement each of its improvised phrases ('She's hitting each note with her body before it is even out so I know what I do through her') is subsumed *into* the music that now constitutes all he can know of the outside world (*CTS*, 138). The woman who once offered Bolden an image of his own expressive nature now blurs imperceptibly into his very being: she comes steadily 'closer' to Bolden, inciting him to 'make it past' his 'old ego' and the image of autonomous selfhood it preserves. In thrall to his Dionysiac vision, Bolden completes this passage by becoming both the dancer and the dance: 'Half dead, can't take more, hardly hit the squawks anymore but when I do my body flicks at them as if I'm the dancer till the music is out there' (*CTS*, 138). It is during this ecstatic transcendence of subjectivity that he finally experiences 'what I wanted, always, loss of privacy in the playing', as he gives himself over to an impersonal plane of becoming (*CTS*, 139).

In the moment of his epiphany Bolden experiences life as a flow of pure intensity. His body 'speeds' in response to the quantities of 'desire' it expresses as temporality collapses into the continuous present tense of an 'eternal' becoming. Bolden's sensation of 'a javelin through the brain and down into the stomach' extinguishes self-consciousness as his identity

dissolves into a series of libidinal drives (*CTS*, 138). The novel, as Douglas Barbour observes, signals this dissolution through the 'growing abandonment of the first-person pronoun in a systematic derangement of sense perceptions, as "my heart ... at my throat hitting slow pure notes" shifts to "the long last squawk" and then to "the stomach, feel[ing] the blood that is real move up bringing fresh energy in its suitcase"'.[13] As the 'red force' of blood pours into Bolden's throat his point-of-view disintegrates into the 'red wade' of singularities that infused Billy the Kid's ecstatic final vision (*CTS*, 139). In the final moments of this section Ondaatje steps outside Bolden's internal chaos to show Willy Cornish catching his stricken friend as he falls; when Cornish does so he glimpses the 'blood spill out' from Bolden's horn 'as he finally lifts the metal from the hard kiss of the mouth' (*CTS*, 140). A portion of blank text subtends this appalling image before we encounter the three words of Bolden's final will and testament: 'What I wanted'. The uninscribed space at the heart of Ondaatje's typescript suggests Bolden's passage from social relation to pure singularity: it symbolises the passage of his traumatised body into a 'kind of ahistorical weightlessness and transparency'.[14] The final pages of *Coming Through Slaughter* will, however, count the cost of Bolden's singular itinerary; in so doing, they mark a defining moment in the development of Ondaatje's aesthetics.

The last phase of the novel begins by exploring what is lost by subjecting singular perception to historical consciousness. The scene of the Labor Day parade is immediately followed by a spare biographical entry which reduces this notorious event to the threadbare notation: 'April 1907 Bolden (thirty one years old) goes mad while playing with Henry Allen's Brass Band' (*CTS*, 141). If this cursory biographical note fails to account for the enigma of Bolden's experience, little has been added to it by more contemporary scrutiny; so much, at least, is clear from Ondaatje's initial trip to New Orleans to research Bolden's story. Ondaatje's visit to Storyville in order to take 'fast bad photographs into the sun' of the barbershop where Bolden 'probably' worked yields little of value or interest; these images, he admits,

merely provide a 'mirror' of his own imaginative investment in Bolden's legend (*CTS*, 143). And although jazz experienced a cultural efflorescence in the years following Bolden's disappearance, the assimilation of Bolden's legacy into a common style quickly obscured what was original in its perception of life (*CTS*, 157). Some of the implications of this observation are comically underlined in the 'Frank Amacker Interviews' conducted in 1965. Throughout this series of academic exchanges with Franck Amacker, a New Orleans jazz veteran, the very qualities of stylistic improvisation that established jazz as a radical break with what came before it consistently elude critical definition. The rags that Amacker plays to the assembled cultural historians in homage to the first Jazz Age are continually remade by the mode of his performance ('He now says that he made up the last song'); much of what he passes down as authentic cultural history proves either to be conjecture or a corruption of the facts (*CTS*, 164). Did Amacker's auditors but know it, his ludic performances actually embody a profound historical truth: what emerges from his restless recreation of inherited tradition is the creative force of jazz as an *event* of cultural difference. Yet in their zeal to make the past conform to its received historical image, the researchers lose this truth from view; entire reels of Amacker's testimony are consequently deemed to contain 'no interesting information' (*CTS*, 166).

But if Ondaatje's novel contests the occlusion of the event of historical difference within narratives of cultural history, it discovers no utopian alternative in the singular transcendence of historical consciousness. Ondaatje's refusal of the redemptive possibility of a purely singular inherence emerges in the scenes describing Bolden's journey towards, and confinement within, East Louisiana State Hospital. Bolden is delivered in these pages from historical consciousness into historical subjection; his passage from a sense of social relationships to the univocal plane of creative intensity leads only to incoherence and blank passivity. Bolden's rejection of subjective coherence may expose him to the pure event of becoming, but it also renders him completely vulnerable to the disciplinary violence of institutional forces.

Ondaatje's unhappy sense that the absolute deterritorialisation of subjectivity merely anticipates its violent reterritorialisation at another level resonates throughout the novel's final pages. It finds its sharpest expression in the stylistic interplay between *intensity* and *narration*: Bolden's beatific insistence upon entering the House of Detention that 'Everyone who touches me must be beautiful' is cruelly contradicted by the history of guard rape of detainees which names him as a recurrent victim (*CTS*, 146). Elsewhere Bolden's aesthetic perception of life as pure becoming is presented as an intolerable burden as well as a mode of creative release. When he is alone in the asylum his brain drives his musician's hand 'up into the path of the circling fan': this self-destructive gesture recurs 'forever and ever in his memory' (*CTS*, 147).

Bolden's train journey from the House of Detention to the State Hospital contains some of the most affecting writing in Ondaatje's entire oeuvre. Affecting and affective: through a series of startling and sharply poetic images Ondaatje invites us to inhabit Bolden's angle of vision as he dissolves the world into a stream of intensities:

> Am walked out of the House of D and put on a north train by H. B. McMurray and Jones. Outside a river can't get out of the rain. Passing wet chicory that lies in the field like the sky. The trees rocks brown ditches falling off the side as we go past. The train in a wet coat. Blue necklace holding my hands together. (*CTS*, 150)

The surreal and unsettling quality of these sentences lies in their failure to maintain any coherent relation between the impressions from which we compose our idea of everyday experience. The instability of Bolden's field of vision becomes clear in his idiosyncratic use of preposition and simile. Thus is the train a 'wet coat' for its passengers, or is it *in* a wet coat? Does the simile 'like the sky' in the sentence 'Passing wet chicory that lies in the field like the sky', imply that the sky is *above* the field or *in* the field? As this unravelling of semantic relations continues, Bolden's thought-patterns appear to be determined by little more than the coincidence of sound between otherwise

unrelated words: 'You see I had an operation on my throat. You see I had a salvation on my throat' (*CTS*, 150). The chiming of these nouns is not without its irony: Bolden's operation, far from gaining him salvation, expunges his last authentic mode of expression from the novel.

The unintended irony of Bolden's perception is, however, lost to him because he can no longer recognise the interplay between different perspectives that irony expresses. What is eliminated from Bolden's point-of-view in the novel's last few pages is any sense of relational difference: he simply gives himself over to the immediately singular nature of sensation in a movement of depersonalisation that leaves him no coherent position from which to discriminate between the forces that play across his body. Where once Bolden's creative decomposition of the real allowed him to experience life beyond the order of time, linear sequence and worldly relation, his final incarnation reveals the involuntary *submission* of the self to the immanent flux of life ('In the morning men were found heels bandaged in their night-shirts and naked when the doors opened … He washed his face in the travelling spokes of light, bathing and drying his mouth nose forehead and cheeks in the heat. All day. Blessed by the visit of his friend' (*CTS*, 160)).

Trying earlier in the novel to communicate the creative intensity of his reinvention of jazz syntax, Bolden observes: 'The right ending is an open door you can't see too far out of' (*CTS*, 98). The significance of this formulation lies in its simultaneous respect for and transformation of narrative structure: the 'right ending' appears when a form is exposed to the virtual possibilities it *contains*. Bolden's subsequent abandonment of any sense of relational difference destroys the creative tension that kept his art alive. Consequently the image of his incarceration in the novel's haunting closing paragraph is imbued with a ghastly metaphorical suggestiveness; the absence of any creative relation between being and the various modes of its becoming is represented as a form of death-in-life:

> I sit with this room. With the grey walls that darken into corner. And one window with teeth in it. Sit so still you

can hear your hair rustle in your shirt. Look away from the window when clouds and other things go by. Thirty one years old. There are no prizes. (*CTS*, 170)

By maintaining such a concentrated focus upon Bolden's creative disorganisation of sense and self-consciousness, *Coming Through Slaughter* can be read as a powerful allegorical reworking of the original Dionysiac experience. This allegory is supplemented, however, by another vision of aesthetic experience which reproduces the Dionysiac force of Bolden's art whilst employing the impersonal resources of irony, tone and narrative perspective to lend formal coherence to its singularising trajectory. We can glimpse this secondary, and properly Apollonian, redemption of Dionysiac experience in those scenes in which narrator and character briefly exchange places:

> The thin sheaf of information. Why did my senses stop at you? There was the sentence, 'Buddy Bolden who became a legend when he went berserk in a parade …' What was there in that, before I knew your nation your colour your age, that made me push my arm forward and spill it through the front of your mirror and clutch myself? Did not want to pose in your accent but think in your brain and body, and you like a weatherbird arcing round in the middle of your life to exact opposites and burning your brains out so that from June 5, 1907 till 1931 you were dropped into amber in the East Louisiana State Hospital. (*CTS*, 144)

In moments like these the creative resonance of Bolden's story for Ondaatje is intensified by the shock of recognition with which he recognises aspects of Bolden in himself: 'When I read he stood in front of mirrors and attacked himself, there was the shock of memory. For I had done that. Stood, and with a razor-blade cut into cheeks and forehead, shaved hair. Defiling people we did not wish to be' (*CTS*, 143). If *Coming Through Slaughter* suggests that fidelity to the transfiguring force of art must involve a commitment to dissolve imaginative relations into the immediately singularising elements that constitute them, it also insists that this singularising itinerary can only

preserve its powers of derealisation by maintaining a relationship with an *idea* of narrative form.[15] The paradoxical movement of 'making and destroying' that Ondaatje discerns at the heart of Bellocq's sensibility is, in this regard, fundamental to his own artistic vision (*CTS*, 55). Leaving behind him the legendary story of Buddy Bolden, Ondaatje's fascination with the often lacerating interplay between the extremes of his own experience led him next to an artistic examination of his own cultural origins. It is to the psychic and cultural tensions of *Running in the Family*, his second prose work, that we now turn.

Running in the Family

Although Michael Ondaatje was born in Sri Lanka into a family of Dutch-Tamil-Sinhalese origin, he left the island at the age of nine in the wake of his parents' divorce and his mother's departure for England five years earlier. After eight years in England, Ondaatje travelled onward to Canada in 1962, where he took out Canadian citizenship, eventually settled in Toronto, and gradually began to be spoken of as a 'Canadian' writer of considerable power and promise. Yet despite Ondaatje's seemingly untroubled transition between these three very different cultures, his imagination remained haunted by the first country he left behind; the persistence in his early work of figures like Billy the Kid and Buddy Bolden who seem both representative of, and marginalised within, the communities in which they live expresses the sense of ambivalence and self-division this negotiation between different cultural traditions was likely to produce. During the late 1970s what had remained implicit in Ondaatje's art became increasingly central to his field of vision; this imaginative process culminated in his return to Sri Lanka, after a twenty-five-year absence, to engage directly with the legacy of his childhood inheritance. *Running in the Family* (1982), Ondaatje's second published prose work, offers an account of his journeys to Sri Lanka in 1978 and 1980 in which he attempts to come to terms with his position between different cultures and within a fissiparous family history.

Neither Ondaatje's title nor the consistently maintained biographical focus of his narrative should deflect our atten-

tion, however, from the broader implications of *Running in the Family*'s examination of colonial identity and culture. While the book presents, on one level, a richly evocative account of Ondaatje's own turbulent family history, his experience of being simultaneously drawn to, and excluded from, any sense of authentic cultural origins also functions as a metaphor for the hybrid, self-divided and ambivalent character of colonial subjectivity. Indeed, the eclectic and intertextual character of *Running in the Family* goes beyond an examination of Ondaatje's personal experience of estrangement and exile in order to explore the hybrid historical origins and internal cultural divisions of modern Sri Lanka. Throughout the text Ondaatje's unsettling apprehension of being both deracinated and profoundly at home comes to personify the perceived discrepancy between represented and lived space endemic to those cultures condemned to articulate their own experience in an imposed tongue. Because the elastic time frame of Ondaatje's narrative permits him to range freely across three generations of family life, his portrait of modern Sri Lanka manages to encompass the history of its pre- and post-Independence politics while bearing witness to the national trauma of establishing a coherent post-colonial identity in the era of decolonisation. Ondaatje's implied correspondence between familial and national history also gains weight and resonance from his artful recreation of the lifestyle and self-perception of the Burgher class to which his family belonged. The ambivalent position of the Burghers between an indigenous culture they sought to transcend and a colonial authority they could never hope to reproduce offers Ondaatje a nuanced perspective from which to consider the possibilities and potential pitfalls of a post-colonial cultural politics. His response in *Running in the Family* is to reject both the narcissistic identification with the imperial imaginary that reduced the Burghers to a ruinous superfluity in their own country and the nationalist demand for ethnic purity that would lead to the catastrophe of civil war in the ensuing years. Instead, Ondaatje ascribes positive content to the perception of life that both these positions repress: the experience of cultural hybridity and ambivalence – those

'in-between' spaces and subjectivities – engendered by the fact of cultural difference.

Ondaatje's tentative acceptance of the double vision that cultural hybridity makes possible is the implied subject of the text's disquieting opening lines. *Running in the Family* begins with an untitled preface in which an elliptical glimpse of Sri Lankan space mutates abruptly into a 'nightmare' suffused with images of dispossession and loss. In this nightmare a hitherto unidentified male figure is forcibly subsumed into an anarchic and predatory landscape which appears to renew its vitality in the act of reclaiming his body: 'Later on, during a fever, the drought still continuing, his nightmare is that thorn trees in the garden send their hard roots underground towards the house climbing through windows so they can drink sweat off his body, steal the last of the saliva off his tongue' (*RF*, 17). Although the encompassing gloom of this nightmare vision is quickly dispelled by a bedroom light which illuminates a male figure now recognisable as Ondaatje ('For twenty five years he has not lived in this country, though up to the age of eleven he slept in rooms like this'), the sinister implication of this scene should give us pause: unexpectedly for a work so preoccupied with motifs of return and inheritance, contact with the 'hard roots' of Sri Lankan soil seems to threaten a *loss* of voice and a retreat into sterility and silence (*RF*, 17). The ambivalent narrative mood persists uneasily throughout the succeeding sentences as Ondaatje's attention flickers between the palpable texture of lived experience and his sense of the historically constituted character of cultural representation. Maintaining its unbroken fidelity to the object of perception, his glance lingers over the visual particularity of a garden emerging into sunlight: 'Dawn through a garden. Clarity to leaves, fruit, the dark yellow of the King Coconut' (*RF*, 17). Yet even as these words evoke the thick materiality of sensuous experience, the passage's teasing metafictive conclusion diverts our gaze from the integrity of the contemplated image towards the larger historical context in which all autobiographical writing takes place: 'Half a page – and the morning is already ancient' (*RF*, 17).

Effortlessly 'postmodern' in its self-referential mode of address, this sentence hesitates uncertainly between two distinct modes of cultural inscription. Building upon a series of childhood memories while transfiguring them in the act of aesthetic apprehension, this 'half a page' of prose offers a microcosm of the larger text in which Ondaatje refashions fragments of the past into a deeply personal narrative of affiliation and belonging. But in a quietly insistent narrative counter-movement, the temporising adjective 'ancient' propels this experience *beyond* Ondaatje's personal angle of vision by relocating it within the entire history of images that have come to define the image of modern Sri Lanka. The subtle interplay between the singularity of perception and the archive of cultural representations is crucial to the narrative structure of *Running in the Family* because it enables what Homi Bhabha has called the 'double temporality' of post-colonial experience to emerge.[1] The limitation of a purely autobiographical reworking of an involved family history is, as Ondaatje's nightmare implies, that it threatens to identify him too closely with the 'hard roots' of a specifically Sri Lankan childhood. Such identification threatens to rob him of his voice because it expunges any trace of the duplicitous play of identities – the persistent dialogue between different cultural locations and histories – that underpins his sense of himself as both a writer and a cultural subject. Ondaatje's response, which is to imbricate autobiography with the impersonal perspective of colonial history, allows him to inscribe his own presence upon the text of Sri Lankan culture while reproducing the antagonism between different histories and traditions that divides it at its core.

The eccentric situation of the preface, a piece of writing both within and outside the main body of the text, offers a formal clue to Ondaatje's fascination with hybrid states and subjectivities. This clue is noteworthy because *Running in the Family* consistently envisages personal and cultural origins as a negotiation between different versions of history and conflicting notions of value. What begins in the book as a quest for a more authentic sense of identity and origin quickly metamorphoses into a literary exploration of the hybridity and ambivalence

engendered by the movement across and between cultures. By finding an analogue in his own history for the shuttling traffic between incommensurable cultural temporalities and world-views, Ondaatje discovers a template for post-colonial subjectivity in the 'narrative ambivalence' between 'disjunctive times and meanings'.[2] This sense of a double temporality demands, as so often in Ondaatje's work, a double writing: his development of hybrid or doubled tropes like pastiche, parody and mimicry is perfectly calibrated to portray the internal division of a subject situated ambivalently within and between the signifying traditions of East and West, mythopoeia and history, archaism and modernity or First and Third World. Style in *Running in the Family* is, then, both a response to experience and a way of perceiving a world: only by thinking the question of origins from a perspective both within and beyond them, Ondaatje reminds us, does it becomes possible to inhabit the 'double and split time' of colonial subjectivity and the modern postcolonial nation.[3]

A connection between styles of representation and modes of perception is established by the book's two epigraphs. These epigraphs juxtapose a 'clearly Orientalist and exotic' glimpse of Ceylon presented by a Franciscan friar of the fourteenth century ('I saw in this island fowls as big as our country geese having two heads') with Douglas Amarasekera's self-deprecating and neo-colonial contemporary native worldview.[4] Uncomfortably aware that the modern cultural image of Sri Lanka has its roots in both these narrative traditions, *Running in the Family* incorporates both modes into its heterogeneous narrative form. The generic elusiveness of a text which is by turns memoir, travelogue, auto-biography, cultural history, confession and experimental novel is caught in John Russell's description of 'Ondaatje's memoir' as a 'literary artefact of great stylistic range, developing a unique structure that carries it beyond the boundaries of the travel genre into those of the nonfiction novel'.[5] If 'nonfiction novel' appears altogether too vague a formulation to explain the sheer stylistic diversity of Ondaatje's literary performance, Chelva Kanaganayakam underscores the importance of such variety to Ondaatje's examination of cultural stereotype and self-image:

The notion of 'running' is particularly appropriate, suggesting as it were several alternative prepositions, all of which define the preoccupation of this work. *Running* is as much about running 'in' as it is about 'to', 'from' or 'against'. The constant shifts in perspective, the foregrounding of textuality, the need to belong and the need for distance, the awareness of history and the self-consciousness about historiography – all combine to create the effect of a complex quest in which the notion of identity needs to be explored in all its multiplicity.[6]

Kanaganyakam's reference to constant shifts in perspective attempts to convey the non-linear, recursive and nomadic movement of Ondaatje's narrative which reproduces the dislocation of a subject unable to recognise itself in the received forms of colonial historiography. This sense of dislocation is exacerbated by the text's oscillation between referential and non-referential modes of discourse: Ondaatje's habitual play between mimesis and metaphor undermines any idea of representation as innocent, neutral or transparent by suggesting that coherent images of colonial subjectivity require the strategic management of cultural ambivalence. His dilatory and episodic progress through Sri Lanka, which draws together an assortment of cultural traditions while seeming to have no fixed purpose or goal, also exudes a subtle political resonance. For there is, as Ondaatje's wry and self-questioning narrative makes clear, no single route through *Running in the Family* or the history sedimented within it: the text's polyphonic structure opens its contents to a multiplicity of readings. In this way Ondaatje's nomadic itinerary refuses to accommodate itself to the established topography of Sri Lankan culture; instead it offers a utopian imaginative alternative to the ethnic, geographical and social divisions enforced upon its polity by its baleful imperial history.

The ambivalent nature of colonial space and subjectivity is the subject of 'Asia', the first of the text's extended prose sections. In keeping with a work preoccupied with cultural hybridity and difference, the 'Asia' chapter actually takes place in Canada, where Ondaatje awakens from a dream of Sri Lanka into the

bleak beginning of an Ontario winter morning. His dream has, however, already transformed his perception of the home place; attempting to dispel the oneiric image of a lush 'tropical landscape', Ondaatje feels himself still to be 'in a jungle, hot, sweating' (*RF*, 21). Ondaatje's 'Asia' is from the beginning an in-between place: a 'dream' of authentic cultural origins, a collection of maps strewn upon a Canadian floor, the vivid, if fragmentary, memories of a dislocated childhood. Settled in Canada but dreaming of Asia, Ondaatje realises that he is 'already running', travelling back in memory towards 'the family I had grown from' (*RF*, 22). Only by revisiting his past can he make sense of his present and future: 'In my mid-thirties I realised I had slipped past a childhood I had ignored and not understood' (*RF*, 22). Later, drunk at a farewell party on the eve of his departure for Sri Lanka, Ondaatje suddenly senses that the exploration of his cultural origins demands a new narrative syntax capable of inscribing the alterity of indigenous experience within Western representations of colonial space:

> *Asia.* The name was a gasp from a dying mouth. An ancient word that had to be whispered, would never be used as a battle cry. The word sprawled. It had none of the clipped sound of Europe, America, Canada. The vowels took over, slept on the map with the S. I was running to Asia and everything would change. It began with that moment when I was dancing and laughing wildly within the comfort and order of my life. Beside the fridge I tried to communicate some of the fragments I knew about my father, my grandmother. 'So how *did* your grandmother die?' 'Natural causes'. 'What?' 'Floods'. And then another wave of the party swirled me away. (*RF*, 22–3)

The connection between styles of representation and modes of being is further developed in 'Tabula Asiae'. The title of this vignette plays knowingly upon the strategic colonial vision of Ceylon as a tabula rasa: a blank space devoid of history, tradition and law. Ondaatje's punning revision of 'rasa' into 'Asiae' reminds us that this 'blank' native space is always also remade in the image of imperial desire. He highlights the privilege

accorded to imperial reconstructions of indigenous space by subordinating his own memories of Sri Lanka to the dubious authority of the 'false maps' – the 'old portraits of Ceylon' – that adorn his brother's wall in Toronto (*RF*, 63). Verisimilitude is a contingent feature of these early modern images: what appear in them as cartographical 'translations' of an extra-discursive reality actually reveal the superimposition of mercantile fantasy upon potentially penetrable spaces. Unreliable though these maps may be in their depiction of contour and coastline, they nevertheless disclose a fundamental truth: the interdependence of the technological mastery of space and the economic mastery of places and peoples. While the maps may begin as 'mythic shapes' to describe new and exotic realities, they are quickly pressed into service as 'routes for invasion and trade'. Upon their borders native space is framed by exotic fantasies of luxury and wealth:

> At the edge of the maps the scrolling mantling depicts ferocious slipper-footed elephants, a white queen offering a necklace to natives who carry tusks and a conch, a Moorish king who stands amidst the power of books and armour. On the south-west corner of some charts are satyrs, hoof deep in foam, listening to the sound of the island, their tails writhing in the waves (*RF*, 63–4).

Ondaatje's preoccupation with early modern imperial discourse about Ceylon offers a sharp insight into its demand that cultural difference be simultaneously *produced* and *managed*. One of the ways in which colonial discourse produces its own cultural authority is its active separation of values: the construction of the Western imperial self-image as the enlightened and rational motor of world history depends upon an *a priori* division between 'Western' and 'non-Western' cultural economies. Because imperial identity is founded upon this ideological distinction between cultural modalities and values, the 'primitivism' of colonial culture must constantly be articulated upon the planes of dialect and speech, fleshed out in the lived relationship between bodies, and performed in the rituals of social custom and religious observance. Irrespective of the phenomena that meet the

imperial gaze, its underlying demand remains the same: what is obscure in native culture must be made visible, what is cultural must be reinscribed in nature, while what is enigmatic must be seen to embody the essence of a disappearing world.

But if definitive features of the imperial self-image are produced through this active separation of values, this image remains equivocally poised between its mercantile and moral dimension. While the presumed primitivism of colonial culture appears to justify in advance the wresting of resources from a people unable to appreciate their commercial value, the material fact of expropriation unsettles the moralising tone of imperial self-representations. It was this incommensurability between material motivation and moral self-image that the idea of the 'civilising mission' of colonialism was intended to resolve. The strategic brilliance of this concept was to underscore the irrefragable otherness of colonial culture while simultaneously portraying it as potentially assimilable to the Enlightenment world. There is little point 'civilising' anyone, after all, if they are not *potentially* capable of inclusion in a civilised polity – the 'Other' turned into the same – but the implied judgement that such a process is necessary in the first place reinscribes the perception of primitivism within the dream of its ultimate disavowal. Such discursive procedures have one overriding ambition: they posit a moment of false identity at the heart of what is otherwise inimical in order to disguise the ongoing violence of the imperial project.

In *Running in the Family* Ondaatje offers a bitingly ironic insight into the conceptual manoeuvre at the heart of the civilising mission: the reinvention of material dispossession as historical destiny. One of the ways he does this is to inhabit the perspective of the imperial gaze as it lingers over its desired object:

> The maps reveal rumours of topography, the routes for invasion and trade, and the dark mad mind of travellers' tales appears throughout Arab and Chinese and medieval records. The island *seduced* all of Europe. The Portuguese. The Dutch. The English. And so its name changed, as

well as its shape, – Serendip, Ratnapida ('island of gems'), Taprobane, Zeloan, Zeilan, Seyllan, Ceilon, and Ceylon – the *wife* of many marriages, *courted* by invaders who stepped ashore and claimed everything with the power of their sword or bible or language. (*RF*, 64; emphasis mine)

What is remarkable about this paragraph is its subtle inter-weaving of two modes of discourse and two visions of impe-rial history. Assuming the impersonal, distanced and objective third-person point of view of 'historical' representation, the first voice rehearses a grimly familiar tale: the gradual consolidation of exotic 'travellers' tales' into maps that double as 'routes for invasion and trade', the arrival of 'invaders' who 'claimed every-thing with the power of their sword or bible or language', and the ensuing imperial scramble for colonial possessions traced by the etymological transition from 'Serendip' to 'Ceylon'. Insin-uating itself into this account, however, is another version of events that studiously reproduces the equivocations and ratio-nalisations of imperial historiography. This supplementary account mimics the language of sentimental romance in order to portray a process of conquest and sequestration as a movement of natural sympathy. Within the terms of this revisionist narra-tive, invasion is refigured as seduction and rape as courtship; elsewhere a nation subjugated by successive imperial masters is merely the 'wife of many marriages'.

While the artful juxtaposition of these two perspectives exposes the strategic recoding of investments that helps to shape imperialist discourse, it also identifies ambivalence at the heart of colonial subjectivity. These two themes come together in the trope of marriage which is both a metaphor in *Running in the Family* for the imbalance of power relations within a system of imperial dominance and a site of miscegenation that produces hybrid cultural forms and subjectivities. Miscegenation is a crucial term here because the imposed 'marriage' between imperial master and colonial 'wife' creates an unstable third term incompatible with the cultural self-representation of either imperial discourse or the colonised space. In a striking passage, the adulterated image of a subject that is *neither here nor there*

is used to invoke the historical origins of the Ondaatje family line:

> This pendant, once its shape stood still, became a *mirror*. It *pretended* to reflect each European power till newer ships arrived and *spilled* their nationalities, some of whom stayed and intermarried – my own ancestor arriving in 1600, a doctor who cured the residing governor's daughter with a strange herb and was rewarded with land, a foreign wife, and a new name which was a Dutch spelling of his own. Ondaatje. A parody of the ruling language. And when his Dutch wife died, marrying a Sinhalese woman, having nine children, and remaining. Here. At the centre of the rumour. At this point on the map. (*RF*, 64; emphasis mine)

From the beginning the name 'Ondaatje' is a parody of the ruling language: mixed within it are two languages, two histories, two different experiences of culture and place. This hybrid inscription of origins, Kanaganyagam notes, serves only to accentuate the irony that '[t]he name, hardly recognisable as Tamil or Sinhalese, with minor changes, means, in the Tamil language, "to become one"'.[7] If we follow Homi Bhabha in understanding hybridity as a problematic of colonial representation in which imperial authority is open to, and unsettled by, the trace of the 'Other' it has assimilated to itself, the ethical and political force of Ondaatje's text becomes clear.[8] Simultaneously interpellated and marginalised by the 'ruling language' of colonialism, Ondaatje exploits the ambivalence of hybridity to give imaginative life to an experience of being that such language seeks to negate or exclude. His defiant repositioning of himself at the 'centre of the rumour' signals his refusal of merely marginal status: the parodic, because doubled, colonial subject now moves centre stage, alive to the moments of non-coincidence or contradiction in the narratives that map its history, and committed to the possibility of thinking differently by thinking the event of difference itself.

Ondaatje begins to explore the relationship between thinking difference and thinking differently in 'Jaffna Afternoons'. The

choreography of these early sections is of considerable thematic importance: where 'Asia' pointedly interposes Western representations of Ceylon between the reader and an encounter with modern Sri Lanka, Ondaatje's first incursion into his former home place forces him directly to confront the island's imperial legacy. Significantly, Ondaatje's record of his return to Sri Lanka does not begin in Colombo, the nation's capital, or in any of his family's homes, but at the governor's house in Jaffna, in the very north of the island, where his Uncle Ned is holding a commission into recent race-riots.[9] This location is well chosen to illustrate the persistence of the imperial inheritance within contemporary Sri Lankan culture. Built by the Dutch around 1700, the governor's house is an isolated, if still redoubtable, monument to imperial authority; wandering through its various rooms, Ondaatje feels himself to be enmeshed in the 'labyrinth of 18th-century Dutch defense' (RF, 25). The building's 'internal vastness' becomes a metaphor for economic and cultural prestige: its walls seem to stretch 'awesome distances' towards the very limits of vision (RF, 24). These interior spaces are described in the following terms: 'The doors are twenty feet high, as if awaiting the day when a family of acrobats will walk from room to room, sideways, without dismantling them from each other's shoulders'. The blithe surrealism of this image should not blind us to its weight of implication: exposure to the imperial residues of Sri Lankan history confirms Ondaatje in the need to reinhabit its legacy upon his own terms. His passage through the 'labyrinth' of the governor's house therefore constitutes a crucial stage in his rethinking of his own cultural origins: a perception reinforced by the conversations he shares there with his Aunt Phyllis attempting to 'trace the maze of relationships in our ancestry' (RF, 25).

The fraught relationship between imperial discourse and indigenous experience remains an abiding theme of Running in the Family. It receives perhaps its most powerful expression in Ondaatje's examination of the Burgher class, the privileged social grouping to which his family belonged. The symbolic significance of Ondaatje's portrait of Burgher society can

scarcely be overstated: located precariously between identification with imperial authority and an unwelcome apprehension of the realities of colonial servitude, the Burgher's febrile social world reflects one aspect of the traumatic experience of cultural change during the era of decolonisation. Condemned to occupy an historical moment when the colonial hierarchies that underpinned their relative social privilege were upon the point of dissolution, the Burghers attempted to escape the social divisions of the pre-Independence period by inhabiting a fantasy world modelled upon the 'Jazz Age' cultural values of the Western leisure class (*RF*, 51).

But for all that the Burgher class strove to separate itself from the colonial realities of interwar Ceylonese culture, it remained firmly excluded from the English and European imperial social milieu. The Burghers' curiously liminal position between different cultures and modes of affiliation is highlighted in 'Historical Relations', a section which, with its studied allusion to the title of Robert Knox's seventeenth-century record of his incarceration upon Ceylon ('An Historical Relation of the Island Ceylon, in the East-Indies'), plangently evokes the experience of cultural estrangement and exile:

> This was Nuwara Eliya in the twenties and thirties. Everyone was vaguely related and had Sinhalese, Tamil, Dutch, British and Burgher blood in them going back many generations. There was a large social gap between this circle and the Europeans and English who were never part of the Ceylonese community. The English were seen as transients, snobs and racists, and were quite separate from those who had intermarried and who lived here permanently. My father always claimed to be a Ceylon Tamil, though that was probably more valid about three centuries earlier. Emil Daniels summed up the situation for most of them when he was asked by one of the British governors what his nationality was – 'God alone knows, your excellency'. (*RF*, 41)

The fragility of the indigenous Ceylonese self-image is nicely caught in this ironic sketch of a community in which everyone

is 'vaguely related' to everyone else, but no one is quite sure of their true identity or origin. This vignette offers a suggestive backdrop to the question Ondaatje poses throughout 'A Fine Romance': what should be the psychological and social response of the Ceylonese subject to its uncertain cultural location *between* European and Asian identities? One possible response to this dilemma is provided by Ondaatje's paternal grandfather Phillip ('Bampa'), who dedicates his life to the attempt to recreate himself as an English gentleman (*RF*, 56).

The riven image of the colonial subject appears in Bampa's vacillation between an enthusiastic embrace of English imperial style and an abiding attachment to native customs and habits. He is uncomfortably aware of inhabiting a persona that is neither 'white' nor Ceylonese ('He was dark and his wife was very white'); this unresolved tension expresses itself in his fluctuation between imperial mimic and sarong-clad indigene (*RF*, 56). Another significant feature of Bampa's cultural location is his fastidious cultivation of his 'empire', the family home Rock Hill. The quintessentially English overtones of the name 'Rock Hill' should not be overlooked: Bampa's jealously guarded estate exudes the ersatz authority of empire while mimicking the success of that empire in transforming native subjects into imperial functionaries. Read in the context of Ceylon's colonial history, Bampa's sedulous expansion of his 'empire' can be read as both a metonomy and a parody of British imperialism. On one hand, his occupation of a tranche of 'prime' land at the centre of Kegalle symbolises the imperial appropriation of indigenous economic and social resources; on the other, the isolation that follows his arrogant refusal to participate in the social life of his home city ('Most people considered him a snob') reflects the terminal prospects of an imperial governing class trying to impose its own authority and image onto a sullenly resentful subject population (*RF*, 55–6).

The full psychological and social effects of colonial identification with imperial codes and values emerge in the tortured personal history of Ondaatje's father Mervyn. Ondaatje's bittersweet memories of his father's erratic and charismatic personality

give *Running in the Family* real emotional depth and resonance; but Mervyn's unstable character is also symptomatic of a more general historical and cultural crisis. The particular nature of the crisis Mervyn embodies is revealed in the temporal shifts in Ondaatje's familial narrative. Despite some similarities of temperament and attitude, Ondaatje's father and grandfather inhabit very different worlds: where Bampa's yearning for assimilation into his own vision of Englishness seemed merely anomalous in the early decades of the last century, Mervyn's narcissistic identification with imperial culture during the throes of decolonisation and upon the eve of a newly independent nation-state has a wholly different significance. Seen in this light, Mervyn's chronic dipsomania, his rage and self-destructiveness, his childish ingenuousness and his almost compulsive desire to please should not be understood as elements of a purely private pathology: each of these traits represents an aspect of the trauma of colonial dispossession for a subject and a culture stranded between the coercive, if sometimes reassuring, mechanism of imperial authority and the uncertain prospect of a post-imperial future.

The opening paragraphs of 'A Fine Romance' offer an intriguing glimpse into the complexities of Mervyn's condition. His troubles began soon after he arrived in England from Ceylon to take up his place at Cambridge University (*RF*, 31–2). Cambridge for Mervyn is simply the backdrop to his fantasy of English aristocratic society; once in England this fantasy becomes confused with the business of everyday life. The suspicion that this fantasy is not Mervyn's alone is supported by his parents' prayer that a sojourn in Cambridge might absolve him of 'that streak of bad behaviour in the tropics': this expression, more commonly applied to the foreign excesses of aberrant scions of empire, reflects their conviction that a spell abroad has the potential to transform him into an English gentleman (RF 31). Mervyn's entire 'English' career never amounts, in fact, to more than a pastiche of ruling-class Englishness, combining as it does a wan aestheticism, a brief engagement to a Russian countess and the obligatory imperial adventure 'to fight against the

rebels' in Ireland (*RF*, 32). His thoroughgoing investment in the class dynamic of social climbing is unsurprisingly shared by his parents, whose fury at his earlier deception is quickly assuaged by news of his engagement to the eligible Kaye Roseleap, who 'leapt from the notable Roseleaps of Dorset' (*RF*, 32).

These early intimations of Mervyn's eccentricity soon acquire a much darker aspect. Mervyn is a profoundly erratic figure in *Running in the Family*: his experience embodies the violent splitting of a subject who can no longer recognise his own image within either imperialist or indigenous discourses of self-identification. Mervyn's brief immersion in upper-class English social life repeatedly confirms to him his irreducible cultural and racial difference from the rest of his milieu; at the same time his imaginative attachment to English class consciousness vitiates his former sense of national belonging. His emotional volatility expresses the historical condition of a man for whom there is now no proper place: the age of English imperial self-confidence for which he feels such nostalgia is steadily drawing to a close; but it was never, strictly speaking, *Mervyn's* age anyway. Although he is recurrently compelled in England to experience the fact of his cultural difference from everyone around him, he can find no way of translating this perception of difference into an idea of autonomy or independence. Mervyn's unpredictable fluctuation between an affiliation to imperial and indigenous Ceylonese culture persists after his departure from England: upon his return to Ceylon he unexpectedly announces his engagement to a local Ceylonese girl, Ondaatje's mother Doris Gratiaen; he then immediately follows this reassertion of his native attachments by joining the Ceylon Light Infantry and identifying himself once again with the neo-colonial insignia of the English ruling class.

Ondaatje's celebrated poem 'Letters and Other Worlds' focuses unflinchingly upon the sheer inscrutability of his father's image. In one famous passage Mervyn drunkenly deranges a religious procession in Ceylon: 'As a semi-official, and semi-white at that, / the act was seen as a crucial / turning point in the Home Rule Movement / and led to Ceylon's independence

in 1948' (*RF*, 25). No longer able imaginatively to locate himself as either an imperial scion or a colonial subject, this semi-white semi-official acts out the agony of his divided cultural inheritance in an orgy of self-destruction. His chronic dislocation is also reflected in his drunken habit of commandeering trains at gunpoint and leading them aimlessly back and forth across the Sri Lankan countryside. One such escapade achieved a minor place in national folklore because Mervyn's luckless passengers included John Kotelawala, who would later become prime minister of Sri Lanka. Despite Mervyn's temporarily crazed condition, his deference to one version of Englishness remains intact: discovering that he has unwittingly hijacked a train-full of sleeping high-ranking British officers, he negotiates his way quietly around the 'English carriage', careful not to disturb the imperial 'rage for order in the tropics' (*RF*, 154). These hallucinatory, and often terrifying, railway excursions offer a metaphor for Mervyn's private emotional state: he can only shuttle back and forth between unthinking prejudice and inchoate modes of feeling without ever making any objective progress beyond them. Mordantly amusing as these tales of drunken anarchy may be, Ondaatje never loses sight of the traumatic origins of his father's behaviour. His emotional disturbance is lent a nightmarish symbolic force in the prose fragment 'The Bone', which opens with the disquieting admission 'There is a story about my father I cannot come to terms with' (*RF*, 181). In this story, Mervyn had drunkenly commandeered another train, stripped off his clothes and paraded naked before his appalled fellow-passengers, before leaping down into darkness and running headlong into the jungle. Having finally tracked Mervyn down, his friend Arthur was confronted with the following sinister vision:

> My father is walking towards him, huge and naked. In one hand he holds five ropes, and dangling on the end of each of them is a black dog. None of the five are touching the ground. He is holding his arm outstretched, holding them with one arm as if he has supernatural strength. Terrible noises are coming from him and from the dogs as if there

is a conversation between them that is subterranean, volcanic. All their tongues hanging out. (*RF*, 181)

Hovering uncertainly between fantasy and reality ('Arthur cut the ropes and the animals splashed to the ground, writhing free and escaping'), this image manages to convey both aspects of Mervyn's psychological and social condition (*RF*, 182). On one side he is haunted by the potentially catastrophic threat posed to his self-image as he seems about to be torn apart by powerful and conflicting forces ('The dogs were too powerful to be in danger of being strangled. The danger was to the naked man who held them at arm's length, towards whom they swung like large dark magnets'); on the other there glimmers his curious sense of himself as a tragic, but redemptive, figure who internalised the agony of colonial dispossession in order to keep future generations from harm: 'He did not recognize Arthur, he would not let go of the ropes. He had captured all the evil in the regions he had passed through and was holding it' (*RF*, 182). His conviction of the redemptive power of his own example recurs in an episode at the very end of the book in which he attempts to explain the nature of his own depressive 'darkness' to two old friends:

> When I saw you come (my father said), I saw poisonous gas around you. You walked across the lawn to me and you were wading through green gas as if you were crossing a river by foot and you were not aware of it. And I thought if I speak, if I point it out it will destroy you instantly. I was immune. It would not kill me but if I revealed this world to you you would suffer for you had no knowledge, no defenses against it ... (*RF*, 200)

If Mervyn's manic mood-swings and internally divided self-image dramatise the social and psychological effects of the colonial relation, his interaction with other Sri Lankans also raises the question of how they might begin to respond to their traumatic imperial history. One of the ways Ondaatje explores this question is by examining indigenous attitudes to the practice of inter-ethnic marriage. This practice accrues considerable symbolic importance in *Running in the Family* because it offers both a symbol of prospective ethnic and social harmony and

a metaphor for the cultural tensions intrinsic to a polity still struggling to come to terms with the divisions of colonial rule. The sections of the book that recount the marriage of Ondaatje's parents provide a perturbing picture of the difficulties that still confront the newly independent nation. Thus the first response of Lalla, Doris Gratiaen's mother, to her daughter's marriage to Mervyn Ondaatje, is one of amused condescension: 'When my mother eventually announced her engagement to my father, Lalla turned to friends and said, "What do you *think*, darling, she's going to marry an Ondaatje ... she's going to marry a *Tamil!*"' (*RF*, 118). She 'continued to stress the Tamil element in my father's background' at every opportunity, and laughed uproariously all the way through the couple's wedding ceremony. This incident has lasting repercussions: Lalla's ethnic snobbery came to mark 'the beginning of a war with my father' (*RF*, 119). At the same time, the sheer banality of this familial struggle – Mervyn, his son recalls, would secretly train his dog to fart in Lalla's vicinity – undermines the implicit claim of either participant to moral or cultural superiority based upon their ethnic heritage. There is nothing essential to the concept of ethnic particularism, Ondaatje suggests, that can serve as an ethical or political ground for cultural identity or value. The political and moral tragedy of the last two decades of Sri Lankan history offers an unhappy testament to this fundamental statement of principle.

The marriage of Doris Gratiaen and Mervyn Ondaatje is culturally significant for other reasons. Whatever their ethnic and temperamental differences, the pair is united in its commitment to the enabling function of fantasy in the expression of interdicted desire and the management of social and psychological trauma. Rosemary Jackson has observed how fantasy operates simultaneously in two ways: it expresses the illegitimate and repressed contents of a particular need or desire, and, in so doing, traces the limits of a cultural order or system of values. By running up against, and frequently transgressing, the limits that define cultural order, fantasy 'opens up for a brief moment, onto disorder, onto illegality, onto that which lies outside the law, that which is outside dominant value systems'. Because the

'excursion into disorder' that fantasy represents can only begin from an imaginative position within the dominant cultural order, it illuminatingly exposes the very limits of that order: 'Its introduction of the "unreal" is set against the category of the "real" – a category which the fantastic interrogates by its difference'.[10]

The relationship between Ondaatje's parents opens up a fantastic space in which the expression of a mode of feeling that transgresses inherited notions of ethnic propriety reveals the violent and repressive nature of these ideas. Unwilling to countenance Lalla's constant emphasis upon Mervyn's 'inferior' ethnic status, the newlyweds create a private fantasy world unmarked by cultural antagonism or racial division. Early evidence of the couple's private fantasy world is provided by their wedding photographs in which they burlesque the habitual poses of romantic love. What lends this burlesque a more than usually subversive force, however, is its capacity to go beyond a parody of romantic expectations and reveal the barely repressed origins of the prejudice that motivates Lalla's contempt for her dark-skinned son-in-law – the imperial stereotype of the primitive colonial savage (RF, 161–2).

Ondaatje is instantly aware of the historical resonance of this subaltern document: 'My Aunt pulls out the album and there is the photograph I have been waiting for all my life' (RF, 161). The significance of his parents' investment in fantasy and theatricality is that it enables them to manage private psychological trauma by subverting imperial representations of colonial subjectivity. Yet the tragedy for the Ondaatje family is that this imaginative resistance to social division and racial prejudice is continually compromised by Mervyn's residual attachment to a fantasy image of the imperial leisure class. While Mervyn's dipsomania and self-destructiveness give poignant expression to the psychological and cultural alienation of the colonial subject, his litany of excess simultaneously reinforces the entrenched imperial stereotype of the ungovernable colonial savage. The emotional cost of Mervyn's self-cancelling identification with the forces that oppress him is movingly portrayed in the scene

where Doris is compelled to rework elements of private fantasy in order to ward off the domestic threat that her husband now represents:

> It was she who instilled theatre in all of us. She was determined that we would each be as good an actor as she was. Whenever my father would lapse into one of his alcoholic states, she would send the three older children (I would be asleep – too young, and oblivious) into my father's room where by now he could hardly talk let alone argue. The three of them, well coached, would perform with tears streaming, 'Daddy, don't drink, daddy, if you love us, don't drink', while my mother waited outside and listened. My father, I hope, too far gone to know the extent of the wars against him. (*RF*, 170–1)

Doris's artful manipulation of these tense familial scenes is an act of war to secure a fragile and temporary peace. Drawing strategically upon her memories of 'every play she had been in or had read', her direction of these little one-act dramas confronts her husband with the domestic legacy of his own emotional violence. (*RF*, 171) Their effect upon her youngest son is more ambivalent: aware that these impromptu performances sometimes win the family a temporary respite from his father's worst excesses, Ondaatje's reworking of these distressing childhood scenes also forces him to experience once more his own equivocal relationship to the image of his father. These fragmentary evocations of an unresolved private tragedy, in which theatricality and resistance to repressive authority are inextricably entwined, retain a lasting significance because they replay in microcosm the trauma implicit in all acts of colonial historiography, where remembering, as Homi Bhabha recalls to us, 'is never a quiet act of retrospection' but a 'painful re-membering, a putting together of the dismembered past to make sense of the trauma of the present'.[11] Painful as this act of aesthetic 're-membering' may be, it also enables us imaginatively to transcend the forms in which the past has been given to us by suspending the 'natural flow' of representation and laying bare the discursive constitution of cultural identities and values.[12] The paradoxical force and

substantive promise of the aesthetic is revealed in this simultaneous presentation and suspension of the merely given: art
awakens us to the fullest sense of who and what we are, and, in
so doing, compels us to transform ourselves through a confrontation with the forces that compose us.

This understanding of the aesthetic as a mode of perception
that permits both affective identification with, and an imaginative
opening beyond, particular states of being has substantial consequences for Ondaatje because it provides the conceptual ground
for a distinctly post-colonial poetics. Condemned, as Ondaatje's
compatriot Robert Kroetsch has observed, to inhabit a language
and a history that appears to be authentically its own but which
in fact retains the imprint of a concealed imperial experience, the
colonial subject is confronted with two choices.[13] The first, which
is expressed in the worldview of Mervyn Ondaatje, is to narrow
the distance between these historical perspectives to a point of
imperceptibility by means of a narcissistic identification with
imperial codes and values. The second is to insist upon the irreducible difference between these perspectives so that the experience of cultural dislocation constitutes the inaugural ground of
post-colonial subjectivity. Rather than attempting to assimilate
itself to a vision of colonial authority for which it was always the
inverse image and bad 'Other', post-colonial subjectivity seeks
to articulate itself in the play of difference *between* cultural
identifications and ascriptions of value. Deliberately adapting
the discriminatory identity effects of imperial discourse for its
own ends – those effects which, in Homi Bhabha's influential
formulation, produce an image of the colonial subject as white,
but not quite – this double inscription of (post)colonial identity as neither one thing nor another exposes imperial discourse
to the repressed cultural forces that challenge its entrenched
authority and opens up its singular version of history to a host
of competing voices.[14]

The perception that post-colonial subjectivity is an effect
of cultural difference inflects Ondaatje's sense of himself upon
his return to Sri Lanka. 'I sit in a house on Buller's Road', he
reflects at one pivotal point in his narrative. 'I am the foreigner.

I am the prodigal who hates the foreigner' (*RF*, 79). Simultaneously occupying the subject position of prodigal and foreigner,
he is unable to recognise himself as either the absolutely determined product of colonialist cultural representations or the
wholly singular exception to such external determination. What
strikes him instead is the way different perceptions of time –
the history of indigenous self-representation, for example, or
the imposed national narrative of imperial historiography –
produce different, and sometimes radically incompatible, forms
of cultural memory. Ondaatje playfully underlines the connection between modes of perception and versions of memory
in his account of his inaugural experience of time: 'About six
months before I was born my mother observed a pair of kaba-
ragoyas "in copula" at Pelmadulla. A reference is made to this
sighting in *A Coloured Atlas of Some Vertebrates from Ceylon,
Vol 2*, a National Museums publication. It is my first memory'
(*RF*, 75). The appearance of a 'memory' that is both internally
marked and externally fashioned underlines the dilemma of
the post-colonial subject who finds itself both central to, and
always already marginalised within, historical representations
of its own origins. For this reason *Running in the Family* returns
obsessively to the problem of establishing one's own proper
place within a Ceylonese cultural history that has become
almost completely inscrutable to the native gaze. Kneeling with
his children upon the flagged stone floor of a Colombo church
while they search for the legend of their forebears, Ondaatje can
only peer uncertainly through 'fading light' as he tries 'to catch
the faint ridge of letters worn away by the traffic of feet' (*RF*,
66). Try as he might, he can discover no uncorrupted remnant of
his historical beginnings: lifting the 'ancient pages' of the church
ledger into 'the last of the sunlight', he discovers 'the destruction caused by silverfish, scars among the immaculate recordings
of local history and formal signatures' (*RF*, 66). Other locations
reveal the same occluded history: 'To jungles and gravestones …
Reading torn 100-year-old newspaper clippings that come apart
in your hand like wet sand, information tough as plastic dolls'
(*RF*, 69).

Standing in the 'coming darkness' of a Sri Lankan evening, Ondaatje is momentarily overwhelmed by the country's portentous colonial legacy (*RF*, 65). Suddenly glimpsing a fragment of his own family history amid the sepulchral gloom of St Thomas's church, he is strangely uplifted, rather than discomposed, by the enigma it presents to ready comprehension: 'What saved me', he reflects looking down upon a series of barely legible letters preserved upon a portion of worn stone, 'was the lack of clarity' (*RF*, 66). Ondaatje's insistence upon the restorative value of forms of inscription that resist unitary determination is intended as a corrective to exclusively political responses to contemporary colonial conditions. This idea deserves a little exploration, because Ondaatje's attitude to the sphere of the 'political' has proved to be a contentious subject of debate. A case in point is his treatment of the tragic Sri Lankan youth uprising of April 1971. This insurgency, ruthlessly repelled by the security services, marked a key transitional stage between the reformist policies of the United Front coalition and the emergence of a more radical leftist Sri Lankan politics during the 1970s. The incipient revolutionary violence of the uprising had one other notable consequence: shaken by the unexpected force of the rebellion, the government rapidly reinforced the counter-insurgency capacity of the police and military, a development which reverberated throughout, and contributed towards, the factional agony of the country a decade later.

The background to the insurgency can be briefly sketched. Although the United Front's 1970 election victory promised both a redistributionist social and economic policy and a 'distinct leftward tilt' in its view of foreign affairs, the combination of high unemployment and rising prices that blighted its first year in office quickly precipitated a period of economic crisis.[15] By the early months of 1971, as K. M. De Silva notes, it was apparent that the government 'faced a deadly threat from the Janatha Vimukthi Peramuna (J.V.P.), an ultra-left organisation dominated by educated youths, unemployed or disadvantageously employed'.[16] To the consternation of the government, which failed to credit intelligence reports of the imminent threat that

the JVP now presented, a full-scale insurrection quickly erupted. De Silva takes up the story:

> The insurrection was from beginning to end a revolt of youth, the first large-scale revolt against government of youth in this country, and also perhaps the biggest revolt by young people in any part of the world in recorded history, the first instance of tension between generations becoming military conflict on a national scale. The creed of generational war was linked to the eradication of a colonial status which had ended two decades previously but was presumed to be still in existence. It was a movement of the new and ultra-left against the established left – the populist S.L.F.P. and the traditional parties of the left, the L.S.S.P. and the C.P. Although the most tenacious and defiant acts of the insurgents and the most serious centres of revolt accurately matched the large concentrations of the depressed castes, the *vahumpura* and *batgama*, caste was not the sole or even a major determinant of the insurrection. It was secondary to the class factor. The insurgents were in general the children of the rural poor, Sinhalese and Buddhist, and the ethnic and religious minorities played no significant role in the insurrection.[17]

These youthful insurgents make a brief, although unforgettable, appearance in 'Kegalle (ii)', one of Ondaatje's bittersweet meditations upon the rise and fall of Rock Hill. Here in a few tense paragraphs he juxtaposes the decline of his grandfather's country seat – Rock Hill would be sold within a year of the rebellion – with a sudden premonition of a new national narrative in which thousands of the marginalised and dispossessed offer a summary challenge to the 'neo-colonial situation' of Sri Lankan life.[18] Having broken into local government offices and acquired the location of every registered weapon in the county, the rebels move from address to address, sequestering weapons, food and equipment, until their progress brings them to the door of Rock Hill. Henceforth this potentially perilous encounter between two competing Sri Lankan worlds becomes increasingly surreal: apparently aware that Mervyn Ondaatje once donated land to be a playground for local children, the rebels treat his remaining

family with courtesy and kindness. The climax of the scene is wholly unexpected: momentarily relaxing their revolutionary vigilance, the young men lay down their arms and embrace a symbol of the despised colonial era by playing cricket with the Ondaatje family.

Chelva Kanaganyakam's judgement upon the surreal image of insurgents with cricket bats is curt and unforgiving: 'The juxtaposition is hardly amusing or convincing'.[19] Reflecting more generally upon Ondaatje's reduction of civil carnage to a succession of polished ironies, he sees this development as symptomatic of Ondaatje's substitution of literary sensibility for an awareness of the exigencies of political realities. Unlike other of his contemporaries who imbricate fact with fiction in order to create subaltern narratives of post-colonial history, Kanaganyakam continues, Ondaatje offers a vision of contemporary Sri Lanka which attempts to transcend the vexed issue of existing political commitments:

> The work's weakness lies in its refusal to participate actively in the referential, in its reluctance to condemn or praise; in foregrounding the 'narrative' at the expense of the 'national', Ondaatje abandons a wonderful opportunity to assert a much needed sense of belonging. Those of his generation, the 'Midnight's Children', many of them exiles and expatriates, had felt the need to create experimental and metafictional structures ... And yet they never fail to confront the immediate and the political. Except for occasional moments, as in the discussion of the poetry of Lakdsa Wikkramasinha, Ondaatje hardly ever shows signs of impassioned involvement with contemporary events. In his failure, Ondaatje shares the shortcomings of the majority of Sri Lankan writing in English which, for the most part, has stayed clear of the upheavals that have transformed a kindly and generous nation into a cruel and mindless battlefield.[20]

Ondaatje's engagement with Lakdsa Wikkramasinha's poetry affords an excellent opportunity to consider the relationship in his work between the 'immediate' and the 'political'. Ondaatje's response to Wikkramasinha is recounted in the

book's third section, 'Don't Talk to Me about Matisse', which takes its title from one of the latter's poems. Wikkramasinha's poem scornfully denounces an imperial culture that either ignores the material depredations of colonialism or else seeks to excuse them in the name of the aesthetic consolations they occasionally make possible. He juxtaposes these two evasive attitudes in the adjectival compound 'white-washed' ('and our white-washed / mud-huts were splattered with gunfire'), which gestures simultaneously to a mode of indigenous style and the history of imperial indifference to native pain and dispossession (*RF*, 86). Despite the considerable emotional charge of these lines, however, their view of a strictly antithetical relationship between 'European style' and indigenous culture is finally, as Douglas Barbour suggests, 'too monologic' for Ondaatje's text.[21] The four poems of Ondaatje's that follow attempt to explore the relationship between the externally perceiving eye and the quiddity of the Sri Lankan interior while inscribing the visual difference of this landscape at the heart of representation itself.

These poems open out upon a landscape where 'everything that is important occurs in shadow' and shadows 'eliminate / the path' from which the interior might be charted and definitively known (*RF*, 88–9). Surveying this land where 'brown men' rise 'knee deep like the earth / out of the earth', Ondaatje peoples his lyrics with a collection of figures whose vivid and irreducible difference one from another resists their presumptive assimilation into what Wikkramasinha calls 'the culture generally' (*RF*, 90). He discovers an aesthetic analogue for this interplay of images in the Sigiri 'communal poem' of the fifth century in which, as the lyric 'Women Like You' phrases it, 'Hundreds of small verses / by different hands / became one / habit of the unrequited' (*RF*, 93). The play between identity and difference that these lyrics institute is retraced in 'The Cinnamon Peeler', one of Ondaatje's most famous poems. Rehearsing the time-honoured imperial trope of the indigenous female body as the image of native cultural space, the poem begins by establishing an implicit correspondence between sexual love and the triumphant incorporation of the 'Other' into one's own sphere of

influence. From its opening lines an erotic fantasy of possession inscribes itself upon the domestic interior: 'If I were a cinnamon peeler / I would ride your bed / and leave the yellow bark dust / on your pillow' (*RF*, 95). Wholly encompassed by her lover's possessive desire, the body of the beloved becomes an extension of his authority and mode of feeling:

> Your breasts and shoulders would reek
> you could never walk though markets
> without the profession of my fingers
> floating over you. The blind would
> stumble certain of whom they approached
> though you might bathe
> under rain gutters, monsoon. (*RF*, 95)

Resolutely breaking the body of his lover down into a series of erotic affects – an 'upper thigh', an 'ankle', the 'crease that cuts your back' – the cinnamon peeler's mastery soon seems unassailable: 'You will be known among strangers / as the cinnamon peeler's wife' (*RF*, 96). But suddenly a narrative counter-movement begins which takes the cinnamon peeler beyond self-possession and asks him to accept the relative limits of his own angle of vision. In a startling reversal of perspective another form of desire now enters the poem: the desire of the native woman for a degree of autonomy and independence. Playfully accusing her lover of selfishness and infidelity, she issues a challenge to his authority that awakens him to a vision of freedom glimpsed as a reciprocal relationship between relatively autonomous bodies ('When we swam once / I touched you in water / and our bodies remained free'). True freedom for the dispossessed indigenous subject, the poem concludes, is not to be found in the absolute negation of external influence but rather by reclaiming the 'trace' of its troubled history upon its own terms (*RF*, 96).

The desire to reclaim a place for oneself within the narrative of a tragic history is the presiding theme of the book's final pages. 'During certain hours, at certain years in our lives, we see ourselves as remnants from the earlier generations that were destroyed', Ondaatje reflects, 'so our job becomes to keep peace with enemy camps, eliminate the chaos at the end of Jacobean

tragedies, and with the "mercy of distance" write the histories'
(*RF*, 179). The task of writing with the 'mercy of distance'
requires a demanding self-scrutiny: like his mother who, after her
divorce, was compelled to learn 'a new dark unknown alphabet',
Ondaatje's unravelling of his father's emotional legacy forces
him to reconcile himself to the 'chaos' of his own family history
(*RF*, 150). This spirit of reconciliation imbues the late section
'Thanikama' in which Ondaatje's narrative art tries to effect the
rapprochement between father and son that history denied them.
'Thanikama' begins by reliving the blank despair of Mervyn's
declining years: the futile meetings with a former wife who will
never return to him; the all-day drinking en route to a home he
can now barely remember. Mervyn's bearing throughout these
pages is of a man already years posthumous ('this corpse'), a
remnant of that Sri Lankan generation who could find no vital
stake in the future (*RF*, 188).

His fearsome isolation is suddenly broached by a strange
roadside meeting. Halting briefly in his car at Warakapola,
'where the dark villages held the future', Mervyn gives a lift
to a young cinnamon peeler, the symbolic representative of
his son's art and craft (*RF*, 187). What might appear to be a
moment of profound 'psychological identification' between the
two men is in fact a more complex movement of identification
and estrangement as Ondaatje reaffirms once more a vision of
post-colonial subjectivity that his father could never share.[22]
Following his father home in his imagination he pictures him
now at the centre of a disappearing world; even the book he is
reading is being destroyed by ravening ants one precious page at
a time. The disintegration of Mervyn's private world symbolises
the collapse of an entire stratum of Sri Lankan culture: unable to
transcend his narcissistic identification with the imperial imaginary, Mervyn is glimpsed finally 'with his back against the wall',
terrified of 'the company of the mirror' (*RF*, 189). Nowhere else
is the contrast between the father's life and the son's art so
poignantly expressed; defiantly rejecting the prior determination of experience by either an image of imperial authority or a
discourse of colonial nostalgia, Ondaatje turns his gaze instead

to the shape of the future-to-come:

> Sweat down my back. The fan pauses then begins again. At midnight this hand is the only thing moving. As discreetly and carefully as whatever animals in the garden fold brown leaves into their mouths, visit the drain for water, or scale the broken glass that crowns the walls. Watch the hand move. Waiting for it to say something, to stumble casually on perception, the shape of an unknown thing. (*RF*, 190)

'You must get this book right', Ondaatje's brother Christopher implored him. 'You can only write it once' (*RF*, 201). But looking back upon his finished manuscript, Ondaatje realises that his diffuse and necessarily incomplete text is the perfect form for the cultural history it narrates: 'While all these names may give an air of authenticity, I must confess that the book is not a history but a portrait or "gesture". And if those listed above disapprove of the fictional air I apologize and can only say that in Sri Lanka a well-told lie is worth a thousand facts' (*RF*, 206). Leaving Sri Lanka temporarily behind him, Ondaatje next prepared to adapt the 'well-told lie' of literary fiction to explore the modern origins of Toronto, his second home.

In the Skin of a Lion

Ondaatje's second novel *In the Skin of a Lion* (1987) inaugurates the mature phase of his fiction. It was also responsible in large measure for the sharp rise in his literary profile and was the first of his works to achieve a degree of commercial success. One reason for the novel's popularity is its exploration of a theme that continues to resonate at the core of our (post) modern condition: the experience of the deracinated individual adrift in the bewildering maze of the metropolis. By focusing upon the interrelated lives and struggles of a group of Toronto workers, both immigrant and native-born, Ondaatje retraces the imaginative terrain of modernist urban classics such as James Joyce's *Ulysses* (1922), John Dos Passos' *USA* (1936) and Ralph Ellison's *Invisible Man* (1952). But where these earlier novels fluctuated between an evocation of the phenomenological contents of subjectivity and an examination of the social and political contexts of modern life, Ondaatje's commitment to the material and communal experience of labour gives his version of this modernist aesthetic credo a distinctive ethical dimension. Deftly recasting the modernist exile as the modern proletarian or immigrant worker, *In the Skin of a Lion* argues that what is central to the history of our times – the process of labour responsible for the buildings and civic spaces that constitute one image of our technological modernity – is the very force that has effectively been repressed from historical consciousness. Like *Running in the Family* before it, *In the Skin of a Lion* presents both a memorial to a lost historical experience and a

complex reworking of collective memory that offers new ways of conceiving the narrative of a nation.

In a teasing prefatory note Ondaatje cautions us that 'This is a work of fiction and certain liberties have at times been taken with some dates and locales'. His playful tone dissimulates a robustly utopian spirit: these 'liberties' are intended as a true measure of freedom because they seek to reinvent the time and the space of cultural memory. They reinvent time and space, in fact, by reinventing time *as* space: at the heart of *In the Skin of a Lion* lies a distinction between the city perceived as the imaginary totalisation of bodies and the city experienced as a lived space of practices and traditions. For the Commissioner of Public Works' Rowland Harris, migrant labour is both economically indispensable and socially invisible: effortlessly transcending the world of physical toil, his monocular urban vision immobilises labour by translating it into the physical fact of the monuments it leaves behind. His lofty perspective evacuates lived experience from civic space by reducing the swarming life of the city to the exclusive demand of the scopic drive. This recoding of the endless self-differentiation of life into a transcendent mode of vision expresses a desire for 'pure' knowledge and the rationalisation of social authority. Michel de Certeau's reflections upon the perspective of the modern 'voyeur-god' who positions himself above and beyond the motility of urban existence offer a brief anatomy of this type of desire:

> His elevation transfigures him into a voyeur. It puts him at a distance. It transforms the bewitching world by which one was 'possessed' into a text that lies before one's eyes. It allows one to read it, to be a solar Eye, looking down like a god. The exaltation of a scopic and gnostic drive: the fiction of knowledge is related to this lust to be a viewpoint and nothing more.[1]

Harris's scopic drive does not, however, go unchallenged. Throughout the novel Ondaatje juxtaposes Harris's transcendent vision with another way of seeing engendered by the habits and spatial practices of everyday life. Turning away from Harris's Olympian perspective, the novel descends to ground

level to explore an experience of urban space that is immanent to, rather than abstracted from, the teeming life of the city. Impervious to the allure of the celestial eye, Ondaatje offers a fragmentary counter-history of social modernity that imagines urban life as the fluid and discontinuous movement between habits and habitus: life expressed, that is, in the passage between work space and home space, home space and neighbourhood, and between neighbourhood and the dream of a new civic and political community. Aware that the particular figure of history inscribed in Harris's authoritarian urban text requires the conversion of lived space into the *idea* of a city, Ondaatje's everyday record of Toronto disperses this ideal location into a series of viewpoints freed from the organising perspective of industrial capital. Behind this transition from idealised to lived space lies the profoundly utopian desire to turn the 'no place' of social representation inhabited by the immigrant worker into the image of a new community:

> To walk is to lack a place. It is the indefinite process of being absent and in search of a proper. The moving about that the city multiplies ands concentrates makes the city itself an immense social experience of lacking a place – an experience that is, to be sure, broken up into countless tiny deportations (displacements and walks), compensated for by the relationships and intersections of these exoduses that intertwine and create an urban fabric, and placed under the sign of what ought to be, ultimately, the place but is only a name, the City. The identity furnished by this place is all the more symbolic (named) because, in spite of the inequality of its citizens' positions and profits, there is only a pullulation of passer-by, a network of residences temporarily appropriated by pedestrian traffic, a shifting among pretences of the proper, a universe of rented spaces haunted by a nowhere or by dreamed-of places.[2]

In this experience of 'lacking a place' and this 'indefinite process' of being 'absent' and in search of a 'proper' civic identity we discover the guiding theme of *In the Skin of a Lion*. This theme is dramatised by the story of Patrick Lewis, the central character

of the novel, whose experiences provide a common thread linking the text's various sections. Before we meet Patrick, however, we must first take account of the novel's two epigraphs, drawn from the Sumerian *Epic of Gilgamesh* and John Berger's metafictional novel *G*.

The epigraph from *Gilgamesh* gives the novel its title: 'The joyful will stoop with sorrow, and when you have gone to the earth I will let my hair grow long for your sake, I will wander through the wilderness in the skin of a lion'. Despite Ondaatje's elliptical handling of the myth – he returns to quote from it in a key scene at the very end of his narrative – *In the Skin of a Lion* develops an important element of the *Gilgamesh* story. The passage Ondaatje quotes here describes a moment in the myth where Gilgamesh mourns the death of his friend and comrade Enkidu. Enkidu begins the story as the wild and untamed man of nature ('He was innocent of mankind; he knew nothing of the cultivated land'): seduced by a harlot from the city, he is separated from and rejected by the natural world.[3] Exiled from his true home, Enkidu challenges Gilgamesh, King of Uruk, to single combat; defeated by him, he becomes Gilgamesh's trusted comrade and defender. Later he is killed as a consequence of Gilgamesh's successful campaign to destroy the evil giant Humbaba and establish himself as the image of a just and omnipotent ruler. In symbolic terms, Enkidu's fateful relationship with Gilgamesh dramatises the cost of social integration: the perilous transition from nature to culture demands the violent renunciation of 'natural' man. In Ondaatje's hands Enkidu's mournful story also provides a template for the modern immigrant experience: marked at once as pre-cultural and pre-modern, the immigrant body too often finds itself excluded from the space of culture that it helped make possible. Like Gilgamesh, Patrick identifies himself with this abject body; and like Gilgamesh he is transformed by his relationship with it. The challenge before him is to translate empathy into political engagement by participating in the collective expression of a new social vision.

The epigraph Ondaatje takes from John Berger's *G* ('Never again will a single story be told as though it were the only

one') couples resistance to totalising points-of-view with a commitment to the recuperation of previously silenced voices and histories.[4] Berger is an important, if intermittently acknowledged, influence upon *In the Skin of a Lion* because his work insistently links modes of perception to forms of social praxis. In a revealing passage early in the novel Nicholas Temelcoff, a daredevil construction worker engaged in the building of the Bloor Street Viaduct, experiences a sudden technological epiphany: 'He floats at the three hinges of the crescent-shaped steel arches. These knit the bridge together. The moment of cubism' (*ISL*, 34). With its sly allusion to Berger's seminal 1968 essay 'The Moment of Cubism', the final sentence crystallises a moment of supreme novelistic self-consciousness: Cubist principles underlie Ondaatje's style of composition as well as Temelcoff's way of seeing.

The influence of Cubism upon Ondaatje's literary style lies in its dissolution of the field of vision into a multiplicity of viewpoints and a series of singular forces. The Cubists refused the perceptual privilege of Renaissance perspective and the omniscient point-of-view: what counts instead is the interaction between the surfaces and objects from which the picture is composed. Nothing else exists except the interrelationship of forms, planes and surfaces. It is no longer possible to 'complete' the picture by imposing a 'unity of meaning' upon it: instead we must find our place in a Cubist painting at the very moment that the discontinuity between its planes and surfaces spatially underscores the partial and located perspective of the viewer who would order it into coherence.[5] To appreciate the revolution in perspective that Cubism represents we must abandon the 'habit of looking at every object or body as though it were complete in itself' and consider in its place the relationship between *material forces* and *forms of perspective*. Through the Cubist reinvention of space, the relation between force and perspective is now inscribed in the structure of the objects themselves.

The extent of Ondaatje's investment in the 'moment of Cubism' becomes apparent as the novel proceeds. Berger's succinct formulation of the interior logic of Cubist form is, however, of

immediate importance: 'We begin with the surface, but since everything in the picture refers back to the surface we begin with the conclusion'.[6] *In the Skin of a Lion* obeys this Cubist injunction by beginning with a brief narrative insert which, relating as it does Partick's journey with Hana to Marmora and a reunion with Clara Dickens, actually constitutes the novel's concluding lines. The conclusion of the novel 'is' the interrelationship of the events that it describes: 'This is a story a young girl gathers in a car during the early hours of the morning' (*ISL*, 1). Form is politics and politics is form: *In the Skin of a Lion* intertwines a narrative about the mode of its own becoming and the tale of the emergence of the urban outsider as a citizen and a political subject. It is a story to be 'gathered', assimilated, and made one's own: a story that defines its characters in social, political and linguistic terms while being continually redefined by the place they make for themselves within its own shifting borders.

'Little Seeds', the novel's first section, charts the gradual emergence of the young Patrick Lewis's personality and worldview. Unsurprisingly Patrick experiences a divided sense of identity and inheritance: he comes from a family of homesteaders whose lifestyle 'typified the ascetic, puritanical industriousness seen as defining national identity by the early Canadian historians', but whose social position has been progressively eroded by the uneven development of industrial modernity.[7] A member of the indigenous community whose presence went largely unrecorded in the national narrative, Patrick's dual position as both prodigal and outsider supplies a nuanced perspective upon the emergence of modern Canada during the interwar years. His passage to Toronto from the remote logging station where he was raised mirrors the broader movement from countryside to city throughout this period; the years he spends amidst the city's migrant community reveal the human cost of the project of civic expansion that helped transform Canada into the image of a 'modern' nation. Much of the novel's emotional power is generated by Patrick's response to the plight of the migrant community; his identification with their struggle for rights and recognition provokes a conflict in him between the private man

of feeling and the public man of action. Every aspect of Patrick's existence is involved in this conflict; the boy who once stood deliberately apart from life is eventually compelled to declare his emotional loyalties and his ethical principles in the white heat of political foment.

Patrick's ambivalent relationship with the world around him is the presiding theme of the novel's opening pages. A solitary and sensitive child brought up in a motherless home, he spends his early years in rapt contemplation of nature: 'Bugs, plant hoppers, grasshoppers, rust-dark moths. Patrick gazes on these things which have navigated the warm air above the surface of the earth and attached themselves to the mesh with a muted thunk' (*ISL*, 9). His abiding sense of isolation is reflected in the separation of his home place from the wider culture: 'He was born into a region which did not appear on a map until 1910, though his family had worked there for twenty years and the land had been homesteaded since 1816' (*ISL*, 10). Lacking any vital relationship to the spaces mapped in his school atlas, Patrick creates instead a private imaginative world from an array of sensuous particulars:

> He longs for the summer nights, for the moment when he turns out the lights, turns out even the small cream funnel in the hall near the room where his father sleeps. Then the house is in darkness except for the bright light in the kitchen. He sits down at the long table and looks into his school geography book with the maps of the world, the white sweep of currents, testing the names to himself, mouthing out the exotic. *Caspian. Nepal. Durango.* He closes the book and brushes it with his palms, feeling the texture of the pebbled cover and its coloured dyes which create a map of Canada. (*ISL*, 8–9)

Like his father Hazen Lewis, the young Patrick is marked by an instinctive watchfulness and reserve. The peace of the boy's world is only disturbed by the appearance of a group of itinerant Finnish loggers; he is immediately drawn to their physical vitality and unassuming mastery of local terrain. Something impalpable about these men is also enigmatically disclosed to

him: he is moved by the way the common bond of fraternity transforms a 'collection of strangers' into a 'strange community' of men (*ISL*, 7). Patrick is both fascinated and appalled by this elliptical movement beyond self-possession; his ambivalent response is dramatised in a curious episode at the conclusion of the opening section. Gazing out towards the fields one winter's night Patrick suddenly detects a constellation of lights flickering across the darkness of the river; what he finds when he investigates this apparition propels him to the very edge of his known world. Arcing across the ice of the frozen river, a group of Finnish loggers illuminate the darkness with sheaves of burning cattails. Transfixed by the scene, Patrick experiences a sudden epiphany: 'But even to the boy of eleven, deep in the woods after midnight, this was obviously benign. Something joyous. A gift' (*ISL*, 21). Enthralled by the balletic grace of these shimmering bodies, he glimpses in their interchange of movement and gesture a minor miracle of creative expression: 'The hard ice was so certain, they could leap into the air and crash down and it would hold them. Their lanterns replaced with new rushes which let them go further past boundaries, speed! romance! one man waltzing with his fire . . '. (*ISL*, 22).

This vision marks a definitive break between two ways of seeing the world: from this moment on 'nothing would be the same' for Patrick (*ISL*, 22). In the skater's harmonious interdependence he senses another way of being in the world; yet he recoils from the challenge it presents to his enclosed and autonomous self: 'But on this night he did not trust either himself or these strangers of another language enough to be able to step forward and join them' (*ISL*, 22). Instead he turns away from the scene and retreats into the trees, 'carrying his own lamp' back into a private darkness (*ISL*, 22).

Part of the narrative burden of 'Little Seeds' is to estrange Patrick from his habitual way of seeing the world. His father works as a dynamiter in the feldspar mine excavations: his occupation lends an expressive image to the novel's abiding interest in the conflict between fixity and flux. Although himself a meticulous workman, Hazen does not attempt to impress a

'base of theory' upon his son: he discovers the truths of human experience in the relationship between the shaping hand and the material fact of the earth (*ISL*, 18). Scorning his father's preoccupation with the grain of material existence, Patrick 'absorbed everything from a distance' (*ISL*, 19). The potentially perilous implications of his indifference to the material world are registered abruptly one evening:

> [Hazen] could assemble river dynamite with his eyes closed. He was meticulous in washing his clothes every evening in case there were remnants, little seeds of explosives on his apparel. Patrick scorned this obsession. His father took off his shirt one evening and threw it onto the campfire. The shirt fizzed and sprayed sparks over the knees of the loggers. There were abrupt lessons like this. (*ISL*, 18–19)

The novel's second section, 'The Bridge', provides another abrupt lesson in the pressure material forces exert upon unprotected human material. Ondaatje's focus shifts now from the imperceptible social margin of national life to the expanding core of the modern metropolis. This shift also marks a transition from 'private lives' to 'public history': the story of the construction of Toronto's Bloor Street Viaduct symbolises a struggle between two antithetical visions of cultural space and tradition.[8] In the eyes of Commissioner Harris the viaduct reflects the power of capital to transcend the world of lived social relations: the bridge translates its human material into a monument of pure civic prestige. But in the eyes of the men who build it the bridge offers a glimpse of a hitherto invisible city: the collective experience sedimented in the experience of alienated labour embodies for them an image of a democratic polis redeemed from exploitation and social division.

'The Bridge' takes as its subject the perennial industrial conflict between labour and capital. What is distinctive about its treatment of this particular theme, though, is its translation of socio-economic forces into spatial relations. Perhaps the best explanatory model for Ondaatje's insistent spatialisation of force and perception is Deleuze and Guattari's distinction between

smooth and *striated* space. A smooth space for Deleuze and Guattari is open, indefinite and potentially unlimited; it lacks both a single organising principle and a set of fixed boundaries. Smooth space cannot be determined by a unitary standard or a transcendent point of vision; it is produced by the continuous variation and self-differentiation of its constituent elements. Smooth space is activated and dynamic space, not merely perceived or represented space, a space that is constituted by the free association of bodies. It is a *nomos*, not a *logos*: a space created by the fluidity of social relations in a particular time and place.[9]

If a smooth space continually opens up new trajectories and forms of becoming, it disappears when it is striated or made to conform to a fixed standard. A striated space, by contrast, expresses a vertical and hierarchical principle of organisation by combining multiple points of connection into a circumscribed territory. Striated space turns smooth space into segmented space: within its domain spaces are delimited, then gridded, and divided into areas of major and minor importance.[10] Striation functions most effectively by imposing a standardised 'work-model' upon every other type of activity. It subjects free action to fixed purposes and quantifies labour as a 'generalised operation' of the state apparatus.[11]

Although not of the same nature, smooth and striated spaces exist only in mixture: smooth space is constantly being stratified; striated space is continually being smoothed.[12] 'The Bridge' maps the first part of this movement by foregrounding Commissioner Harris's vision of a civic space purged of social relations. Ondaatje's bluffly declarative prose mimics Harris's subtraction of the human from the field of vision: 'The bridge goes up in a dream' (*ISL*, 26). Lifted free from the 'limitations' of human detail by the transcendence of the scopic drive, Harris's dream transforms a living city into an idea of pure form: 'The wind moved like something ancient against them. All men on the bridge had to buckle on halter ropes. Harris spoke of his plans to this five-foot-tall Englishman, struggling his way into Pomphrey's brain. *Before the real city could be seen it had to*

be imagined, the way rumours and tall tales were a kind of charting' (*ISL*, 29; emphasis mine).

Ondaatje's portrait of Harris's careworn and alienated workforce scrupulously resists his presumptive elimination of human detail. He also challenges Harris's visionary transcendence of social relations by incorporating an emergent paradigm of cultural subjectivity into his narrative: the story of the modern immigrant experience. The migrant worker embodies a paradoxical position in early twentieth-century Toronto, being at once integral to its mode of industrial production and extrinsic to the self-representation of its public sphere. Bound together, though, by the performance of a common action, these workers define the image of a nomadic society: a social formation defined by the immanent and continuously evolving relations between its constituent elements rather than its proscribed place within the state apparatus. To be nomadic in this sense is not to be constantly in transit between one point and another, but to renounce the stratification of enclosed and bounded spaces. A nomadic trajectory smooths space and overcomes the social division of settlements and subjects by dissolving the monumental figure of the city into the network of its constituent practices.

The story of the Macedonian construction worker Nicholas Temelcoff develops important aspects of this new spatial imaginary. Unlike Commissioner Harris, whose optical transcendence of the mundane sphere of labour reflects the social invisibility of the migrant body, Nicholas immerses himself in the near-at-hand and locally given world. His world is encountered close-up rather than seen from a distance: his field of vision is composed from multiple points of connection between material forces. The significance of what Ondaatje calls Nicholas's 'moment of cubism' is that it links an immanent practice to a new vision of collective experience by illuminating the material forces that form and deform the social body: 'He is happiest at daily chores – ferrying tools from pier down to trestle, or lumber that he pushes in the air before him as if swimming in a river … It does not matter if it is day or night, he could be blindfolded. Black space is time' (*ISL*, 34–5).

Despite his exclusion from the offical historical record ('Even in archive photographs it is difficult to find him'), Nicholas lives at the heart of the Toronto migrant community (*ISL*, 34). His imperceptibility highlights Ondaatje's distinction between two forms of historical ontology: unlike Harris, whose visionary gaze subordinates social relations to an impersonal idea of life, Nicholas perceives the tissue of living history in the social construction of space: 'Black space is time'. This tension between an immanent and a transcendent vision of social relations is symbolised in one of the novel's most dramatic scenes. One night in April 1917, five nuns stride out onto the unfinished bridge. As Harris watches in mute horror, a gust of wind lifts one of these women off her feet and flings her headlong into the vacant air. Falling towards certain death, she is saved at the last moment by Nicholas, who, swinging in mid-air beneath the central arch, reaches out to catch the 'black-garbed bird' as she spills out of the sky towards him (*ISL*, 32).

The vertiginous experience of the woman who will become Alice Gull is of signal thematic importance. In simple narrative terms, the incident brings together two characters who will each exert a profound and continuing influence upon Patrick Lewis. But the nun's fall also marks a moment when two worlds collide; from this moment she begins to exchange her investment in a redemptive vision of mankind for a commitment to collective social struggle. Recovering with Nicholas from their joint ordeal in the Lake Ohrida Restaurant, she envisages its twilight interior as 'another country' full of tactile pleasures and sensuous possibilities; suddenly catching sight of her habit in a hallway mirror she turns decisively away from her own spiritual image (*ISL*, 39). Her first faltering steps towards the world outside are also explicitly figured as a passage beyond the self into a new mode of becoming: 'What she will become she becomes in that minute before she is outside, before she steps into the six-A.M. morning' (*ISL*, 41). Nicholas, too, experiences her fall as a moment of rupture and change; upon waking he now sees the world 'from the point of view of the woman' (*ISL*, 48). What passes between them in the uncertain space between the

bridge and the mundane world is the premonition of a common destiny; for the rest of his life Nicholas will be haunted by the memory of the 'twin' whose breath is now partly his own.

Entering the subterranean world of the Lake Ohrida Restaurant the nun is bereft of voice and name; when she leaves she is reborn as 'Alice', having adopted the name of the restaurant parrot Alicia. Her self-reinvention is one small example of a broader revision of cultural origins; all over North America immigrants are becoming hybrid versions of themselves. The 'event' that 'will light the way for immigration in North America', Ondaatje wittily suggests, is the introduction of the talking picture; the dialects and gestures played out on screen provide these newcomers with a new language and a new set of social conventions (*ISL*, 43). Before this technological breakthrough most immigrants learned English by memorising popular songs or 'mimicking actors on stage'; plays in Toronto frequently ground to a halt when the entire crowd bellowed phrases from speeches heard at earlier performances (*ISL*, 47). Although Nicholas finds learning English 'much more difficult than what he does in space', he is brought to Canada in 1914 because of a 'spell' cast upon him by language: living in a Macedonian village, he is entranced by 'a fairy tale of Upper America' relayed to him by 'those first travellers who were the judas goats to the west' (*ISL*, 33–4). This 'fairy tale' offers Nicholas a compelling imaginative counterpoint to the existential hell of Europe on the brink of the First World War; he hurriedly leaves Macedonia after his village is burned when war breaks out in the Balkans. Later he discovers the cost of cultural translation to be the necessary repression of his own tragic history; like so many migrants before him, he becomes 'a vault of secrets and memories' (*ISL*, 47).

Nicholas's sense of anomie is reproduced in the social alienation felt by a number of the novel's main characters. The scale of social exclusion under modern industrial capitalism from the centres of wealth and privilege is explored in 'The Searcher', a section which brings all of these figures into relation with one another. The experiences of migration and internal exile are now part of a common narrative: arriving in Toronto at the age

of twenty-one, Patrick Lewis has become 'an immigrant to the city' (*ISL*, 53). Standing alone beneath the vast arches of Union Station he feels cut off from his former life: 'Now, in the city, he was new even to himself, the past locked away' (*ISL*, 54). All around him newly arrived immigrants call out in foreign tongues; unable to make themselves understood, they hover uncertainly within the 'safe zone' of the station 'as if one step away was the quicksand of the new world'. Contemplating this sequence of anguished and anonymous gestures, Patrick gains a sudden insight into the fate of the industrial masses in the age of monopoly capitalism: 'Patrick sat on a bench and watched the tides of movement, felt the reverberations of trade. He spoke out his name and it struggled up in a hollow echo and was lost in the high air of Union Station. No one turned. They were in the belly of a whale' (*ISL*, 54).

Patrick's encounter with the huddled masses at Union Station confronts him with a continuing dilemma: is the life of the individual a private story, expressed in defiance of the everyday world, or does it contribute to a 'human order' beyond itself, leaving all that it touches transformed (*ISL*, 145)? The boundaries of Patrick's private world are first tested by his role in one of the most curious episodes of modern Canadian history: the nationwide search for the Toronto theatre magnate Ambrose Small. By the end of the First World War Small owned a chain of theatres stretching the length and breadth of Canada. On 2 December 1919, he sold his chain to Trans-Canada Theatre Ltd for 1.7 million Canadian dollars. Leaving his wife Theresa to deposit the cheque in Toronto's Dominion Bank, Small spent the afternoon settling his outstanding business affairs, left his office, and was never seen again. Despite a nationwide manhunt and the offer of a $50,000 reward, no trace of Small was ever found. Because of Small's reputation as a philanderer, suspicion initially fell upon his mistress Clara Smith, beguilingly described by one commentator on the case as 'a vivacious brunette with an infectious smile and a way of walking that would stir the sensual desires of any male'.[13] After Smith was absolved of any involvement in the affair, the focus of the investigation switched to

Small's secretary and business manager John Doughty. Although Doughty was later convicted of bond-theft from Small's estate in 1921, no connection to his employer's disappearance could be established. By this time the entire country was consumed with the bizarre tale of the missing millionaire: Small was 'sighted' in Mexico, the United States and several Canadian cities, but he resolutely failed to materialise. In unwitting parody of the international obsession with the now mythic Ambrose Small, an escaped patient from the Wisconsin Asylum for the Insane contacted the Chicago *Tribune* in 1926 claiming to be the missing mogul; an avid reader about the case, he had 'digested all the dates, names and locations and when at last he made his escape he was ready to take Small's place'.[14] Ten years later the Small case ended in the courts when the burden of his estate was released to his wife. It proved to be the final act in a collective drama that had excited the hopes and fantasies of a generation.

With its inventory of implausible characters and its thoroughgoing pulp-fiction sensibility, the strange case of Ambrose Small demonstrates the imbrication of fact with fantasy in the making of popular history. Ondaatje meticulously recreates the fever of the time when 'over 5,000 men claimed to be Ambrose Small' (*ISL*, 55). In his version of the story Small becomes the subject of a national passion-play in which the erotic fetishisation of death offers a momentary respite from the banality of everyday life: 'A woman in Hamilton saw Ambrose with his throat cut. She woke one morning to feel blood on the pillow, looked up and saw someone was sawing her neck, and she said I am Ambrose Small. Then she woke up again'. Ondaatje highlights the fantasy element in the public obsession with Small by tailoring facts with abandon and recasting the entire story in mythic terms. He amends contemporary newspaper accounts of the case and alters the date of Small's disappearance, while supplying lurid and unsubstantiated gossip about the 'appalling parties' that Small never actually threw at his Glen Road home (*ISL*, 57). The effect of his historical revisionism is to transform Small into the superhuman embodiment of amoral 'bare-knuckle capitalism', a 'hawk who hovered over the whole

province, swooping down for the kill, buying up every field of wealth, and eating the profit in mid-air' (*ISL*, 57).

A year after arriving in Toronto, Patrick becomes a 'searcher' for Ambrose Small (*ISL*, 59). His search for, and struggle to the death with, Small dramatically changes his circumstances and encourages him to imagine life in wholly new terms. The precondition for Patrick's transformation is his meeting with Small's mistress Clara Dickens. By altering Clara Smith's surname to 'Dickens' Ondaatje hints slyly at his literary rewriting of the historical record; Patrick's instant attraction to Clara also captures something of his bookish retreat from the world into 'novels and their clear stories' (*ISL*, 82). Patrick's relationship with Clara is pivotal in the true sense: like the idea of remorse, as she expounds it to him, it involves 'a turning around on yourself' (*ISL*, 67). At certain moments Patrick's feeling for Clara seems to anticipate a new mode of social relation; entranced by the 'spell of her body' he finds himself enfolded within 'the complex architecture of her past' (*ISL*, 66). But although Clara challenges Patrick's solipsistic withdrawal from the world by 'bullying his private nature', he continues to shelter behind a self-protective silence (*ISL*, 72). This barrier is ultimately breached not by Clara, but by her actress friend, the former nun Alice Gull, whose performative reworking of her personal history encourages Patrick to emancipate himself from the shackles of his own past. Looking back upon the days he spent with the two women at Alice's farmhouse, Patrick accepts it was then that the horizons of his world first started to shift: 'He feels more community remembering this than anything in his life' (*ISL*, 79). This experience of emotional communion is unmercifully brief: refusing either to break with Small or provide clues to his location, Clara leaves Patrick, abandoning him to his romantic image of himself as the luckless victim of a pitiless fate. It takes Patrick two years to escape the shadow cast by Clara's disappearance; such respite as he is able to find demands a symbolic rapprochement with the emotional legacy of his own childhood. To open oneself to the future, Ondaatje suggests in *In the Skin of a Lion*, one must first unlock the past. The full force of this conviction is brought home

to Patrick by Clara's mother's admission that her daughter has hidden with Small in the one place – Patrick's childhood home Bellrock – that he would never wish to revisit: 'But he knew then. Knew exactly where they were. He had been the searcher who had gazed across maps and seen every name except the one which was so well-known it had remained, like his childhood, invisible to him' (*ISL*, 91).

Patrick's retreat from the public world into the private space of childhood places him in a position of considerable peril. His vulnerability is underlined by his near-fatal encounter with Ambrose Small, now mysteriously made flesh, who emerges from hiding long enough to attempt to burn Patrick to death. The mortal threat Small poses to Patrick is reinforced by a moment of profound psychological identification: gazing into his rival's eyes, Patrick glimpses the terrifying reflection of his own emotional isolation. In symbolic terms, Small's fantasmic reappearance in Patrick's home place forces him to acknowledge that there is no space untouched by the reified social relations of monopoly capitalism. For too long Patrick has existed as an unreflective 'creature of habit' that 'belonged with the last century' (*ISL*, 98). Following his struggle with Small he is 'less neutral now', prepared at last to try and define his own role within the troubled history of his time (*ISL*, 98).

Fittingly the next section, 'Palace of Purification' explores Patrick's emotional and political response to modern industrial society. Its title wittily juxtaposes Commissioner Harris's image of the 'ideal city' served by his new Lake Ontario Waterworks and the struggle of the migrant workers to be cleansed of the marks of their oppression and seen as something other than mute industrial hands (*ISL*, 109). In the east end of Toronto a tunnel is being built under Lake Ontario to lay intake pipes for the new Waterworks. Through what he calls elsewhere the 'irony of reversals', Ondaatje examines this episode by envisaging the construction of the Waterworks from the inhuman point-of-view of modern urban history itself (*ISL*, 133). With its combination of subjectless sentences and staccato verb-phrases, Ondaatje's prose poignantly evokes the anonymity of a group

of men who exist beneath the threshold of historical visibility: 'Work continues. The grunt into hard clay. The wet slap' (*ISL*, 105). Having effectively eliminated the identity of these workers from the novel's field of vision, Ondaatje assimilates their history to a technological image of urban life whose condition of possibility is the reification of lived experience:

> In the tunnel under Lake Ontario two men shake hands on an incline of mud. Beside them a pickaxe and a lamp, their dirt-streaked faces pivoting to look towards the camera. For a moment, while the film receives the image, everything is still, the other tunnel workers silent. Then Arthur Goss the city photographer packs up his tripod and glass plates, unhooks the cord of lights that creates a vista of open tunnel behind the two men, walks with his equipment the fifty yards to the ladder, and climbs out into sunlight. (*ISL*, 105)

For a moment, while the film receives the image, everything is still, the other tunnel workers silent: somewhere in this proliferation of subordinate clauses a defining image of the modern city comes into focus. This image derives elements of grandeur from its classical inheritance: descending like Prometheus, the photographer casts transfiguring light upon the dull sublunary world. Something else is, however, illuminated by the flash of the camera eye: the no-time of historical representation in which the migrant workers live. In a staged picture to celebrate the tunnel's completion two men with dirt-streaked faces shake hands upon a muddy incline; everything that sustains the stubborn resistance of proletarian tradition to social authority is effaced by the false image of reconciliation the image projects. Technology, not labour, now creates the 'vista' of open tunnel that its products work to preserve, while far away beneath the sunlight, the 'cut of the shovel into clay' persists in immemorial darkness (*ISL*, 105).

Goss's photographic social history of modern Toronto offers an interpretative clue to the novel before us: we must look beyond the 'white lye' of established civic history to the social forces its representations obscure (*ISL*, 111). To do so would

mean to detect signs of redemptive promise in the 'unfinished world' these images describe: the promise of a coming community whose emergence expresses itself through its potential to become other than it is. Working upon the Lake Ontario Tunnel Patrick takes his place within just such a community: a community within which the common fear of death puts each man *in the position of his neighbour* and inscribes this image of reciprocity at the very heart of life. While Harris continues to dream of his ideal city, Patrick's sense of time and space is transformed by his participation in the collective becoming of this new social grouping. Working amongst the migrant community he is estranged from every aspect of his former existence; finding himself an 'alien' among this group of outsiders, Patrick tries desperately 'to leap over the code of languages between them' (*ISL*, 113). Soon, however, he comes to perceive the possibility of freedom in his 'deliriously anonymous' new circumstances (*ISL*, 112). Making common cause with migrant workers with whom he can exchange only elementary fragments of language, Patrick is compelled to improvise a role for himself in the collective performance of everyday life.

The idea of performance is central to the novel because it expresses a mode of social relation that is defined by the relations it establishes between its constituent parts rather than by subjecting life to the tyranny of a general rule or an organising point of vision. Performance creates the medium of its own existence without reference to external norms, laws or boundaries; it smoothes striated space by opening up new points of connection within the spatial organisation of social experience. Ondaatje underlines this point in the scene in which Patrick is invited by his fellow workers to a clandestine meeting in the half-built Waterworks. Two features of this scene are noteworthy: this nocturnal gathering takes place outside the law and beyond the watchful eyes of the authorities; and it employs the idea of performance to expose the determining conditions of social existence. The irreducibly political character of theatrical performance in this context is encapsulated by the allegorical puppet-play enacted before the assembled spectators. The ensuing drama performs a

utopian vision of social assimilation and the migrant experience: the costumes of the forty puppets represent 'a blend of several nations' that expresses their desire for political representation upon the 'dangerous new country of the stage' (*ISL*, 116). This residue of utopian thinking resonates at the core of the play itself, which dramatises the struggle of a nameless 'hero' – an allegorical image of the anonymous immigrant body – to assert his autonomy and independence in the face of social authoritarianism and political repression. The hero's humiliation before civic authority affords the crowd an image of its own dispossession; its collective identification with his fate transforms social anomie into the beginnings of political resistance:

> A plot grew. Laughing like a fool he was brought before the authorities, unable to speak their language. He stood there assaulted by insults. His face was frozen. The others began to pummel him but not a word emerged – just a damaged gaze in the context of those flailing arms. He fell to the floor pleading with gestures. The scene was endless. Patrick wanted to rip the painted face off. The caricature of a culture. His eyes could not move away from that face. (*ISL*, 117)

During the performance of the puppet play art becomes a vehicle for political dissent by reinventing the relationship between lived space and everyday practice. This dissent is expressed by the recoding of space (the play transforms a space of work and subjection into a zone of recreation and social solidarity), the refusal of interdiction (its performance requires secret entry into previously forbidden territory) and the reassertion of native tradition and folk memory. Watching the play Patrick makes the transition from social outsider to the representative man of the crowd: emotionally overcome by the spectacle of the hero's silent suffering, he steps out from the audience and becomes a part of the drama. What he finds when he reaches the exhausted figure on stage confounds all his preconceptions: the 'hero' is in fact a woman, Alice Gull. Patrick's shock at this revelation is part of the scene's broader revaluation of roles and responsibilities: 'What had been theatrical', Patrick reflects as

he moves uncertainly backstage, now seems a part of a more general 'metamorphosis' (*ISL*, 120).

Patrick is transported by his experience of communal performance because it affords him a vision of the world unconstrained by the repressive social relations of industrial modernity. This capacity of art to offer a vision of life beyond the social determination of human experience informs every level of Patrick and Alice's exchanges about the nature of political commitment and ethical action. Throughout their discussion Patrick evinces a distrust of the 'language of politics' which he sees as too narrow and prescriptive to encompass the scope of our ethical nature (*ISL*, 122). Political rhetoric misses what it means to be human, he implies, at the very moment that it tries to translate thought into the dogmatic repetition of a fixed principle. Although Alice recognises nothing more in Patrick's remarks than a solipsistic withdrawal from any political commitment to a just society, his refusal to allow social relations to be the subject of a general determination nonetheless maintains a singular fidelity to the event of experience. In contrast, Alice's revolutionary politics subordinates life to the presumptive terms of an ideological decision: despite her commitment to the political potential of art ('You reach people through metaphor'), art remains inadequate in her view to effect lasting social change (*ISL*, 123). In a world where the pursuit of 'truth' and 'justice' means nothing more than to 'name the enemy and destroy their power', politics, rather than ethics or aesthetics, becomes for her the determining ground of every genuine human value (*ISL*, 124).

It is a measure of Ondaatje's aesthetic integrity that the terms of this debate remain equivocally poised. The purpose of the exchange is not unquestioningly to privilege either participant's position: each is made aware during the course of the conversation of an inconsistency in their own view of the world. There is undoubtedly a certain justice in Alice's charge that Patrick invests too heavily in a reactive 'image of compassion': to be just it may sometimes be necessary to move beyond moral rhetoric and intervene in the sphere of political action (*ISL*, 124). At the same time, Alice's militant commitment to an ideological

version of truth takes little account of the interior space where part of our humanity resides. Certainly the novel exhibits scant sympathy for Alice's absolutist belief in the ethical primacy of her ideological 'grand cause' (*ISL*, 125). Ondaatje's distaste for the ideological circumscription of private feeling expresses itself in the bleak irony of one of the novel's most tragic incidents. Attempting to convert Patrick to her unsparing political vision, Alice adapts a line from the journals of the Canadian poet Anne Wilkinson to suggest how revolutionary action reveals 'the extreme looseness of the structure of all objects' that constitute the horizon of any particular social system (*ISL*, 135). While this remark, as Glen Lowry points out, usefully illuminates the 'chain of loosely related, seemingly coincidental events' that brought Alice and Patrick together – her vertiginous fall from the Bridge, Temelcoff's miraculous rescue, Alice's friendship with Clara Dickens, Patrick's sudden move to Toronto – it also anticipates Alice's violent demise at the hands of unseen ideological forces: she will be literally taken to pieces when a terrorist bomb she is unknowingly transporting explodes in a public thoroughfare.[15]

Alice's tragic story crystallises a broader point about the relationship between ideology and aesthetic experience. Her insistence upon the need for direct political action demonstrates how very much more urgent ideological imperatives often appear than the call of what Ondaatje calls elsewhere the events of art. Ideology speaks to our need for an explanatory narrative to make sense of everyday life; art, on the other hand, seems somehow too slow in its response to the pressure of reality, always lagging behind the events it purports to describe. But it is, Ondaatje maintains, the very slowness of art – the quality that may make art appear superfluous or merely ornamental – that enables it to transcend the raw force of contingency and provide an imaginative structure with which we might understand the 'chaos' of our historical experience: 'Official histories, news stories surround us daily, but the events of art reach us too late, travel languorously like messages in a bottle ... The first line of every novel should be: "Trust me, this will take time but

there is order here, very faint, very human"'(*ISL*, 146).

While certainly no artist, Patrick's openness to aesthetic experience enables him to maintain an imaginative distance from 'official histories' without seeking to replace them with an ideological image of life. Often this aspect of Patrick's nature reveals itself in fleeting moments of sensuous responsiveness: listening to the strains of Puccini's *La Bohème* in a communal bathhouse, he is granted sudden insight into the 'clarified world of passion' that art sometimes manages to redeem from the pressure of the workaday world (*ISL*, 136). Puccini's opera achieves its 'clarity', Ondaatje implies, through its extra-subjective dimension: his music embodies the singularity of modes of feeling – it performs *this* or *that* person's desire or despair – in a sensory medium that recalls us to that quality of imaginative sympathy we each hold in common. The potential of art simultaneously to enact and transcend the singularity of lived experience is crucial to *In the Skin of a Lion*; it is by means of this capacity that Ondaatje makes a connection between modes of perception and ways of reinterpreting the historical world. Patrick has an abiding sense of the enigma of aesthetic experience: avidly consuming novelistic romances as a child, he had 'never believed that characters lived only on the page. They altered when the author's eye was somewhere else' (*ISL*, 143). His intuition that the meaning of these stories is in part determined by the reader's angle of vision informs his later historical research into the history of the Bloor Street Viaduct. Poring over surviving newspaper accounts of Commissioner Harris's visionary project, Patrick begins to imagine another kind of history which would inscribe the exigencies of immigrant labour at the heart of modern social experience. Like Lewis Hines's photographic record of American child labour, which exposed the brute fact of material exploitation that 'official history' works so hard to dissemble, Patrick's counter-history of modern Toronto seeks to illuminate the hidden 'interactions' by which a community defines an ethos and a place (*ISL*, 144). This subaltern idea of history has an avowedly ethical dimension: it aims to make each member of the community aware of how they are sustained 'by the strength of something

more than themselves' (*ISL*, 144). As Patrick emerges one day from his archival labours in the Riverdale Library, his footsteps begin surreptitiously to merge with the rhythms of a street-band of musicians. Entranced by the interrelationship between musical phrase and structure, Patrick sees in art a template for the historical imagination: 'His own life was no longer a single story but part of a mural, which was a falling together of accomplices. Patrick saw a wondrous night web – all of these fragments of a human order, something ungoverned by the family he was born into or the headlines of the day' (*ISL*, 144–5).

The novel explores the relationship between art and temporality in both formal and thematic terms. Stunned by Alice's untimely death, Patrick consoles himself by recomposing her memory in sequences of broken phrases. What these phrases unexpectedly reveal to him is the 'real gift' of literature: literature gives us the opportunity to 'turn the page backwards' and experience the past in all its singular force (*ISL*, 148). The force of literature, upon this reading, lies in its power to reinvent the experience of historical time: art permits us a 'retreat from the grand story' so that we might revisit those 'fragments of memory' which encapsulate the particular history of an individual or a people (*ISL*, 148). Desperate to fill the void left by Alice's disappearance, Patrick's imaginative recreation of her image inaugurates a double temporality in which she is simultaneously alive and dead, given to us in both the continuous present tense of her life with Patrick and as a stream of memories and sensations that gradually dislocate him from the surrounding world. Patrick's experience in this regard is typical of the novel's larger recursive structure in which events repeatedly reveal unknown facts about the past that transform the way a character conceives of his or her present circumstances. Reminiscing about Cato, the father of her daughter Hana, Alice tells Patrick how the night he was born his father had to skate three miles for a doctor across a frozen lake with only lit cattails for a guide. Not only does this anecdote unlock one of the enigmatic images with which the novel begins ('Now in his thirties he finally had a name for that group of men he witnessed as a child'); it also reveals to Patrick the

buried immigrant experience concealed in his formative child-hood memory (*ISL*, 151). Patrick returns this gift of renewed and extended memory when he gives Alice's friend, the Macedonian baker Nicolas Temelcoff, a newspaper photograph depicting him as one of the 'daredevils' suspended from the Viaduct Bridge (*ISL*, 34). Talking to Patrick, Nicolas is suddenly reminded of the night he reached into the sky to catch a falling nun; only now, amid Nicolas's dreamy recollection, is the nun revealed to be Alice Gull. 'Talk, you must talk', Nicholas implores the stricken woman in the Lake Ohrida Restaurant, 'and so mockingly she took a parrot's name. *Alicia*' (*ISL*, 148). Reflecting later upon the rupture with memory that the 'pleasure of recall' produces, Nicholas realises that this capacity to reinterpret the meaning of one's own life is part of what 'history' means:

> This is what history means. He came to this country like a torch on fire and he swallowed air as he walked forward and he gave out light. Energy poured through him. That was all he had time for in those years. Language, customs, family, salaries. Patrick's gift, that arrow into the past, shows him the wealth in himself, how he has been sewn into history. Now he will begin to tell stories. (*ISL*, 149)

The need for individuals to lay a narrative claim to the past – to sew themselves back into history – is one of the novel's strongest themes. Nicholas's epiphany suggests one way in which the cultural outsider may imaginatively integrate himself into a new national narrative. At the same time, Ondaatje never abandons his understanding of historical process as an effect of material struggle and social transformation: his commitment to the view that history, in Fredric Jameson's pithy phrase, is what hurts.[16] Certainly Patrick is never allowed to lose sight of this salutary truth: the job he takes at Wickett and Craig's tannery soon after arriving in Toronto exposes him to some of the very worst conditions in which migrant labour is forced to sustain itself. These tannery sections expose the folly of those who would ignore Alice's injunction that, 'It is important to be close to the surface of the earth' by forgetting the material condi-tions of social existence (*ISL*, 141). Stationed on the tannery

floor Patrick is perfectly placed to observe the work of the dyers, those men who give rolled leather its borrowed colour and gloss. Immersed up to their necks for hours in circular pools of dye, the dyers are paid a dollar a day to perform a task that will eventually kill them of consumption. Ondaatje's haunting rendition of their plight offers a caustic reproof to the idealised image of the New World as the melting pot of nations – these men appear literally to be melting as the toxic dyes seep into their body – while reminding us of the human cost of the dream of self-transcendence we call the immigrant experience. Such knowledge renders absurd the utopian metaphor which blithely envisages migration as the successful entry into the skin of another culture: pulling wet hides from the circular pools, the dyers appear to have 'removed the skin from their own bodies' (*ISL*, 130). For a moment Ondaatje's prose reproduces the immigrant dream of cultural assimilation almost upon its own terms ('They had leapt into different colours as if into different countries'); but even as this vision begins to materialise it is undermined by the punning correspondence between 'dyeing' and 'dying' that runs throughout the scene. What these workers are offered, Ondaatje insists, is a mere shadow of the freedom they crave: leaving the tannery each day they enjoy the 'erotica of being made free'; each night, though, they must prepare themselves to receive the visible mark of their subjection once again (*ISL*, 132).

The unresolved political tension between freedom and servitude dominates the second half of the novel. Reading Cato's letters recounting his role in the murderous struggle for union recognition in Canadian lumber camps, Patrick is shamed by his previous indifference to an entire stratum of his nation's social history. Humbled by Cato's sacrifice, he perceives himself by contrast to be a timorous citizen of 'Abashed, Ontario' who gazed into the darkness of his own country and saw nothing there but the spectral outline of his own image (*ISL*, 157). Reflecting upon his own self-absorption, Patrick is struck once more by the failure of empathy – what the narrator calls a 'gap of love' – that held him for so long aloof from the concerns of the wider community (*ISL*, 157). But recrimination about the past is futile:

what he must do, he realises, is 'become a searcher again' for a way of life incompatible either with solipsism or subjection to established social interests (*ISL*, 156). Ondaatje underscores the co-existence of these two imperatives by reworking one of the novel's central metaphors. Recalling Alice's description of a theatrical performance in which the redistribution of social power and prestige was symbolised by the circulation of a cloak composed of animal pelts, he invokes this image to underline a connection between ethical responsibility and participation in the collective figure of political struggle: 'Each person had their moment when they assumed the skins of wild animals, when they took responsibility for the story' (*ISL*, 157). Patrick's moment of decision arrives when Alice's death leaves Hana an orphan: by taking responsibility for her story he discharges a debt to the past while beginning to claim his own stake in the creation of a common future.

The nature of our inheritance from the past is only fully revealed when we learn to turn our gaze to the future: this is the difficult wisdom Patrick must labour to acquire. The implications of this enigmatic lesson elude him in the terrible aftermath of Alice's obliteration: his subsequent incineration of the Muskoka Hotel in the section entitled 'Remorse' merely reaffirms the logic of terrorist violence that sent Alice to her grave. Patrick's actions during his self-destructive flight from Toronto express remorse in its most pernicious form: a violent turning against the self that prevents the self from becoming other than it is. In keeping with Ondaatje's commitment to the irony of reversals, the peril of Patrick's situation is revealed to him by the advice of a sight-less woman in the Garden of the Blind: he must refuse to 'resent his life' by making thought and feeling conform to a predeter-mined series of ideological gestures (*ISL*, 170). Watching the woman negotiate a sensual passage through the flower garden, Patrick becomes aware of another mode of perception: a way of 'seeing' which refuses to subordinate the flows of perception from which we organise our image of the world to a single point or principle. When he leaves this magical space hours later he has become somehow 'unhistorical': a creature whose experience

of the world can no longer be exhausted by the ideological plane from which we judge and order life *(ISL,* 172).

Patrick's fragile experience of 'unhistorical' being is unmercifully short-lived: when Part Three of the novel begins he is incarcerated in Kingston Penitentiary for his earlier incendiary crime. Yet the notion of the 'unhistorical' is meant to evoke a particular mode of perception rather than an entire way of life; consequently the force of this experience continues to resonate through each of the novel's final two chapters. It makes itself felt in the contrast between Patrick's angle of vision and the worldviews of three very different characters: the thief Caravaggio, Ambrose Small and Commissioner Harris. To talk of incommensurability between the points-of-view of Patrick and Caravaggio might appear, at least at first glance, to swim against the novel's emotional current. For not only does the penultimate chapter – tellingly entitled 'Caravaggio' – present a wry and sympathetic account of its eponymous hero's life and crimes; it also seems to prepare us for Patrick's subsequent accession into Caravaggio's sphere of influence. On the surface of things this observation is not without merit: 'Caravaggio' begins, after all, by describing Patrick's awed witness of Caravaggio's miraculous escape from prison and takes for one of its central episodes an incident in which Patrick attempts to save the thief from a savage jailhouse beating. Caravaggio's influence upon Patrick is also implied in those retrospective passages that explore Caravaggio's background and criminal apprenticeship. When reading these sections it is difficult to escape the impression that much of the writing has taken on a slightly tangential quality; it is almost as if the characters portrayed here had stepped fully formed from the pages of another novel. This impression, while well attested, is also somewhat misleading: Ondaatje's interest in Caravaggio, in the penultimate chapter at least, is not confined to the role he might play in the development of a plot or the unfolding of a narrative. Instead, his rootless existence beyond social norms and conventions embodies a way of seeing the world liberated from the organising perspective of everyday life. The emergence of a mode of vision irreducible to the embodied

and located perspective of everyday perception is the subject of
those scenes that chart Caravaggio's nomadic movement across
the Lake Ontario landscape:

> He was running, his boots disappearing into grey bush.
> Away from Lake Ontario, travelling north where he knew
> he could find some unopened cottage to stay quietly for
> a few days. Landscape for Caravaggio was never calm. A
> tree bending with difficulty, a flower thrashed by wind,
> a cloud turning black, a cone falling – everything moved
> anguished at different speeds. When he ran he saw it all.
> The eye splintering into fifteen sentries, watching every
> approach. (*ISL*, 182–3)

But here we have to be careful: what is glimpsed in this passage
is a potential in Caravaggio to see the world otherwise that is
nowhere productively sustained in any other aspect of his life.
In these terms his criminal career is a perversion of his singular
gift of vision: implicit in his virtuoso displays of pelmanism –
that extraordinary mastery of space revealed in his ability to
empty a room and then return each object to its place in perfect
darkness – is the corruption of an expansive mode of becoming
for narrow and selfish ends (*ISL*, 189). It is difficult, with this
in mind, to concur with Douglas Barbour's generous conclusion
that Caravaggio emerges in these pages as 'the spokesman for a
marginalised awareness of the various and subtle demarcations
in society'.[17] Instead what begins in lyrical exorbitance ends in
perceptual limitation: 'As a thief he had a sense of the world
which was limited to what existed for twenty feet around him'
(*ISL*, 189).

The contrast marked implicitly in 'Caravaggio' between self-
limitation and self-transcendence becomes the explicit theme of
'Maritime Theatre', the novel's final chapter. Ondaatje's narrative
now moves abruptly forward in time, switching its focus from
Caravaggio's joyous reunion with his wife Giannetta following
his Kingston jailbreak to Patrick's own return to Toronto in 1938,
five years after he attempted to incinerate the Muskoka Hotel.
Slowly accommodating himself to the noise and bustle of Toronto's Union Station, Patrick acknowledges that this 'cathedral-like

space' has gradually become 'the nexus of his life' (*ISL*, 209). Life in this image, in sharp contradistinction to the boyish worldview of 'Little Seeds', is no longer the expression of a self-enclosed point-of-view: it is a collective 'space' defined by the connections it makes possible between different subjects and practices. The implications of Patrick's epiphany are subsequently borne out in his own experience: arriving back in Toronto he inherits another legacy of his relationship with Alice – he formally assumes the mantle of Hana's father – that alters the trajectory of his entire future (*ISL*, 211). This image of life as a proliferation of possible connections which potentially expose the present moment to a new perception of time is reinforced by the recursive structure of Ondaatje's prose. As the narrative moves towards Patrick's climactic confrontation with Commissioner Harris at the Waterworks, its momentum is interrupted by Clara's telephone call to Patrick from Marmora asking for his assistance following the death of Ambrose Small. Narrated in the present tense, this exchange at once constitutes an analeptic reference back into the past time of reading – it precipitates the journey with which the entire novel 'began' in the narrative insert prior to the beginning of 'Little Seeds' – and a proleptic leap into the future beyond this particular textual moment: for Patrick actually to hold this conversation he must have survived his potentially catastrophic encounter with Harris in the novel's final pages. Here as elsewhere Ondaatje presents writing as an event in time that continually expands our sense of what time can be; a sequence of perceptions that can always extend itself beyond any merely subjective perspective to open up a new image of life.

Ondaatje's fascination with perception as a 'becoming-imperceptible', or an impersonal sequence of images from which single images of life are composed, resurfaces in the haunting passage describing the death of Ambrose Small.[18] This brief and enigmatic scene, which suddenly interrupts the story of Patrick's homecoming to Toronto while seeming to belong to an entirely different world, is, in fact, of central importance to the novel's progression of themes. Progression, in this instance, is emphatically an effect of the forcible juxtaposition of perspective:

where Patrick's experience has taught him how each moment contains a virtual power of becoming capable of being actualised in the future in many different forms, Small's existence is dominated by the need to subordinate life to the demand of his own point-of-view. This demand took an extreme form even in the days when he remained an active participant in Canadian business circles: 'Ambrose Small, as a millionaire, had always kept the landscapes of his world separate, high walls between them' (*ISL*, 213). Rejoining him during the years of his self-imposed exile from public life, Clara discovers a man who can now only perceive the world as an expression of his own interests and needs: 'But during the years that she lived with Ambrose she would know him only as he wanted to be known by her. There was no other road towards him' (*ISL*, 213). The suspicion that what looks like a triumphant assertion of self is instead a death-in-life is confirmed in both emotional and symbolic terms by the record of Small's final days. Waiting for death in his home in Marmora, Small's defiant self-image finally dissolves into a stream of singularities: 'So as he talked and muttered towards Clara, events fell against each other – a night with a lover, a negotiation at the Grand Opera House. Strangers and corpses of his past arrived in this sparse room with its one lamp lit during the day, so the shadows were like moon-tides around it' (*ISL*, 213–14).

What Small dimly apprehends in the temporal chaos of this passage is the virtual power of life: a multiplicity of potential points of connection from which he has fashioned his own particular image. But unlike Patrick, who senses in this virtual power the potential to imagine his life differently, Small can only experience it as the death of the autonomous self. Ondaatje captures Small's inability to perceive anything but catastrophe in this exposure to the 'diverse worlds' of his own past by portraying him as one of the suicidal herons of his early poetry, those creatures who can only preserve their identity by effecting a violent recoil from life:

> Clara crouched in front of Ambrose and now he could not see her. He was sitting lotus, bare-chested, his hands

moving over his face sensuously rubbing the front of
his skull, as he revealed the mirrors of himself, his voice
slowing as his fingers discovered his right ear. Then he
bent forward as he sat so his head would touch the floor
in a long grace-attempted bow, ascetic. A heron stretching
his head further underwater, the eyes open within the cold
flow, open for the fish that could then be raised into the
air and dropped moving in the tunnel of the heron's blue
throat. (*ISL*, 214)

The forcible juxtaposition of perspective is also the structural
principle of the novel's last extended narrative movement. It is
now the summer of 1938, the time of the Spanish Civil War
and the ascension of anti-Leftist hysteria in capitalist North
America. From a stolen boat on Lake Ontario, Patrick, acting in
concert with Caravaggio and Giannetta, prepares to sabotage the
filtration plant of Commissioner Harris's Waterworks in protest
at the material inequity of existing social conditions. Unbalanced
by the shock of Alice's death, Patrick wants nothing more than to
obliterate all trace of the past in a presumptive act of violence. To
the last, though, *In the Skin of a Lion* resists an idea of the political that seeks to transcend the continuing antagonism between
different sectional interests. The force of this refusal is visited
explicitly upon Patrick, whose conception of political resistance
as the violent abrogation of historical time is itself undermined
by the story of his clandestine journey into the heart of the
Waterworks. What he experiences here, despite himself, is an
imaginative reversion to his past with Alice and that period in
his life when political struggle was still understood as a dream
of collective emancipation. Such, however, is the complexity of
the novel's final pages that this memory affords Patrick both
a momentary reprieve from emotional self-enclosure and the
prospect of a political dead end: Alice was, after all, the unintended victim of an act of political violence that left only ruin
and desolation in its wake.

At once propelling Patrick forward in time while looping back
to a series of earlier scenes, the recursive structure of 'Maritime
Theatre' crystallises one of the novel's principal themes: how can

we open ourselves once more to the emancipatory potential of the past without conceiving the future in the past's own image? This question, posed implicitly by Patrick's involuntary memory of Alice Gull, haunts his climactic encounter with Commissioner Harris. Although nothing is definitively resolved by this confrontation, part of its meaning lies in the dialogical form it takes: Patrick's exchange with Harris encourages him to rethink his commitment to an apocalyptic version of history and to see politics instead as a struggle between competing social forces and visions of the future. The sense of tense dialectical struggle is underpinned by the aporetic structure of judgements the scene unfolds, in which each protagonist's point-of-view encounters a challenge that casts doubt upon its authenticating claims. Reflecting scornfully upon Harris's obliviousness to the workers whose labour consolidated his reputation, Patrick reminds him that 'Your goddamn herringbone tiles in the toilets cost more than half our salaries put together' (*ISL*, 236). Responding later to Harris's claim that he fought 'tooth and nail' to make the Waterworks a symbol that would give the city 'something to live up to', Patrick counters furiously, '*You* fought? *You* fought? Think about those who built the intake tunnels. Do you know how many of us died in there?' – to which Harris makes the laconic reply, 'There was no record kept' (*ISL*, 236). Yet if, as Patrick maintains, political power inevitably corrupts the social bond for selfish ends, the blithe renunciation of authority, Harris rejoins, is a solipsistic gesture that has pernicious political consequences. Harris's recognition of the impossibility of establishing an idea of the social uncontaminated by relations and hierarchies of power – a perception that simultaneously confirms Patrick's image of his antagonist and exposes that image as necessarily partial and inadequate – makes itself felt in his recurring dream of all those potential civic spaces left undeveloped for lack of political will:

> You must realise you are like these places, Patrick. You're as much of the fabric as the aldermen and the millionaires. But you're among the dwarfs of enterprise who never get accepted or acknowledged. Mongrel company. You're a

lost heir. So you stay in the woods. You reject power. And this is how the bland fools – the politicians and press and mayors and their advisers – become the spokesmen for the age. You must realize the trick is to be as serious when you are old as when you are young. (*ISL*, 237)

In the final moments of their exchange Patrick attempts once more to evade the implications of Harris's voluntarist rhetoric by ascribing a redemptive value – a value evoked powerfully by the Christ-like stigmata of the 'wound at her side' displayed by Alice's torn and broken body – to the mere fact of suffering itself (*ISL*, 240). But the novel's unwillingness to endorse this conclusion manifests itself both at the level of action – Patrick lapses into unconsciousness and fails to fulfil his threat to blow up the Waterworks – and by Ondaatje's decision to cede Harris the last word. Looking down upon the prone figure of his rival, Harris's brief valedictory judgement sees Patrick as a modern version of Gilgamesh, the man who must accept the realities and responsibilities of power by staking his claim amongst the common things of the earth: 'He stood over Patrick. "He lay down to sleep, until he was woken from out of a dream. He saw the lions around him glorying in life; then he took his axe in his hand, he drew his sword from his belt, and he fell upon them like an arrow from the string"' (*ISL*, 242).

In the Skin of a Lion presents a fascinating counter-history of Canadian civic modernity. Ondaatje's next project extended his subaltern critique of modern social and cultural conditions by exploring aspects of the mind of Europe during a time of political darkness. For this we have to turn to *The English Patient* and the chaos of the final days of the Second World War.

The English Patient

If the success of *In the Skin of a Lion* helped Ondaatje secure an international audience for the first time, his next book *The English Patient* propelled him to world fame. The novel won the Booker Prize in 1992, an award Ondaatje shared with the British writer Barry Unsworth, guaranteeing him international celebrity and prestige. In the same year *The English Patient* also received the Canadian Governor General's Award and the Trillium Award. The novel's appeal and popularity was reinforced by the appearance, in 1996, of Anthony Minghella's film adaptation which went on to win nine Oscars at the Academy Awards. Such was the success of *The English Patient* that the Picador paperback edition alone had sold more than three-quarters of a million copies in the first decade after its publication.

The novel opens in Italy in April 1945 during the chaotic final phase of the Second World War. Ondaatje's choice of date is not arbitrary: *The English Patient*, like the world it describes, is poised uncertainly between two worlds and two visions of international (dis)order. This division is symbolised at its conclusion by the detonation of the atom bomb over Hiroshima, an event that marks the transition from full-scale military conflict to the beginning of the Cold War. But if *The English Patient* is concerned on one level with the transition between two phases of modern international history, it is also a novel about the nature of *Englishness*. In order to grasp the full implications of this statement, we need to understand 'Englishness' as a mode of cultural authority rather than a repertoire of social

conventions. Englishness in this sense does not merely imply citizenship of a nation and culture; it also describes a power to write and *define* the cultural self-image of other nations. Just as maleness and whiteness were often historically perceived as 'unmarked' positions which determined the universal content of what it meant to be human, 'Englishness' was often seen within colonial discourse as a synonym for civilisation, humanity, reason and enlightenment in general rather than the expressive content of a particular national tradition. Although Ondaatje is at pains to explore the nature of national differences through the developing relationships between his main characters, these particular differences are always interpreted within the context of a history which takes Englishness as its principal subject. This tension between cultural difference and interpretative context goes to the very heart of the novel because the need of each of Ondaatje's protagonists to establish the true identity of the 'English' patient reflects the novel's broader preoccupation with Englishness as the unmarked but legitimating term in national and imperial relations.

The venue for the encounter between Ondaatje's four protagonists is the Villa San Girolamo, just north of Florence. We are first introduced to Hana, Patrick Lewis's adopted daughter from *In the Skin of a Lion*, now serving as a nurse during the Allied Italian campaign. While the First Canadian Infantry Division continues its agonising progress through Northern Italy, Hana remains at the villa to care for one particular individual, a figure burned beyond recognition who claims to have forgotten his true identity and comes to assume the name of the 'English patient'.[1] This pair is joined by David Caravaggio, the thief from *In the Skin of a Lion*, who hears of the unlikely couple at the villa during his convalescence in a military hospital in Rome following his mutilation by the Gestapo, and journeys there in order to confirm his suspicions about whom each of them might be. Completing the quartet is Kirpal Singh, or 'Kip' as he is renamed during his wartime service in England, a Sikh sapper with the Royal Engineers travelling through Italy defusing bombs left by the Germans. The effect of Kip's entry

into, and eventual renunciation of, the villa community is to push the novel beyond its local borders by staging a confrontation between the colonial outsider and the geopolitical imperatives of the Anglo-American imperium.

In an interview conducted a week after *The English Patient* won the Booker Prize, Ondaatje reflected upon some of the novel's principal themes:

> It is a book about very tentative healing among a group of people. I think it is that most of all. It's also two or three or four versions of a love story. There's the love of Caravaggio towards Hana, and Katharine towards the Patient, and Kip towards Hana. Even Kip towards the Patient. For me, it primarily concerns *situation*, as opposed to theme. That's how I imagined the book, and how I see the book. They're barely spoken relationships. For instance, I worked a lot on the association between Kirpal Singh and the English Patient, erasing the background, erasing oversaid things.[2]

The 'situation' of the novel is clearly crucial to its psychological and cultural terrain. *The English Patient* explores the situation of a group of embattled and war-weary exiles attempting to make sense of their lives in the absence of any supervening law or established social structure. The character and cultural location of the Villa San Girolamo extends the symbolic resonance of this situation in a number of ways. Located close to Florence, one of the treasure houses of Renaissance art, the mined and disfigured villa provides a grim reminder of the fragility of European cultural humanism in the face of political barbarism. At the same time, its apparent archetypal significance as a modern version of the Garden of Eden ('The Villa San Girolamo, built to protect inhabitants from the flesh of the devil, had the look of a besieged fortress, the limbs of most of the statues blown off during the first days of shelling') gives it a potentially utopian dimension (*EP*, 43). Ondaatje underscores the villa's archetypal quality earlier in the same interview: 'One of the things I discovered in the book was that I thought that this was an Eden, an escape, a little cul-de-sac during the war, and this was where healing began'.[3]

The English Patient develops several themes that have preoccupied Ondaatje from as far back as *The Collected Works of Billy the Kid*. These themes include the idea of cultural hybridity; the continuing tension between private and political or molecular and molar life; the dehumanising consequences of an imperialist *Weltanschauung* that can only maintain its own integrity and prestige by effecting a violent division between the 'West' and a series of cultural, racial and linguistic Others; the complexities of familial and cultural inheritance; and the pervasive modern experience of migrancy in which individuals often feel themselves to be both deracinated and at home. Linking these concerns one to another is the grand theme of betrayal which, as John Bolland observes, 'exemplifies the conflict between personal commitment to individual or group and the more abstract allegiance to nationhood and state'.[4] This theme recurs in many guises throughout the novel: Hana feels betrayed by history, having lost all three of her parents to various acts of political violence; Caravaggio is convinced that the patient betrayed the Allies by collaborating with the Nazis; Clifford is betrayed by the love affair between Katharine and the patient; the patient feels betrayed by Katharine's temporary return to Clifford; Kip feels betrayed, on behalf of all 'the brown races of the world', by the Allied bombing of Japan; while Hana experiences Kip's ultimate renunciation of the villa community as a betrayal of her love for him (*EP*, 286).

In the searing image which first formed the book in Ondaatje's imagination a man falls burning to the desert from a flaming aeroplane. Nothing is known about this man: his identity and his past are precisely what remain to be determined by the experience the novel unfolds. In the responses they offer this human conundrum Hana, Caravaggio and Kip are forced to confront unexamined aspects of their own lives. Reflecting upon the genesis of *The English Patient*, Ondaatje testifies to the enigmatic power of this formative image: 'I usually begin books in a dream-like – no, that's too esoteric. But I had this little fragment of a guy who had crashed in the desert. I didn't know who he was, or anything'.[5] Returning in another interview to this

uncanny beginning, he presents the patient as a site of temporal disturbance, the culmination and ruined consequence of a situation that has somehow, through the act of its complex retelling, still to be lived through:

> Certainly [the patient] was the character who began the book for me. About the first image I had was of this man who was a complete mystery to me. I had to find out who he was. And then a lot of the landscapes and situations that had been in my mind for a long time, that had to do with the desert and with exploration, entered the book.[6]

If the enigma of the patient's origins served as a stimulus to Ondaatje's literary imagination, the question of his identity is for Hana, Caravaggio and Kip a puzzle whose solution might help them make sense of their current circumstances and reclaim a lost aspect of their own lives. Consequently the desire to name and to know the patient intensifies as the novel proceeds; but absolute certainty of his background remains tantalisingly out of reach. Although considerable evidence is amassed to suggest that the patient is Count Ladislaus de Almásy, a Hungarian aristocrat accused of spying for the Germans in North Africa, the truth of this conviction is never decisively established. One reason for continuing uncertainty is the patient's inability to guarantee the nature of his identity for any length of time: he is, at different points in the novel, variously 'I', 'he' and 'Almásy', and this (pro)nominal slippage necessarily undermines the possibility of secure self-identification upon which the value of confession depends. Denied the possibility of interaction with a subject who might explain himself and account for his own actions, his interlocutors have little choice but to forge narratives and invent scenarios to supplement his occulted reminiscence. Reading, narrativisation, and self-revelation therefore become elements in a complex textual economy: in Ondaatje's idiosyncratic version of the talking cure, the patient's three housemates read and rewrite his image in order to bring elements of their own existence into focus.

The insistent demand that the patient's subjectivity be turned to narrative account is underscored by the symbolic

function he comes to play in unblocking the traumatic histories of each of the villa's inhabitants. This function is crucial because subjectivity in *The English Patient* is constituted by the relationship between a self and an Other who comes to represent another version of the self precisely because it symbolises repressed elements of its experience that cannot be lived out in any other way. This relationship appears in various guises. For Hana the patient represents an aspect of her lost paternal relation; for Caravaggio his image symbolises the body of the war and his own war-torn body; while for Kip the patient's blackened remains offer a ghastly evocation of the ruined colonial body: a body fought over and ceaselessly remade in the image of its antagonists. The persistently doubled nature of the patient's image is further accentuated by his suspension between life and death as he prepares to become one more memory among all the others that circulate throughout the novel.

The integrity of the patient's image is therefore both crucial and curiously beside the point: its continuing life is inseparable from its fantasmic appropriation by others. Certainly the question of who the patient 'is' will not be resolved from his own lips: his identity will instead be reinvented by a communal act of storytelling. This sense of a life no longer lived on its own terms emerges as early as the second page of the novel with the intimation of the patient's imminent death: 'He whispers again, dragging the listening heart of the young nurse beside him to wherever his mind is, into that well of memory he kept plunging into during those months before he died' (*EP*, 4). But even this early in the narrative, the patient's image has already been remade by the young nurse sitting beside him: gazing down at his 'black body' with its 'destroyed feet' and the 'hipbones of Christ', she transforms him into her own vision of a 'despairing saint' (*EP*, 3). Crucial to this mythopoeic conversion of flesh into symbol is its recasting of the patient's body as a *redemptive body*: her solicitude of the prone figure before her offers Hana the chance to transcend the chaos of a catastrophic history. The extent of Hana's symbolic reworking of the patient's blackened form becomes clear during her first encounter with him

in the hospital at Pisa. What she sees in the 'ebony pool' of the patient's charred face is not the profile of a despairing saint but the erasure of all visible signs of distinction (*EP*, 48). Tenderly scrutinising the remains of 'a man with no face', Hana reluctantly concedes that 'there was nothing to recognise in him' (*EP*, 48). But emptied of individual significance, the black hole of the patient's face becomes a blank canvas upon which any new image may be projected. The instability of the patient's identity is partly an effect of this continual translation of a physical body into a textual space. The same process inflects his first account of his burning fall into the desert:

> I fell burning into the desert.
> They found my body and made me a boat of sticks and dragged me across the desert. We were in the Sand Sea, now and then crossing dry riverbeds. Nomads, you see. Bedouin. I flew down and the sand itself caught fire. They saw me stand up naked out of it. The leather helmet on my head in flames. They strapped me onto a cradle, a carcass boat, and feet thudded along as they ran with me. I had broken the spareness of the desert …
> Who are you?
> I don't know. You keep asking me.
> You said you were English (*EP*, 5).

This passage of descriptive prose is crossed by two different impulses: the patient's desire to obfuscate his own origins and Hana's determination to confirm him as a particular type of subject. It is a mistake merely to perceive the patient as the passive victim of external projection: 'No less than the other characters', Stephen Scobie points out, 'Almásy projects a fiction of identity onto the blank screen of his own burned body'.[7] The fiction he projects here abruptly dissolves history into myth: neither English nor Hungarian, he becomes the protagonist of his own epic drama, falling like Lucifer from the sky following a Miltonic 'war in heaven' (*EP*, 5). The patient's eagerness to present himself as an archetypal, rather than merely historical, figure is countered by Hana's need to read him as an *English* patient. Her claim, nowhere substantiated by the rest of the

novel, that 'You said you were English' underpins one version of the patient's identity; although challenged resolutely by Caravaggio it is never completely displaced. By establishing, to herself at least, that the patient is 'English', Hana makes him both a tragic symbol of Allied sacrifice and a substitute for her stepfather Patrick Lewis, who died burned and alone, an anonymous victim of the battle for France. 'He was a burned man and I was a nurse and I could have nursed him', Hana later writes despairingly of Patrick to Clara Dickens. 'Do you understand the sadness of geography?' (EP, 296). It is just this openness to interpretation that confirms the importance of the patient to each of the other protagonists. Anonymous, initially unreadable and consistently enigmatic, he is a constant hermeneutic lure and temptation: his presence demands to be translated into recognisable codes of cultural and political affiliation. Proclaimed simultaneously Hungarian and English, the patient is always also a problem *of* English: a metaphor for the types of libidinal investment at stake in the process of reading itself. Reading, as the patient's experience in the Villa San Girolamo demonstrates, can always outrun its proper object in its attempt to invest a particular world with form and coherence. Or, as the patient puts the matter himself in an uncharacteristic burst of defiance: 'You must talk to me, Caravaggio. Or am I just a book? Something to be read, some creature to be tempted out of a loch and shot full of morphine, full of corridors, lies, loose vegetation, pockets of stones?' (EP, 253).

The link the patient implies here between reading and the desire to interpret the world according to one's own interests and needs is a staple theme of his relationship with Hana. When the novel begins Hana has emotionally withdrawn herself from the ravages of wartime Italy into a private literary universe. Literature affords her an imaginative consolation for the diremptions of contemporary experience by providing a fantasy space apparently untouched by current geopolitical and ethnic division. But Hana's imaginative distinction between word and world can survive neither Ondaatje's irony nor his insistence upon the textual mediation of all our historical experience. While

her taste for nineteenth-century colonial romance – an enthusiasm reflected in her predilection for novels like *Kim, The Last
of the Mohicans* and *The Charterhouse of Parma* – offers her
a temporary refuge from the prison house of modern history,
her subsequent relationship with Kip forces her to confront the
trauma of colonial experience: a trauma too often sublimated or
repressed by the literary narratives she devours. The impossibility of maintaining an absolute distinction between textuality
and history becomes apparent in the scene where Hana reads her
favourite novels aloud to the drowsing patient. As he drifts in
and out of consciousness, the patient can no longer distinguish
between gaps in literary narrative and the violent erasure of civic
spaces. For him the novel *is* the villa and the villa *is* the novel:
both are texts to be read and spaces to be mastered, imaginative
structures whose fragmentary form opens everything within
them to reappropriation and revision: 'The villa that she and
the Englishman inhabited now was much like that. Some rooms
could not be entered because of rubble. One bomb crater allowed
moon and rain into the library downstairs – where there was in
one corner a permanently soaked armchair' (*EP*, 7-8).

If Hana uses literature to construct a private refuge set
apart from the carnage of wartime experience – Ondaatje finds
a marvellous image for this in her physical dependence upon
piles of books to replace a missing staircase between the villa's
upper and lower floors – the novel also portrays literature as an
unstable and potentially explosive force with the power to blast
open the walls of this sanctuary and expose her once more to the
world outside (*EP*, 13). However, what is for Hana a metaphor
for the possibility of imaginative self-transformation exists for
the sapper Kip as a continuing existential threat: throughout the
booby-trapped villa and grounds '[b]ombs were attached to taps,
to the spines of books, they were drilled into fruit trees so an
apple falling onto a lower branch would detonate the tree, just
as a hand gripping the branch would. He was unable to look at a
room or field without seeing the possibilities of weapons there'
(*EP*, 75; emphasis mine). Books, *The English Patient* implies,
may be the catalyst for historical upheaval as well as a potential

escape from it: at one point Caravaggio recalls how the German spy Eppler 'used a copy of Daphne du Maurier's novel *Rebecca* as a code book to send messages back to Rommel on troop movements' (*EP*, 164). Elsewhere the rehearsal of a passage from Herodotus's *Histories* opens up a new world of passion to the patient and his lover Katharine Clifford that sets in train one of the tragic events upon which the novel turns. Hana herself acknowledges the irreducible public force of the 'private' scene of writing when she imprints the trace of her own desire upon the pages of the book she is reading, opening it in the process to new contexts of interpretation, altering, if only ever so slightly, the relationship between two different historical worlds:

> She opens *The Last of the Mohicans* to the blank page at the back and begins to write in it.
>
> > *There is a man named Caravaggio, a friend of my father's. I have always loved him. He is older than I am, about forty-five, I think. He is in a time of darkness, has no confidence. For some reason I am cared for by this friend of my father.*
>
> She closes the book and then walks down into the library and conceals it in one of the high shelves. (*EP*, 61)

Hana's implicit, although powerfully suggestive, recognition of the interpretative play between text and context is reinforced by the novel's explicit emphasis upon the intertextual basis of historical and cultural discourse. No individual, text or cultural structure, *The English Patient* reminds us, ever has its meaning alone: its meaning exists in its relation to the history of discourse that constitutes its general interpretative context.[8] All too aware that the formal unity of a particular text or worldview is a carefully cultivated fiction, *The English Patient* works tirelessly to open up each of its various versions of history to a range of alternative interpretative possibilities. Its thoroughgoing subversion of the formal unity of the text is evident in its own flagrantly intertextual origins: Ondaatje incorporates into the novel a series of allusions to texts as diverse as *Kim, The Tempest, Paradise Lost, The Charterhouse of Parma, A Passage to India, Anna Karenina*, the poetry of Christopher Smart and

Anne Wilkinson, Herodotus's *Histories*, Caravaggio's painting of David and Goliath, and his own *In the Skin of a Lion*. Diverse these texts may be, but their presence alerts us to a constellation of themes crucial to the novel's structure of feeling and range of political resonance. These themes include the experience of cultural difference and the effects of the colonial relation, the troubled nature of inheritance, and the conflict between public morality and private feeling. No reading of *The English Patient* can ignore the interpretative dilemmas posed by these shifting intertextual relations: in order to make sense of the novel we have to impose a fragile provisional order – a narrative, in other words – upon this network of allusions.

Ondaatje's fascination with intertextuality also inflects the novel's inquiry into the status and function of historical knowledge. This theme finds a symbolic locus in the figure of the classical historian Herodotus of Halicarnassus. For years the patient has carried with him one particular book, a copy of Herodotus's *Histories*, which comes to represent for him the *ne plus ultra* of writing in general: 'No more books', he says to Hana as she arrives in his bedroom fresh from the villa library. 'Just give me the Herodotus' (*EP*, 118). Earlier in the novel she glances at the notebook on his bedside table: 'It is the book he brought with him through the fire – a copy of *The Histories* by Herodotus that he has added to, cutting and gluing in pages from other books or writing in his own observations – so they are all cradled within the text of Herodotus' (*EP*, 16). Later the patient explains the interest Herodotus holds for him in the following terms:

> I have seen editions of *The Histories* with a sculpted portrait on the cover. Some statue found in a French museum. But I never imagine Herodotus this way. I see him more as one of those spare men of the desert who travel from oasis to oasis, trading legends as if it is the exchange of seeds, consuming everything without suspicion, piecing together a mirage. 'This history of mine', Herodotus says, 'has from the beginning sought out the supplementary to the main argument'. What you find in him are cul-de-sacs within the sweep of history – how people betray each other for the sake of nations, how people fall in love … (*EP*, 118-19)

Known as both the 'father of history' and the 'father of lies', Herodotus offers, in his anti-imperialist account of the conflict between the Persian Empire and the Greek city states, a model of historical writing that embraces, rather than disavows, the status of history as a type of narrative.[9] His work presents material drawn from an eclectic range of sources: autopsy (the evidence of things directly seen), folklore, military report, traveller's tale, local anecdote, dreams, oracles, details drawn from poetical histories as well as the reproduction of textual fragments and other forms of recognisably written evidence. As the plural title of his account suggests, Herodotus's concern throughout *The Histories* is to replace a monolithic conception of 'history' with a sense of the enduring struggle between competing perspectives and interests that lies behind the emergence of any definitive historical point-of-view. This connection between the particularity of perspective and the consecration of historical value is consistently maintained: 'Herodotus presents his work', Aubrey de Sélincourt reminds us, 'as a collection of oral traditions, and his method is frequently to allow native spokesman to present their case: "the Persians say", "the Athenians do not agree", "the Spartans alone maintain", and so on. More than once he refers to his role explicitly as "to say what is said" and he cautions that he reports more than he believes'.[10]

Another defining feature of Herodotus's corpus is his imbrication of 'historical' with extra-historical material: he often frames his description of an historical episode with a literary device to draw out aspects of its broader thematic significance. *The Histories* opens with the tale of Candaules and Gyges – the story of the king who tempted his servant to spy upon his own naked queen and was murdered by the pair as a consequence – and this reminder of the nemesis that so often attends hubris in all its forms is the perfect prologue to a text absorbed by imperial over-reaching, military retribution and political vengeance. The same story subsequently plays a vital role as an erotic catalyst in the patient's occulted version of his own history. He falls in love with Katharine Clifton when she reads this story aloud to him during their sojourn in Egypt, imagining her as the queen

and himself as Gyges, the usurping and victorious lover; but as his story unfolds he comes to realise that he has also to play the part of Candaules, the slain king, who pays a terrible price for getting too close to the flame of his own uxorious passion.

The pivotal role of Herodotus in *The English Patient* underpins Ondaatje's challenge to the presumed distinction between literary and historical writing. The patient's habit of pasting passages from other documents into his copy of Herodotus shows that for him 'history' is not a closed book but a continuing dialogue: its borders are permeable and its contents perpetually in process. By placing in question the formal distinction between the inside and outside of a text, the patient's ceaseless supplementary labour offers an intriguing way of thinking about a novel preoccupied by a number of experiences that cannot be represented within its own borders. These textual absences may take the form of personal encounters and memories too painful to dwell upon, such as Hana's loss of her father or the death of Katharine Clifton, or the ideological suppression of material incommensurable with the presuppositions of a particular Western version of history, such as the erasure of the colonial presence from accounts of the Allied campaign or the loss of Indian freedom under British imperial rule. What results is a kind of unrealised or abruptly cancelled potentiality: a mode of historical possibility or feeling that can find no authentic expression in its own contemporary world. Confronted with this fragmentary and self-cancelling mode of disclosure, the question becomes how to make sense of a text that so studiously represses the historical conditions of its own possibility.

The question of how to read is broached directly by the novel on a number of occasions. Perhaps the most suggestive example appears in the scene in which the patient, irritated by Hana's breathless rendition of the opening of Kipling's *Kim*, imparts to her his 'first lesson about reading':

> 'Read him slowly dear girl, you must read Kipling slowly. Watch carefully where the commas fall so you can discover the natural pauses. He is a writer who used pen and ink. He looked up from the page a lot, I believe, stared through

his window and listened to birds, as most writers who are alone do. Some do not know the names of birds, though he did. Your eye is too quick and too North American. Think about the speed of his pen. What an appalling, barnacled old paragraph it is otherwise'. (*EP*, 94)

Central to the patient's lesson is the injunction to see in the particularity of literary style a suspension of the habitual flow of events during which something of the buried nature of an experience is revealed to us. This exhortation, however, is as remarkable for what it dissembles as for what it brings into view. By focusing Hana's attention solely upon Kipling's style, rather than *Kim*'s complex ideological portrait of imperialism and the Anglo-Indian colonial encounter, the patient proves himself to be an inadequate guide to the issues raised by the novel: issues which, although effaced by his style of reading, continue to resonate in the intertextual relation between *Kim* and *The English Patient*. *Kim* is, we recall, the story of Kimball O'Hara, a young white 'English' orphan of Irish descent living in Lahore (then in India, now in Pakistan), who becomes the *chela* or disciple of a Tibetan Lama and follows him in his quest to free himself from the 'Wheel of Things' and merge his soul with the 'Great Soul' that transcends all earthly experience.[11] While undertaking his service to the Lama, Kim is also engaged upon his own quest to discover the meaning of a prophecy that 'Nine hundred first-class devils, whose God was a Red Bull on a green field, would attend to Kim, if they had not forgotten O'Hara'.[12] The furtherance of these two quests will take him the length and breadth of India, involve him in a series of confrontations and accommodations with the reality of British rule, and induct him into the 'great game' of British imperial policy. In the adventures that follow Kim, a figure who is neither 'Eastern' nor 'Western' but a curious hybrid of the two, must try and forge an identity for himself in the wake of this experience of social displacement and cultural self-division.

Ondaatje's reading of *Kim*, unlike the patient's, pays attention to the ideological, as well as aesthetic, implications of Kipling's style. He delves beneath the novel's narrative surface in order to

explore the points of tension implicit in its complex ideological structure. What interests Ondaatje is the way in which *Kim* manipulates literary style and narrative form to manage a series of conflicts in its account of the effects of the British imperial presence in India. These conflicts emerge with unsettling regularity: while Kipling's novel is often critical of the ignorance, racism and cultural prejudice of British attitudes towards Indian mores and values – 'The talk of white men is wholly lacking in dignity' remarks the Lama contemptuously of his treatment at the hands of the British Army and clergy – it continues to reinforce those imperialist attitudes in its broader vision of its native characters.[13] Despite his challenge to the presumption of imperial rule, the Lama is also portrayed as a naïve and ingenuous figure still dependent upon the cultural authority of the colonial outsider. This dependence is clearly marked in the novel's opening paragraph, where the Lama, although a Buddhist adept, still needs to be instructed in the history of his own religion by the white curator of the Lahore Museum, whom he refers to gushingly as 'O Fountain of Wisdom' before 'compos[ing] himself reverently to listen to fragments hastily rendered into Urdu'.[14] Kim's own relation to the Lama, his guide and helpmeet, does not escape this colonial prejudice: 'The Lama was his trove', Kim reflected with cool calculation, 'and he purposed to take possession'.[15]

Unsurprisingly, Kim's position as both a type of the colonial subject and an agent of imperial policy recruited into the British Secret Service precipitates a crisis in his identity. Yet because this crisis threatens to undermine the cultural distinction between imperial and colonial subjectivity that underpins Kipling's wider political vision, the question of Kim's identity must be resolved before the novel can reach its conclusion. Kipling achieves this resolution by suggesting that Kim's life as an 'Indian' native represents the *sublimation* of his true European self whose rediscovery represents the real culmination of his quest. Literary style is the vehicle for the revelation and ideological management of cultural misrecognition: the very terms that confirm Kim's youthful immersion in the culture

and street life of Lahore ('It was intrigue, of course … but what he loved was the game for its own sake – the stealthy prowl through the dark gullies and lanes, the crawl up a water-pipe, the sights and sounds of women's world on the flat roofs, and the headlong flight from housetop to housetop under cover of the hot dark') subsequently underwrite his acceptance of a defined and productive role within the economy of imperialism:

> Well is the Game called great! I was four days a scullion at Quetta, waiting on the wife of the man whose book I stole. And that was part of the Great Game! From the South – God knows how far came up the Mahratta, playing the Great Game in fear of his life. Now I shall go far and far into the North playing the Great Game. Truly, it runs like a shuttle through all Hind.[16]

Ondaatje's ironic and intertextual reworking of *Kim* expressly resists Kipling's ideological resolution of the trauma of colonial history. Where Kim's blithe acceptance of a fantasy image of imperial politics translates cultural dispossession into the plot of a boy's adventure tale, his counterpart Kirpal Singh's rejection of the imperial presuppositions of 'western wisdom' uncovers the violent antagonism at the core of Kipling's novel. Singh's resistance to the imperial paradigm is indirectly signalled by the nickname 'Kip' given to him upon his arrival in England: 'Kip' is both an abbreviation of 'Kipling' and a linguistic corruption of 'Kim', who might otherwise be his namesake. Ondaatje accentuates Kip's hostility to Kipling's ideological investments by an effect of ironic reversal in which a culturally dislocated young Indian now attends upon a dying European totem. Hana notes the intimacy of the relationship between Kip and the patient in one of her earliest glimpses of the two of them together: 'In recent days, Hana had watched him sitting beside the English patient, and it seemed to her a reversal of *Kim*. The young student was now Indian, the wise old teacher was English' (*EP*, 111). But what looks at first glance like the reinscription of a colonial stereotype is actually a prelude to the renunciation of political domination: the only truth Kip eventually detects in the patient's 'history lesson' is its silent complicity with the crimes

of imperial history (*EP*, 285). While Kim responds to the uncertainty of his cultural affiliation by pledging his future to the imperial project, Kip's horrified recoil from news of the nuclear bombing of Japan underlines his ultimate political repudiation of the imperial culture he serves: 'In the tent, before the light evaporated, he had brought out the photograph of his family and gazed at it. His name is Kirpal Singh and he does not know what he is doing here' (*EP*, 287).

Kip's epiphany at the end of *The English Patient* – an epiphany that suddenly reveals the unacknowledged truth of his existence as a member of one of 'the brown races of the earth' – is the exception in a novel in which so much that is crucial to the meaning of its characters' experience is repressed in the very instant of its recollection (*EP*, 286). In fact, even Kip's abrupt realisation of the humanitarian catastrophe wrought by imperial geopolitics is inseparable from this general structure of dissimulation: it actually signals his eventual and unwilling acceptance of his brother's claim – a claim relayed in flashes through the novel and given additional force by his incarceration in a British prison in India – that no just and lasting international settlement is possible without the discontinuance of colonial servitude. This form of occulted reminiscence is lent a more than usual significance by its reproduction of what Cathy Caruth has described as the experiential structure of trauma. Trauma, she writes, is 'the response to an unexpected or overwhelmingly violent event or events that are not fully grasped as they occur, but return later in repeated flashbacks, nightmares, and other represented phenomena'.[17] Because 'the most direct seeing of a violent event may occur as an absolute inability to know it', Carrie Dawson continues:

> Traumatic experience involves a complex and paradoxical relationship between knowing and not knowing. Literature that is concerned with the nature and the experience of trauma re-enacts this dialectic by simultaneously engaging the reader's desire to know and circumscribing the limits of his or her knowing. While the act of reading about a traumatic experience cannot, of course, be straightforwardly

equated with the lived experience of trauma, reading can nevertheless function as a mode of bearing witness to an event that is repeatedly relived as and through its forgetting.[18]

The idea that literature can reflect the structure of a traumatic experience by bearing witness to an event repeatedly relived in and through its forgetting has enduring implications for both the readers and the characters of *The English Patient*. It finds expression, as we have seen, in each protagonist's relation to a defining feature of their own history, and this paradoxical relationship between knowing and not knowing comes to characterise the novel's own mode of narrative disclosure. To speak or write of trauma is to put into question the relationship between narrative and experience. Indeed, such writing puts into question the very possibility of turning experience *into* narrative; the literary representation of traumatic experience necessarily involves us in complex deliberations about the nature of responsibility and the status of truth. What is at stake in these deliberations may turn, as Shoshana Felman has argued, upon what is made possible by a distinction between two modes of narrative: *confession* and *testimony*. For Felman confession appears as an act of referential witness to the unfolding of a secret; testimony by contrast is produced whenever there is a *crisis of truth*, whenever 'the facts upon which justice may pronounce its verdict are not clear, when historical accuracy is in doubt and when both the truth and its supporting elements of evidence are called into question'.[19] As a relation to events, 'testimony seems to be composed of bits and pieces of a memory that have been overwhelmed by occurrences that have not settled into understanding or remembrance, acts that cannot be constructed as knowledge, nor assimilated into full cognition, events in excess of our frames of reference'.[20] Implicit in these definitions is a distinction between two modes of truth: a truth that is 'transparent to itself and actually known, given in advance, prior to the very process of its utterance' and a truth that is experienced as a mode of access *to* the truth, a truth that is born *in* the referential process of testimony itself.[21]

Felman's reading of testimony as a performative speech act that is constitutive of its subject and that can possess itself neither as a settled truth nor the self-transparency of knowledge perfectly encapsulates the nature of the patient's relation to his own history. Because testimony, unlike confession, compels the speaking subject to bear witness to a truth that escapes it and that is not of itself available to its own speaker, it comes gradually to involve *both* parties, the speaker and the listener, in the search for the meaning of the narrative it unfolds. At some point in this process, however, a tension may develop between two conflicting demands: while the speaker's halting, inconclusive and elliptical testimony asks its audience to bear witness to and assume its own share of the burden of a traumatic experience, the listener yearns to speak *for and through* the Other, turning testimony into history by interpreting it from the perspective of their own interests and needs. In such circumstances, Felman suggests, a certain question becomes unavoidable: 'Is the testimony, therefore, a simple medium of historical transmission, or is it, in obscure ways, the unexpected medium of a healing?'[22]

This understanding of testimony as a crisis of historical truth which demands a new way of thinking the past sets the textual scene for each of the stories *The English Patient* tells. When the novel begins Hana is wholly unable to cope with the trauma of her own wartime history: 'She cannot bear to talk of or even acknowledge the death of Patrick' (*EP*, 92). Unwilling to accept the reality of her loss, she retreats into a private fantasy in which her father's death never really happened. Her first conversation with the patient in the hospital at Pisa offers her an opportunity to substitute this fantasy for the brute facts of history. In response to his enquiry, 'What does your father do?' she banishes the thought of Patrick's death from the domain of utterance: 'He is in … he is in the war' (*EP*, 42). Nursing the patient, answering his questions, filling in his silences with her own memories and desires allows Hana to take imaginative responsibility for the lost parental body: 'I love him', she informs a startled Caravaggio of the patient, as the two images coalesce in her mind (*EP*, 45). Upon his arrival at the Villa Caravaggio

is quickly unnerved by the way Hana 'has chained herself to the dying man upstairs' (*EP*, 40). The same insight, more empathetically rendered, accompanies the patient's first glimpse of her at the military hospital: 'The burned man noticed the young nurse, separate from the others. He was familiar with such dead glances, knew she was more patient than nurse' (*EP*, 95-6).

Listening meanwhile to the patient's narrative, Kip experiences once more the contentment and peace bestowed upon him by his relationship with his mentor Lord Suffolk, who inducted him into his very 'English' family before being blown up at Erith in 1941. But if his two housemates insist, with varying degrees of emphasis, upon the 'Englishness' of the 'English' patient, Caravaggio insists with more than equivalent force that the dying man is none other than Count Ladislaus de Almásy, the traitor who led the German spy Eppler into Cairo, thereby lending invaluable assistance to Rommel's desert campaign. Terribly tortured by the Gestapo in Italy and haunted by a confused memory that he betrayed military secrets during his ordeal, Caravaggio scrutinises the patient's speech for signs of a confession that might account for his suffering, restoring a sense of its value and purpose, while exculpating him from his abiding sense of his own continuing guilt: 'Caravaggio sits there in silence, thoughts lost among the floating motes ... He watches the man in the bed. He needs to know who this Englishman from the desert is, and reveal him for Hana's sake. *Or perhaps invent a skin for him*, the way tannic acid camouflages a burned man's rawness' (*EP*, 116–17; italics mine). This passage captures Caravaggio's need both to reveal and reconstruct the patient's identity in order to guarantee his own moral self-image. But although he begins by demanding a confession from the 'Englishman' before him, even injecting him with morphine in the hope of securing a drug-induced admission, Caravaggio slowly discovers that the meaning of his own traumatic history is not to be found *in* the patient, concealed there like a secret, but *through* his encounter with the patient's indirect and occulted speech: an encounter that unlocks aspects of his own past and enables him to translate his experience back into narrative.

Despite being flooded with morphine as he abandons himself to his agonised account of his affair with Katharine Clifton, the patient's testimony resolutely refuses to confirm the identity of its own narrative subject. It establishes no clear distinction between the Englishman and the Hungarian: sometimes the patient speaks as if he were Almásy; sometimes he refers instead to 'Almásy' in the third person:

> During those final nights in Cairo, months after the affair was over, we had finally persuaded Madox into a Zinc bar for his farewell. She and her husband were there. One last night. One last dance. Almásy was drunk and attempting an old dance step he had invented called the Bosphorus hug, lifting Katharine Clifton into his wiry arms and traversing the floor until he fell with her across some Nile-grown aspidistras.

Who is he speaking as now? Caravaggio thinks. (*EP*, 244)

The subject of the patient's narrative is displaced at the very moment Caravaggio hopes to grasp it as he encounters a mode of truth's realisation irreducible to confession. What may be glimpsed instead through this flickering play of pronouns and points-of-view is the outline of a *collective subject* of trauma and loss, a subjectivity that potentially includes Caravaggio's own and in which he finds a shadowy reflection of his own image. Adrift in the patient's narrative, Caravaggio slowly begins to detach himself from the carapace of his despairing cynicism and perceive the historical dimension of his own dispossession. The effect upon him of this experience is marked: by the conclusion of the patient's story Caravaggio has already decided that it 'no longer matters which side he was on during the war' (*EP*, 251). When Hana later asks him 'Is he what you thought he was?' Caravaggio replies gently, 'He's fine. We can let him be' (*EP*, 265).

Caravaggio's ultimate indifference to the truth or falsity of the patient's story suggests that in choosing to emphasise the issue of his innocence or guilt we are asking the wrong question of the novel. No satisfactory solution to the problem of reading

the patient, Ondaatje implies, can be found in the purely private realm of individual pathology: the opacity of his image signifies instead a historically constituted problem of knowledge and authority. Ondaatje underscores this wider historical dimension by suspending the patient's image between a particular and a general relevance. While on one level the patient's narrative relates the personal tragedy of an individual who relentlessly disengages himself from the world, it also tells the story of a more general collapse in the relation between 'Englishness' as a discourse of imperial power and the political realities of twentieth-century history. For when the events of the novel are returned to their broader historical context – the interwar decades of the 1920s and 1930s which saw the eclipse of British imperial hegemony and the emergence of the new American imperium – the inscrutability of the 'English' patient's image marks the symbolic terminus of one way of mapping the world and the point of transition between two rival versions of the imperial narrative. It is the patient's double life as character and symbol – as a figure who has to define himself in relation *to* English culture and values but who comes to represent to others a crisis *in* English imperial history – that links the novel's private and public worlds and makes reading *The English Patient* such an unsettling experience.

The suspicion that the patient's elliptical narrative conceals a historically constituted problem of knowledge and authority is reinforced by the novel's curious temporal structure. Although *The English Patient* concerns itself directly with the years between 1939 and 1945, this period is not the patient's primary focus. Unusually for what is ostensibly a war novel, he experiences the war as a form of dead time, history having stopped for him with the death of Katharine Clifton in 1939. Thus while Caravaggio busies himself with trying to establish exactly what 'Almásy' did during the war, the patient turns his own gaze to the 1920s and 1930s, a period of what is for him still living history, when he was one of a small group of European explorers attempting to chart the interior of the Libyan desert. In the context of the patient's years of desert exploration the phrase

'living history' is useful rather than happy: his quest to discover the lost oasis of Zerzura offers him an experience of time no longer governed by a Western conception of history. The reason the desert comes to dominate his imagination is that he sees it as a place in which time and space are liberated from their inherited historical meanings. For the patient, the desert is 'that pure zone between land and chart between distances and legend between nature and storyteller' whose shifting and shimmering surface exceeds any particular mode of cultural inscription and, in so doing, reveals the historically constituted character of every enforced territorial claim (*EP*, 246). His inhabitation of this 'pure zone' enables him to see with renewed clarity the connection between the narcissism of Western political culture and the demands of imperial cartography:

> The ends of the earth are never the points on a map that colonists push against, enlarging their sphere of influence. On one side servants and slaves and tides of power and correspondence with the Geographical Society. On the other the first step by a white man across a great river, the first sight (by a white eye) of a mountain that has been there forever. (*EP*, 141)

Imperial power inscribes the world in its own image, enforcing divisions of labour ('servants') and distinctions of caste and race ('slaves'), reproducing its authority through the phalanx of representations it mobilises to confer a spurious legitimacy upon its physical seizure of resources. But as Elizabeth Bishop's delicate ironic reworking of the language of cartography famously demonstrated ('Land *lies* in water; it is *shadowed* green'), the fact that maps are continually open to historical revision demonstrates the extent to which they reflect a particular set of political imperatives rather than an objective truth about the world.[23] In a similar spirit, the patient's own image of desert cartography restores a sense of the historicity of every image of colonial space: 'The desert could not be claimed or owned – it was a piece of cloth carried by winds, never held down by stones, and given a hundred shifting names long before Canterbury existed, long before battles and treaties quilted Europe and the East' (*EP*, 138–9).

Into the desert comes an unlikely band of European explorers, some drawn by the desire to indulge one last imperial fantasy of colonial space, others by the wish to escape the tragic burden of European political history. The tensions within the group become increasingly pronounced as they begin their expedition to trace Zerzura and the lost army of Cambyses. For some members of the party the narcissistic wish to imprint their own image upon the unmapped interior proves impossible to resist. Fenelon-Barnes, in particular, 'wanted a tribe to take his name'; later his colleague Bauchan outdid him by 'having a type of sand dune named after him' (*EP*, 139). Such narcissism reaches its apogee in the figure of the Englishman Geoffrey Clifton who translates every new and alien experience into the language of English ruling-class gentility (*EP*, 237). 'I name this site the Bir Messaha Country Club,' he announces upon his arrival in El Jof; always a great one for empty ceremonials, he even 'named his plane the *Rupert Bear*' (*EP*, 142–3). Standing resolutely apart from all such acts of imperial inscription, the patient perceives in this apparently harmless extension of the 'family name' one more example of territorial acquisitiveness: 'Erase the family name! Erase nations! I was taught such things by the desert ... But I wanted to erase my name and the place I had come from' (*EP*, 139).

This conflict between cultural imperialism and the desire to renounce the colonial inheritance is fought out over the body of Katharine Clifton, who arrives in Egypt on honeymoon with her husband, and with whom the patient soon embarks upon a tempestuous love affair in Cairo. As befits her contested status, Katharine is an ambivalent figure continually drawn to the romantic possibilities of North Africa while nostalgic for English customs and manners. 'Her passion for the desert was temporary', the narrator informs us, 'she loved family traditions and courteous ceremony and old memorised poems. She would have hated to die without a name. For her there was a line back to her ancestors that was tactile, whereas [the patient] had erased the path he had emerged from' (*EP*, 170). Katharine's emotional attachment to family traditions and the family name marks her

out from the beginning as a very different personality from the patient, who experiences in love an expression of subjectivity so intense that it abrogates all domestic ties and social obligations. As he writes in his diary of their affair: 'A love story is not about those who lose their heart but about those who find that sullen inhabitant who, when it is stumbled upon, means the body can fool no one, can fool nothing – not the wisdom of sleep or the habit of social graces. It is a consuming of oneself and the past' (*EP*, 97).

The patient's lack of possessiveness and his insistence that love 'burns[s] down all social rules' dooms their affair from the start (*EP*, 155). Katharine rejects his attempts to break down the 'walls of her class' and overthrow the imperial values of the 'English machine', sensing in them a solipsistic refusal to accept the world on anything else but his own terms (*EP*, 237). 'You slide past everything with your fear and hate of ownership, of owning, of being owned, of being named', she tells him just before ending the affair. 'You think this is a virtue. I think it is inhuman' (*EP*, 238). Her conviction of the inhumanity of his fear of being owned or named is later tragically confirmed when his failure after her plane crash to supply her married name to the investigating British soldiers leads directly to her death. 'I was yelling Katharine's name. Yelling the Gilf Kebir', the patient sorrowfully recalls, 'whereas the only name I should have yelled, dropped like a calling card into their hands, was Clifton's' (*EP*, 251).

Katharine's insistence upon the inhumanity of the patient's rejection of social relationship illuminates one of the novel's key themes: the prohibitive cost of a purely singular vision of life. The patient is unswerving in his conviction that the meaning of worldly experience lies in its transcendence of every external form of relation; by subjecting our experience to determination in social, historical or national terms we rob it, he believes, of its intrinsic value and significance. Historical being is, for the patient, a fundamentally *limited* form of being: in order to grasp the truth of our experience we must first renounce every external claim upon us. Nothing that is crucial to our experience,

he maintains, is reducible to the explanatory context of political circumstance or bourgeois morality; the vitality of life is
a pure flow of becoming that expresses itself in a momentary
configuration of bodies or the fleeting interaction between an
eye and the landscape that seduces it. Behaviour that seems,
from Katharine's point of view, to embody an inhuman lack of
sympathy is perhaps better understood as a movement *beyond*
the human in which all life, not merely human life, takes its
place upon a single plane of being that is not enclosed within
the interested viewpoint of a specific individual. This dissolution of the boundary between human and inhuman life is most
poignantly portrayed in Katharine's death scene in the Cave of
Swimmers, where the patient, confronted with the spectacle of
his lover's crippled body, attempts to render her 'immune to
the human' by covering her skin in the revivifying colours of
earth and sunlight (*EP*, 248). Looking down upon her brightly
bedaubed flesh, the patient surrenders himself to the force of
his singular vision: 'When I turned her around, her whole body
was covered in bright pigment. Herbs and stones and light and
the ash of acacia to make her eternal. The body pressed against
sacred colour ... All I desired was to walk upon such an earth
that had no maps' (*EP*, 260–1).

The integrity – indeed the possibility – of this vision is,
however, challenged by the outbreak of the Second World War.
The patient hates the war, not for reasons of political dissidence
or humanitarian sympathy, but because it exposes the hollowness of his conviction that the desert cannot be claimed or
owned. The war, in fact, swallows everything: 'In 1939 the great
decade of Libyan Desert expeditions came to an end, and this
vast and silent pocket of the earth became one of the theatres of
war' (*EP*, 134). Consistently hostile to the territorial ambitions
of the Western nation-states, the patient realises that European
history, in defiance of the developing phase of decolonisation
underway since the end of the previous century, is once again
re-establishing itself as the motor of world history by projecting
its expansionist desires upon a series of non-Western cultures
and spaces.[24] But committed as he is to his own mode of existence,

he remains wholly indifferent to the play of world-historical forces, turning his back upon the war and abandoning himself to his own singular vision. Historical consciousness is sacrificed to the immediacy of each passing sensation; the meaning of his story is therefore identical, in the patient's eyes, to the story of 'how one falls in love' (*EP*, 229). However, his indifference to social and political pressures leaves him vulnerable to reappropriation by the very forces he despises: irrespective of the ambiguity of his background, he is always recodified as 'English' *or* 'Hungarian' according to the specific interests of his interlocutors. Although the patient responds by maintaining an exuberantly ironic relation to the external determination of his origins – his own particular brand of 'Englishness' is a wonderful pastiche of national characteristics, combining a love of cricket, a taste for pastoral landscape, reverence for Kew Gardens and a voice capable of mimicking the 'flutter of the English wood thrush he said was found only in Essex' – irony and pastiche are no match for the forces that now define him (*EP*, 112). Nowhere is this clearer than in the scene that symbolises the destruction of all the patient's hopes and dreams: a threat he first glimpses as metaphor – the 'English machine' of Clifford's social class and manner – subsequently materialises as the deathly cargo plane that kills Clifford and Katharine and obliterates everything the patient ever loved or valued (*EP*, 237).

'Kip and I are both international bastards', the patient tells Hana, 'born in one place and choosing to live elsewhere. Fighting to get back to or get away from our homelands all our lives. Though Kip doesn't recognize that yet. That's why we get on so well together' (*EP*, 176–7). Yet whatever the patient's confidence in this shared background and destiny, his continuing indifference to the pressure exerted upon the self by world-historical forces suggests that his own experience of deracination has little in common with that of the Indian sapper by his bedside. The difference in their respective situations is underlined in the scene where Kip is inducted into the British Army in Lahore. Shuffling forward towards his medical inspection, Kip, like each of his compatriots, is marked with chalk on his skin by a British officer;

later he will use the same yellow chalk to identify unexploded bombs in London. Unlike the patient, who refuses to believe against all available historical evidence that the contents of our experience are partly 'owned' or determined by external forces, the body of the colonial subject is always marked – and marked as inferior – by the fact of its ethnic and racial difference (*EP*, 261). Kip's initial response to the experience of colonial subjection is deeply revealing: unmoved by his brother's militant call for a confrontation with imperial authority, he searches instead for what he calls 'the overlooked space open to those of us with a silent life' (*EP*, 200). What this response fails to recognise – a fact ironically indicated by the adjective 'overlooked' – is that this apparently invisible world is already circumscribed and coded by the products of imperial ideology. The story of *The English Patient* is, in one sense, the story of Kip's gradual recognition that there is no private space untouched by the 'public battles' between imperial power and the emerging forces of colonial independence. This recognition, when it arrives, will tear the world of the villa apart, revealing Kip to be the very thing his Lahore markings inadvertently implied: the unexploded bomb concealed at the heart of the novel.

Before this explosive denouement, Kip's 'trick of survival' manifests itself as a profound emotional identification with English culture and customs (*EP*, 201). The force of this identification suggests that this 'trick' should be read as an expression of the cultural ambivalence felt by the colonial subject whose home space has been overwritten by the presiding imperial presence. A familiar imaginative response to the disorientation of finding oneself torn between competing national interests and identifications is, after all, to embrace aspects of imperial culture as one's own. Such is Kip's response when he enters the British Army at the outbreak of the war. He inhabits English culture as if it were simply a continuation of his previous life: he is 'a man from Asia who has in these last years of war assumed English fathers, following their codes like a dutiful son' (*EP*, 217). During the fraught but happy period he spends serving in Lord Suffolk's bomb disposal squad, Kip feels as if he has 'stepped into a family,

after a year abroad, as if he were the prodigal returned' (*EP*, 189). Kip's identification with all things English is reinforced by his tutelary relationship with Lord Suffolk, who takes him on trips to the Devon countryside which he spends 'introducing the customs of England to the young Sikh as if it was a recently discovered culture' (*EP*, 184). Captivated by his new surroundings and grateful for the kindness shown to him by Lord Suffolk and his assistant Miss Morden, Kip realises that he is 'beginning to love the English' (*EP*, 190). His assimilation intro Lord Suffolk's surrogate family affords him a ready compensation for the loneliness he sometimes feels as 'a result of being the anonymous member of another race, a part of the invisible world' (*EP*, 196). Gradually his quiet self-sufficiency earns him more widespread acceptance to the point where he is lampooned, renamed, turned into an English version of himself:

> The sapper's nickname is Kip. 'Get Kip'. 'Here comes Kip'. The name had attached itself to him curiously. In his first bomb disposal report in England some butter had marked his paper, and the officer had exclaimed, 'What's this? Kipper grease?' and laughter surrounded him. He had no idea what a kipper was, but the young Sikh had been thereby translated into a salty English fish. Within a week his real name, Kirpal Singh, had been forgotten. (*EP*, 87)

The death of Lord Suffolk in an explosion in 1941 robs Kip of his English father and exposes him as an outsider in an alien culture. When the reality of his situation finally strikes him, he concludes his work in the bomb disposal unit and rejoins the British Army as it heads overseas towards the Italian theatre. Kip's calculated retreat into the 'anonymous machine' of the army ends the moment he enters the Villa San Girolamo in search of unexploded bombs (*EP*, 195). Not only does he take responsibility for the safety of the villa's inhabitants – at one point saving Caravaggio's life when the Canadian accidentally dislodges a fusebox from a shelf – his presence plays a pivotal role in reclaiming Hana from her emotional isolation and reconciling her to the sudden loss of her father. The evolving relationship between Kip and Hana is exquisitely rendered in the scene

in which Kip, defusing a bomb in the villa grounds, unexpect-edly finds himself holding two live wires without the safety of a descant chord. Desperate for a 'third hand' to extricate him from his deadly predicament, his salvation only arrives when Hana rushes from the villa to pluck one of the wires from his grasp. If this gesture represents in one sense the culmination of the death drive that has gripped her ever since Patrick's death ('I thought I was going to die. I wanted to die. And I thought if I was going to die I would die with you'), it nevertheless propels her beyond self-absorption into a renewed engagement with the world (*EP*, 103).

Looking back upon the moment when Hana came coura-geously to his aid, Kip is wryly amused by the intrinsic literari-ness of this gesture: 'The successful defusing of a bomb ended novels' (*EP*, 105). However, the gentle irony of this remark comes to assume an altogether more forbidding tone in *The English Patient*'s concluding pages. For the event that tears the villa community apart is the successful detonation, rather than defusing, of an explosive device: the dropping of the Atomic Bomb over Japan in August 1945. Although news of the nuclear blast enters the novel in quietly unemphatic fashion ('One bomb. Then another. Hiroshima. Nagasaki'), Kip is brought to his knees by the radio report of this 'tremor of Western wisdom' (*EP*, 284). An event of world-historical proportions, the detonation of the nuclear bomb retains for Kip an unbearable cultural inflection and significance: 'If he closes his eyes he sees the streets of Asia full of fire' (*EP*, 284). Pausing only to collect his rifle, he rushes indoors from his tent in order to confront the 'English' patient, now summarily reconstituted in Kip's eyes as the barely living symbol of Western imperial culture: 'You stood for precise behaviour. I knew if I lifted a teacup with the wrong finger I'd be banished. If I tied the wrong kind of knot in a tie I was out. Was it just ships that gave you such power? Was it, as my brother said, because you had the histories and printing presses?' (*EP*, 283).

Alarmed by the potentially murderous consequences of Kip's identification of the patient as English, Caravaggio insists once more upon the enigma of his origins: 'You don't know who

this man is ... He isn't an Englishman' (*EP*, 285). The implications of Caravaggio's intervention – that 'Almásy' is, in fact,
Hungarian, not English – is irrelevant to Kip, for whom ethnicity,
rather than the internal geopolitical divisions of Europe, is now
the heart of the matter. Kip's indifference to the subtleties of
European national distinctions is clear from his angry rejoinder
'American, French, I don't care. When you start bombing the
brown races of the world, you're an Englishman', which explicitly figures 'Englishness' as a mode of imperial domination
rather than a particular cultural tradition (*EP*, 286). Caravaggio
is, in any event, quick to concede the essential justice of Kip's
position: 'He knows the young soldier is right. They would
never have dropped such a bomb on a white nation'. Consumed
by images of nuclear annihilation and convinced of the moral
bankruptcy of the Western powers, Kip angrily renounces his
English name and the last vestiges of his Anglo-Indian identity: 'In the tent, before the light evaporated, he had brought
out the photograph of his family and gazed at it. His name is
Kirpal Singh and he does not know what he is doing here' (*EP*,
287). Withdrawing from all contact with Hana and Caravaggio,
Kip silently departs the Villa San Girolamo, setting his course
due south in a symbolic attempt to reverse the entire historical
narrative of the Allied invasion of Italy.

Some critics have seized upon Kip's violent act of renunciation to suggest that this markedly anti-Western aspect of the
novel offers an impoverished response to the political realities
confronting the Allies in the war's final months. For Morton A.
Kaplan, Kip's undiscriminating rhetoric about Western attitudes
to the 'brown races of the earth' fails to account for either the specificity and strength of Japanese resistance in the summer of 1945
or the moral case for a military campaign initiated in response
to a virulently nationalist and racist form of politics.[25] What
this criticism ignores, however, is the fact that Kip's perspective
upon world affairs is not necessarily identical with *The English
Patient*'s broader pattern of judgements: although the novel
registers the full force of Kip's political dissent, it also subjects
his point-of-view to qualification and critique. Thus while Kip's

ultimate recoil from the culture of 'English' imperialism is anticipated and amplified by Caravaggio's contempt for 'English wars', his undifferentiated response to the traumas of colonial history is also seen as a potential obstacle to the development of new and more inclusive forms of cultural exchange (*EP*, 122). Ondaatje's abiding sense of the political futility of a monolithic distinction between 'Asian solidarity' and 'Western aggression' is vividly rendered in the scene in which Kip, fleeing south, is thrown from his motorcycle and almost drowned in the Ofanto River. Coming hard upon the heels of his absolute repudiation of Western values and motives, his unfortunate fall serves, according to Mark D. Simpson, as a 'plangent chastisement of such overly speedy or driving fixations and historical leaps'.[26]

The novel's imaginative distance from Kip's rebarbative politics is underlined in its final pages. Following an enigmatic passage in which the candlelight illuminating the dying patient begins slowly to fade, the narrative of *The English Patient* suddenly propels itself fifteen years into the future where it brings two images into apposition. Kip, now married, is a father and a doctor in India; while Hana is now returned to Canada, where her idealism and vivacity burn as brightly as before (*EP*, 301). In a scene that revisits the novel's opening lines, Kip, sitting alone in his Indian garden, senses an abrupt shift in the emotional weather. Looking around the garden he suddenly discovers traces of Hana in everything he sees ('He sees her always, her face and body'): what is restored to him, he realises, in these unexpected 'moments of revelation' is a buried part of his own nature (*EP*, 300). The novel's final sentences develop this restorative impulse by hinting at both 'a synchronous overlapping of spaces' and a potential reconciliation of cultural differences.[27] Alone in her apartment in Canada, Hana drops a glass from her kitchen cupboard; in the same moment, and as if in completion of the same movement, Kip bends in his Indian kitchen to catch his daughter's dropped fork:

> And so Hana moves and her face turns and in a regret she lowers her hair. Her shoulder touches the edge of a cupboard and a glass dislodges. Kirpal's left hand swoops

down and catches the dropped fork an inch from the
floor and gently passes it into the fingers of his daughter,
a wrinkle at the edge of his eyes behind his spectacles.
(*EP*, 301–2)

Unlike the final words of one of *The English Patient's* intertexts, Forster's *A Passage to India* – a novel that concludes with
the foreboding sense of a potentially unbridgeable gulf between
its Indian and non-Indian protagonists – the rhyming of these
gestures tentatively suggests a point of common vision shared
by the inhabitants of two very different worlds. Because the
value of such a vision is precisely what cannot be determined in
advance, Ondaatje tactfully removes the supervening authority
of authorial omniscience from this scene of potential reconciliation ('She is a woman I don't know well enough to hold in
my wing, if writers have wings, to harbour for the rest of my
life'), leaving his characters to take responsibility for their own
futures on their own terms (*EP*, 301).

Ondaatje's decision to conclude the novel with the interdependence of these two images offers an implicit rebuke to those
who seek to impose a unitary narrative upon the open field of
'postcolonial' history. Like Kip, *The English Patient* seems to say,
we should resist the reduction of world history to the expression
of specifically Western interests and imperatives; but *unlike* Kip
we should refuse to accept cultural particularism as a price worth
paying for this anti-colonial commitment. The novel develops
this appeal for a more fluid and dynamic exchange of cultural
perspectives in those moments when the image of the colonial
body returns as a spectre to haunt the Western gaze, opening
it despite itself to a sense of its own historical contingency and
cultural location. Years after returning to Toronto, Caravaggio
will hold the door of a taxi cab open for an 'East Indian' only
suddenly to 'think of Kip' and the world he left behind (*EP*, 208).
This uncanny sense of another presence, however sublimated or
repressed, at the core of one's own life is hauntingly evoked in
the novel's final image of the 'English' patient:

Around three a.m. he feels a presence in the room. He
sees, for a pulse of a moment, a figure at the foot of his

bed, against the wall or painted onto it perhaps, not quite discernible in the darkness of foliage beyond the candle-light. He mutters something, something he had wanted to say, but there is silence and the slight brown figure, which could be just a night shadow, does not move. A poplar. A man with plumes. A swimming figure. And he would not be so lucky, he thinks, to speak to the young sapper again. (*EP*, 298)

Although the patient will not be so lucky to speak to the young sapper again, others will continue to have their lives changed by him. The lasting effects of Kip's presence in the Villa San Girolamo are evident in the scene in which he prepares a celebratory meal for Hana's birthday. Taking advantage of this brief respite from the pressures of war, Kip 'beg[ins] to talk about himself' while asking his guests for 'stories about Toronto as if it were a place of peculiar wonders' (*EP* 268). Encouraged by the sapper's sudden expansiveness, Caravaggio relates the story of a younger and more self-confident Hana singing the 'Marseil-laise'. When Kip, entranced by the story, begins his own halting rendition of the same song, Hana is brought abruptly back to life. Listening amazedly to Hana's sudden outpouring of song, Caravaggio 'realized she was singing with and echoing the heart of the sapper' (*EP*, 269). Singing to Kip and singing *for* Kip, Hana momentarily exchanges positions with the man she loves: 'She was singing it as if it was something scarred, as if one couldn't ever again bring all the hope of the song together. It had been altered by the five years leading to this night of her twenty-first birthday in the forty-fifth year of the twentieth century. Singing in the voice of a tired traveller, alone against everything' (*EP*, 269). If Hana's lyrical identification with the figure of the cultural outsider unlocks a buried element of her own nature, enabling her to write to her stepmother Clara Dickens and imagine a future beyond her grief at her father's death, this symbolic forging of a common cause is consolidated by Kip's miraculous rebirth from the waters of the Ofanto River. Haunted by images of cultural violence and nuclear apocalypse, *The English Patient* ultimately retains little faith in the redemptive promise of a utopian poli-

tics. What it offers instead is the uncertain beginnings of its own 'new testament': the song of a traumatised and war-torn young woman who, within the fragile light glimpsed from the edge of an enveloping darkness, finds a place for the Other at the heart of herself (*EP*, 269).

Anil's Ghost

> Violence is now [1989] so widespread that it is often diffi-
> cult to establish with authority who the agents of specific
> killings were – or even to identify the victims whose
> bodies are sometimes grossly mutilated, burned to ashes
> or transported by distances from the scenes of arrests or
> abductions before being dumped.[1]

> What you decide to write about is where the morality comes
> into it, as opposed to what you say about people ...
> (Michael Ondaatje)[2]

Anil's Ghost (2000), Ondaatje's fourth novel, returns, like *Running in the Family*, to his native Sri Lanka. But although these
texts share a common location, they describe two very different
countries. The event that radically transfigured Ondaatje's
writing between his research trips to his former home in 1978
and 1980 and the publication of his fourth novel twenty years
later was the outbreak of the Sri Lankan civil war in July 1983.
The impact of the civil war upon Ondaatje's writing is plain to
see: where *Running in the Family* offers a measured and often
playful meditation upon the emergence of Sri Lanka as a post-
colonial nation, *Anil's Ghost* charts the descent of this nascent
polity into catastrophic and seemingly interminable sectarian
conflict. The novel begins with a bleak prefatory note:

> From the mid-1980s to the early 1990s, Sri Lanka was in
> a crisis that involved three essential groups: the govern-
> ment, the antigovernment insurgents in the south and the
> separatist guerrillas in the north. Both the insurgents and

the separatists had declared war on the government. Eventually, in response, legal and illegal government squads were known to have been sent out to hunt down the separatists and the insurgents.

Anil's Ghost is a fictional work set during this political time and historical moment. And while there existed organizations similar to those in this story, and similar events took place, the characters and incidents in the novel are invented.

Today the war in Sri Lanka continues in a different form.

A few preliminary contextual remarks are required in order to understand the complexity and provocation of Ondaatje's response to the Sri Lankan civil war. In its initial phase the war took the form of a struggle between the government and the Liberation Tigers of Tamil Eelam (LTTE) who demanded an independent Tamil Eelam state for the Tamil minority population in the north-east of the island. Although the ensuing conflict was routinely portrayed in the Western media as a battle played out exclusively between these two forces, the war had, at least for the fifteen years before a provisional ceasefire was agreed in 2002, three main protagonists: the government, the LTTE in the north, and the JVP (Janatha Vinukthi Peramuna or People's Liberation Front) in the south. The JVP was desperate to preserve the privilege enjoyed by the Sinhala majority since Independence in 1948, and the government was often suspected of being in collusion with it. Two primary phases of the civil war can be distinguished in broad terms: the period between 1983 and 1987 when the conflict was fought out solely between the LTTE and the government; and the period after 1987 when the JVP entered the conflict in an attempt to resist the Tamil insurgency and safeguard the political hegemony of Sinhala nationalism. *Anil's Ghost* is set during this second phase of the war, when the struggle between the Tamil minority and the state – a struggle that encompassed appalling terrorist atrocities by the LTTE and savage and often indiscriminate acts of government reprisal – threatened to plunge the entire country into a modern-day inferno.

The historical origins of the civil war are to be found in the gradual exclusion since Independence of the Tamil minority from political power and positions of civic authority. In the eyes of the Sinhalese the Tamils had always fared disproportionately well under British colonial rule – they pointed to what they believed to be Tamil over-representation in the civil service, medicine, law and other emerging middle-class professions – and they saw in the post-imperial settlement an opportunity to redress this perceived imbalance and assert the rights of the margina-lised majority population. A defining moment in the realign-ment of Sri Lankan politics arrived in 1956 with the passing of the Sinhala Only Act, which enshrined Sinhala as the sole official national language, restricted government jobs to Sinhala speakers, and imposed changes in university admissions policies which debarred many Tamils from entering higher education. As political tensions grew between the two communities, increasing numbers of Tamils began to revive their historical dream of an independent and self-governing Tamil homeland. This dream was given political expression by the Tamil United Liberation Front (TULF), a collection of parties that came together during the 1977 national elections to campaign for an independent Tamil state. Although the TULF achieved significant electoral gains following this campaign, its representatives were subse-quently prevented from taking their parliamentary seats as a punishment for advocating a separatist political programme. From this moment Tamils began to look beyond the established parliamentary system for the fulfilment of their political aspira-tions.

A full-scale civil war erupted in the summer of 1983. Following the gang-rape of a Tamil doctor by members of the Sri Lankan Army, the LTTE ambushed the military, killing thirteen soldiers with a land mine. What began as a series of isolated skirmishes soon became a national catastrophe: riots exploded in Colombo and a number of other Sri Lankan cities leaving several thousand Tamils dead and sparking a mass exodus of their ethnic community to the north of the country. Gradually the LTTE assimilated other Tamil factions to its own organisation and

began a campaign of bombing and guerrilla insurgency against government positions. As the violence continued to paralyse the country, peace talks between the LTTE and the government were convened in 1985; upon their collapse the violence intensified, with civilians now routinely being targeted by both sides. In one attack in May 1985, LTTE guerrillas disguised as government soldiers went on a rampage in Anuradhapura, attacking the Bodhi Tree shrine, a site sacred to the Sinhalese Buddhists, and killing 150 civilians. By 1987 government forces had succeeded in confining the LTTE to the northern city of Jaffna, but the military situation remained highly unstable. The violence peaked once again in April of that year, when the Sri Lankan Army and the LTTE committed bombings in Jaffna and Colombo respectively, resulting in large numbers of civilian casualties. In an attempt to curtail the LTTE insurrection, the government signed a series of accords creating new councils for Tamils in the north and east, and reached agreement with India on the deployment of an Indian peacekeeping force (IPKF). Alarmed by these concessions to the LTTE, the Sinhalese nationalist JVP quickly began an insurrection in the south to destroy the Indo-Sri Lankan agreement. Despite some initial success in their peacekeeping effort, the presence of the IPKF was challenged militarily by LTTE rebels and politically by the mobilisation of Sinhalese nationalist sentiment. As the violence in the north escalated and its causalty list steadily mounted, India withdrew its troops in March 1990. Any residual Indian enthusiasm for the Indo-Sri Lankan agreement disappeared in May 1991, when a female suicide bomber commonly believed to be an LTTE member assassinated ex-Indian prime minister Rajiv Ghandhi in Tamil Nadu. Following the Indian withdrawal, the LTTE increased its stranglehold upon large parts of northern Sri Lanka while the Government intensified its campaign to extirpate the rebels and regain undivided control of the country. Its failure to achieve this aim was dramatically exposed in May 1993 when an LTTE suicide bomber assassinated the Sri Lankan president, Ranasinghe Premadasa, at a political rally in Colombo.

These tragic events form the backdrop to *Anil's Ghost*. The

novel opens in March 1992 with the return to her native Sri Lanka of thirty-three-year-old Anil Tissera, a Western-trained forensic anthropologist, who has spent her career investigating human rights abuses in a number of war-torn countries. Her visit takes place on behalf of a United Nations human rights group that wants to examine the political record of the Sri Lankan premier President Katugala. Unsurprisingly, her presence in the country is unwelcome to the government, which grants her a cursory seven-week period to complete her research while insisting that she is supervised throughout her stay by a local archaeologist, Sarath Diyasena. Apart from potentially hampering her investigation, these restrictions are intended to reinforce the government view that Anil is a cultural dilettante who, in the words of Sarath's brother, the doctor Gamini, arrives seeking the vicarious thrill of an encounter with raw third-world 'reality' before flying home to write a bestselling book and 'hit the circuit' of a fawning liberal press (*AG*, 286). This picture is complicated, however, by Anil's status as a Sri Lankan national returning home after fifteen years in the United States and Latin America. The motif of the returning prodigal is crucial to Ondaatje's design: the contrast between the relative tranquillity of Anil's childhood memories and the devastated contemporary landscape that awaits her underscores the speed and scope of the country's descent into political and moral barbarism.

From the beginning of her visit Anil is sceptical about what her investigation can realistically achieve: 'Forensic work during a political crisis was notorious', she reflects, 'for its three-dimensional chess moves and back-room deals and muted statements for the "good of the nation"' (*AG*, 28). Her scepticism is compounded by her involuntary partnership with Sarath, whom she considers a mere government placeman; he, in his turn, is unconvinced about the real extent of her commitment to the daunting task before her, worrying that she will end up 'like one of those journalists who file reports about flies and scabs while staying at the Galle Face Hotel' (*AG*, 44). Each of their preconceptions is confounded by the events that begin to unfold when Sarath persuades Anil to help him examine some bones

recently unearthed from a sixth-century monastic burial ground concealed in one of the government's archaeological preserves. Despite her initial lack of enthusiasm for the task ('Well, she hadn't come here to deal with the Middle Ages'), Anil quickly realises that some of these bone fragments are not medieval at all, but the remains of a recently buried body (*AG*, 20). This discovery has profound and potentially perilous implications. Because the bones were interred in the Bandarawela caves, a state-protected zone to which access is rigorously restricted, here appears at last to be irrefutable proof of the government's complicity in political abduction and murder. The task before Anil and Sarath is to gain physical access to the burial site in the hope of unearthing more conclusive evidence of what has been taking place in one of the government killing fields.

At Bandarawela this evidence is quickly unearthed. Excavating in the far reaches of one of the caves Anil comes across a recently buried skeleton whose bones are held together by partially burned dried ligaments. Upon closer inspection these bones reveal a mixture of trace elements and evidence of 'transverse cracking' or possible signs of violence which suggest the body was tortured, killed, buried, then disinterred and removed to its present secluded location. 'Do you see?' Anil entreats Sarath. 'He must have been buried somewhere else before. Someone took precautions to make sure the skeleton was not discovered. This is no ordinary murder or burial. They buried him, then later moved him to an older gravesite' (*AG*, 51). Like all good archaeologists, Sarath 'can read a bucket of soil as if it were a complex historical novel', but his experience during the last unspeakable decade has taught him circumspection in drawing elaborate political conclusions from fragmentary empirical evidence (*AG*, 151). Replying to Anil's unequivocal insistence that the disinterred skeleton represents the remains of a 'murder victim', Sarath carefully measures his words: 'A murder ... Do you mean any murder ... or do you mean a political murder?' (*AG*, 51). Two worlds collide here: what appears from Anil's perspective as equivocation or disingenuousness is, from Sarath's point-of-view, the only possible ethical response

to a political situation in which heedless speculation leads all too often to 'new vengeance and slaughter' (*AG*, 157). Already suspicious of Sarath's institutional allegiances, Anil sees nothing more in his sensitivity to political circumstance than a lack of firm principle: 'I don't really know, you see, which side you are on – if I can trust you' (*AG*, 53). The difference between these unlikely colleagues is starkly presented: while Sarath is haunted throughout his examination of the skeleton by questions of political context and consequence, Anil remains convinced these bones will reveal 'permanent truths' about human behaviour that are 'the same for Colombo as for Troy' (*AG*, 64). United in a common purpose but divided in their response to the situation in which they find themselves, the pair removes the skeleton they call 'Sailor' to Colombo. There they set up a research laboratory aboard the ship *Oronsay* located at the end of the symbolically apposite 'Reclamation Street' and continue their reading of its enigmatic remains.

But despite their best efforts Sailor's true identity continues to elude them, forcing Sarath to conclude that they require outside assistance to complete their investigation. Discounting Anil's reservations, he decides that the pair should travel north to the spiritual retreat known as 'The Grove of Ascetics' in order to consult Palipana, Sarath's former teacher and guide. The epigraphist Palipana was 'for a number of years at the centre of a nationalistic group that eventually wrestled archaeological authority in Sri Lanka away from the Europeans' and he plays a crucial role within the novel's economy of themes (*AG*, 79). If in general terms Palipana's intellectual example implies a distinction between Western and non-Western modes of knowledge, his initial function is to bring Anil and Sarath one step closer to recovering Sailor's historical image. The best way to identify Sailor, Sarath suggests to Papliana, is to humanise him by reconstructing his facial image from the contours of his skull; but neither he nor Anil possesses the necessary skills to accomplish such a feat. Palipana responds by telling them of the tradition of Nĕtra Mangala – the tradition of painting eyes on the Buddha image – and giving them the name of Ananda Udugama,

a local artist and gem-worker, who might help them identify the skeleton by rebuilding its face. Encouraged by this information, Anil and Sarath prepare to leave for Ananda's village, but not before Palipana's remarks about the rewards customarily bestowed upon the painters of eyes involve him and Anil in a terse exchange about the nature of truth:

> 'The King would endow all those responsible with goods and land … He directed the artificer to be allowed thirty *amunu* of seed-paddy, thirty pieces of iron, ten buffaloes from the fold and ten she-buffaloes with calves'.
>
> 'She-buffaloes with calves', Anil said quietly to herself. 'Seed-paddy … You were rewarded for the right things'. But he heard her.
>
> Well, kings also caused trouble in those days', he said. 'Even then there was nothing to believe in with certainty. They still didn't know what truth was. We have never had the truth. Not even with your work on bones'.
>
> 'We use the bone to search for it. 'The truth shall set you free'. I believe that'.
>
> 'Most of the time in our world, truth is just an opinion'. (*AG*, 101–2)

Anil's evangelical faith in the emancipatory power of truth will be sorely tested by the end of the novel. As if in preparation for the trials ahead, the narrative suddenly changes direction to explore the effects of the war upon the living as well as the dead. Travelling back to Colombo after taking leave of Papliana, Anil and Sarath are confronted with a ghastly image of the depraved times in which they live: a truck driver lies crucified upon the road before them as an arbitrary sacrifice to the amoral exhibitionism of insurgent authority. Trying desperately to keep Gunsena, the driver, alive, the pair rush him to Colombo Emergency Services where he is treated by Gamini, Sarath's younger brother, the enigmatic 'family secret' with whom the archaeologist has contended since childhood (*AG*, 130). But to their horror Gamini is completely unsurprised by this fresh evidence of barbarity. 'There are no beds left here tonight. Not for this level of injury', he calmly relates. 'See, even crucifixion isn't a

major assault nowadays' (*AG*, 130). Implicit in Gamini's affect-less response is despair at the condition of a society in which compassion can no longer keep pace with the relentless produc-tion of pain. Gamini is the living embodiment of such despair: exhausted by a relentless diet of mortified flesh, he spends his days strung out on amphetamines while seeking relief in profes-sional routine from the carnage of the world outside. Abducted at one point by Tamil terrorists and compelled to care for their stricken comrades, he is sustained throughout his ordeal by his belief that the practice of medicine transcends every political consideration. This sense of medicine as a redemption from political chaos defines Gamini's attitude to his life in emergency services:

> The mothers were always there … There were not too many fathers around then. He watched the children, who were unaware of their parents' arms. Fifty yards away in Emergency he heard grown men scream for their mothers as they were dying. *'Wait for me!' 'I know you are here!'* This was when he stopped believing in man's rule on earth. (*AG*, 119)

An unhappy consequence of Gamini's abrogation of political consciousness is that it leaves him no position from which to distinguish between the motives of the various warring factions. 'Anyway, these guys who are setting off the bombs are who the Western press call freedom fighters', Gamini reminds his companions over a meal of *lamprais* on Galle Face Green. 'And you want to investigate the *government*?' (*AG*, 133). When Sarath gently replies that '[t]here are innocent Tamils in the south being killed too', Gamini answers impassively, 'We're all fucked, aren't we. We don't know what to do about it' (*AG*, 133). Unwilling to accept such a pitiless conclusion, Anil and Sarath eventually locate Ananda and set him to work reconstructing Sailor's human likeness. When Ananda finally produces his clay model of Sailor's features, Anil and Sarath realise that the face upon which they are gazing is not the exact reproduction of a lost original, but a younger, more serene image of anonymous human restfulness, the type of image Ananda might create to

confer a benediction upon the dead and express the 'peacefulness he wanted for any victim' (*AG*, 187). Yet the time they spend working with Ananda is not wasted. Watching Ananda at work, Anil notices that his crouching posture has left a permanent indentation upon his ankle bone. Exactly the same strictures were evident upon Sailor's ankle bones: when Ananda reveals that his injuries arose from hours spent squatting in the gem mines, Anil is convinced that Sailor must have worked in the same underground location. Convinced that these 'markers of occupation' will ultimately give their skeleton a name, the pair goes to enquire of Sailor in the villages where plumbago-graphite mines once flourished (*AG*, 205). They discover Sailor's identity in the third village they visit: he is Ruwan Kumara, a former toddy tapper, who was abducted from the mines by government agents for a reason now lost to memory.

Leaving Anil at the country estate in Ekneligoda that served as their base of operations, Sarath returns to Colombo to search for Ruwan Kumara's name on a list of government undesirables. When he has been incommunicado for a week, Anil nervously contacts Doctor Perera, a friend of her late father's, who arranges for her to be brought back quietly to the capital. A day later Anil finds herself in the Armoury Auditorium expected to elaborate her findings to a hostile audience of military and police personnel trained in 'counter-insurgency methods' (*AG*, 271). To her consternation Sailor, the skeleton upon which all her conclusions depend, has mysteriously disappeared, and another one has been set in its place. Realising that her evidence is now useless, Anil confronts her sneering audience with an unequivocal and implicating judgement: 'I think you murdered hundreds of us' (*AG*, 272). All too aware of the mortal danger in which Anil now finds herself, Sarath, watching unobserved at the back of the auditorium, begins suddenly to heckle her, wondering aloud if she possesses even the rudimentary forensic skill to distinguish between a fresh and an ancient skeleton. Seemingly oblivious to Anil's uncomprehending fury, Sarath then has a two-hundred-year-old corpse wheeled into the hall and challenges her to determine its provenance. Still

reeling from Sarath's apparently motiveless treachery, Anil and the skeleton are abruptly dismissed from the room, while her onetime colleague speaks soothingly behind her back to the newly appreciative gathering.

It is only when she returns to the *Oronsay* with these unwanted remains that Anil discovers that the ancient corpse lying on the table before her is the lost skeleton of Ruwan Kumara. A tape-recorded message artfully concealed between its ribs reveals how Sarath managed to reunite her with this crucial evidence of the operation of government death squads. It is imperative, Sarath's recorded voice implores her, that she complete her investigation overnight, erase all trace of Sarath's complicity, and be ready to leave by air early next morning. These precautions are vital to Anil's escape; but Sarath's fate is already sealed. As an archaeologist, Sarath believes in truth as the ethical basis of life; he would 'have given his life for the truth if the truth were of any use' (*AG*, 157). By compromising his own safety to safeguard Anil's forensic research, he is forced to accept the terrible burden of this altruistic principle. His nemesis, when it arrives, is absolute and unforgiving. Working his way through the fresh photographs of recent murder victims brought each Friday to his office by a civil rights organisation, Gamini suddenly recognises his brother's mutilated body by the traces of its childhood scars and 'innocent' wounds (*AG*, 287). Leaning over Sarath's corpse while he dresses its wounds, Gamini experiences an epiphany that shakes him to the core of his being; unless he finds a way to reverse his withdrawal from the world and hold the dead in his memory 'his brother would disappear from his life' now and forever (*AG*, 288). Alone in a hospital ward in the 'slow, scrambled state' of grief, Gamini attempts the beginning of a 'permanent conversation' with Sarath (*AG*, 288). He is still playing his part in this agonised 'pietà between brothers' when the bodies start to flood into emergency services in the wake of President Katugala's assassination (*AG*, 288).

If Gamini's 'pietà' concludes with a moment in which violence once again breaks in upon contemplation, this impulse is both marked and reversed in the novel's final chapter, 'Distance'. It

is impossible to deduce from this casually unspecific title when exactly the novel's closing events take place; although 'Distance' clearly describes a period some time after Anil's disappearance and Sarath's murder, the political terror in the country still persists. Certainly enough time has elapsed for Ananda to return to the art of Nĕtra Mangala: he has been commissioned to paint the eyes of a half-destroyed and ransacked Buddhist statue whose fractured form offers 'monumental evidence of the violence of contemporary history in Sri Lanka and its embeddedness in communal politics'.[3] At work in the fields of Buduruvagala, 'where Buddhism and its values met the harsh political values of the twentieth century', Ananda begins to recompose the outline of another shattered image (*AG*, 300). It had been assumed when he began his labour of restoration that he would be working under the guidance of foreign specialists; but because of the 'political turmoil' in the area these celebrities failed to appear: 'They were finding dead bodies daily, not even buried, in the adjoining fields' (*AG*, 301). Contemplating the profile of the ruined statue, Ananda gradually relinquishes his plan to 'homogenize the stone' and fuse the rock into an image of tranquillity and composure; the Buddha's real composure, he realises, lies in its power to absorb traces of the suffering of the Sri Lankan people into its serene expression of spiritual transcendence (*AG*, 302). Consequently Ananda's newly restored Buddha deliberately retains the 'pure sad glance' of the 'great scarred face' abandoned by the scavengers amid the mounds of damaged stone (*AG*, 307). The scars left by Sri Lanka's recent history of violence also appear upon Ananda's own body. As he mounts the steps to paint the Buddha's eyes, he wears one of Sarath's shirts beneath his sarong, in silent acknowledgement that '[h]e and the woman Anil would always carry the ghost of Sarath Diyasena' (*AG*, 305).

The novel's poignant closing sentences offer one possible explanation of the question posed by its title: how can the story Ondaatje's novel unfolds be thought to embody *Anil's ghost*? In one sense, of course, the answer is obvious: during her investigation Anil will assume responsibility for the remains and the

memory of Ruwan Kumara. Yet if Anil is haunted by the need to secure a measure of posthumous justice for Kumara, the spectre invoked by Ondaatje's title also implicates her in a relationship with a lost part of herself. For her journey back to Sri Lanka is also a journey of self-discovery; during her first days in Colombo 'buried senses from childhood' once more become 'alive in her' (*AG*, 15). Adrift among cultural traditions and trapped within a past she no longer recognises – from the moment of her return she is instantly labelled 'the swimmer' in homage to an adolescent sporting triumph – Anil faces continual problems of translation as she fixes the world with her 'long-distance gaze' (*AG*, 11). These problems become critical when she is confronted with the ghastly evidence of Sailor's abduction and murder. Looking down upon Sailor's burnt remains, Anil repeats to herself the mantra of human rights workers the world over: 'One village can speak for many villages. One victim can speak for many victims' (*AG*, 176). But although ethical fidelity to the victims of political terror may require the recovery of an idea of universal humanity from the ruins of damaged life, it must also preserve the integrity of individual memory from the global language of 'human rights'. Sarath's suspicion that Anil's universal commitment to human rights risks effacing the very subject it claims to represent is evident in one of their opening exchanges: 'You know, I'd believe your arguments more if you lived here. You can't just slip in, make a discovery and leave' (*AG*, 44).

Reflecting scornfully upon her first meeting with Sarath, Anil is contemptuous of his rigorously empirical procedure: 'Most of what Sarath wished to know was in some way linked to the earth', Ondaatje writes: 'She suspected he found the social world around him irrelevant' (*AG*, 29). For Anil the phrase 'linked to the earth' indicates a disabling narrowness of vision: to remain enclosed within the world-at-hand is, for her, to become impervious to the universal conditions of human experience. Conversely her own rhetoric of rights prescribes the universality of truth by treating each particular victim of state violence as a representative *example* of anonymous human suffering: 'In her work Anil turned bodies into representatives of race and age

sequences telling the story of the break-up of a marriage and a way of life, the poet's own near break-down and, finally, after what the section calls 'Rock Bottom', his recovery and return through the love of another woman'.[25] Certainly the poems that comprise 'Rock Bottom' mine a very deep vein of desolation and despair: 'In the midst of love for you / my wife's suffering / anger in every direction / and the children wise / as tough shrubs / but they are not tough / – so I fear / how anything can grow from this' (*SL*, 147). Ondaatje's acute sense of emotional dislocation in the early 1980s was undoubtedly one of the factors that led him to return once again to Sri Lanka to see if he could establish a closer relationship to his family roots. *Running in the Family*, the book that emerged from this trip, is a playful semi-autobiographical account of his family history that seamlessly interweaves different modes of cultural inscription – poetry, photographs, folklore, gossip, anecdote and so on – into an eclectic national narrative. In formal terms the book's characteristic interpolation of surreal and fantastic elements into biographical memoir has clear affinities with the techniques of 'magic realism' associated with writers like Gabriel Garcìa Márquez. These surreal and fantastic elements lend Ondaatje's prose a freshness and exuberance perfectly attuned to the story of a revenant experiencing the strangeness of his homeland as if for the first time. But they are shadowed throughout by the persistence of a much darker theme: the idea of the absent father who cuts himself off from his family and ends his life isolated and alone.

In retrospect *Running in the Family* affords a tantalising glimpse of a vanishing country; barely a year after its publication Sri Lanka descended into the inferno of civil war. Ondaatje's next book, *In the Skin of a Lion*, would extend his preoccupation with cultural memory and modern civic nationhood by describing the emergence of the city of Toronto as an urban metropolis. When Ondaatje began the novel in 1980 its subject was the life of the Canadian theatre magnate Ambrose Small, who mysteriously vanished in 1919 at the height of his fame, provoking an international manhunt that discovered no trace of his whereabouts.

Yet Ondaatje soon tired of Small's petty egomania and widened the novel's focus to create a panoramic vision of the modern immigrant experience: the story of all those exiles and émigrés who, like him, had come to another country and worked to make it their own. Employing teasing metafictive techniques similar to those being developed by writers like Salman Rushdie, Robert Kroetsch and Peter Carey, Ondaatje's 'historical' novelisation of the civic origins of modern Toronto sought to recover the lost stories of those marginalised citizens who have been written out of the official national narrative. Here as elsewhere Ondaatje's 'postmodern' preoccupation with narrative form retains a latent political edge as a critique of the relationships of power that structure contemporary society.

Upon its appearance in 1987 *In the Skin of a Lion* was a major critical success; it won a succession of prizes over the next year including the Toronto Book Award, the Toronto Arts Award, the Trillium Book Award and the Best Paperback in English Award, and was a finalist for the Ritz Paris Hemingway Literary Prize. Ondaatje was also the recipient of the Wang International Festival Prize, but made a point of donating the $7,500 prize money to a fund for young writers.[26] His solicitude for young and unrecognised writers was a familiar refrain since his involvement with Coach House Press twenty years earlier; its most substantive public expression came in 1990 when he edited *Ink Lake*, an anthology of new Canadian writing designed to bring its contributors to a much wider audience. Ondaatje's commitment to the literary arts in their broadest form was further underlined a year later when with Linda Spalding he co-edited *The Brick Reader*, a representative selection from the arts magazine for which he had been a contributing editor since 1984. Nothing in Ondaatje's literary career to date, though, could have prepared him for the international chorus of praise that greeted the appearance of *The English Patient*, his third novel, in 1992. With this book he made the transition from a national to a world writer. Ondaatje's new celebrity status was confirmed in October of that year when *The English Patient* shared the prestigious Booker Prize with the British writer

Barry Unsworth's *Sacred Hunger*. The novel's international success was subsequently confirmed when it later received the Governor General's and the Trillium Award for fiction.

Such has been the success of *The English Patient* that it now defines Ondaatje's literary image in the eyes of the reading public. This image was consolidated four years later by the extraordinary reception given to Anthony Minghella's film adaptation of the novel, which went on to win nine Oscars at the 1997 Academy Awards. What is remarkable about Ondaatje's novel in artistic terms is its subtle integration of several of his most persistent themes. 'There are a lot of international bastards roaming around the world today', Ondaatje remarked soon after the novel's publication. 'That's one of the book's main stories. These migrants don't belong here but want to belong here and find a new home'.[27] In the interlinked stories of four embattled survivors brought together at the Villa San Girolamo in Rome, Ondaatje presents an unforgettable image of cultural deracination and dispossession. At the same time his postmodern – or at least flagrantly intertextual – narrative style suggestively probes the nature of subjectivity, the relationship between history and memory, the effects of imperial intervention upon colonial history and the establishment and erasure of national boundaries and traditions.

The last words uttered by Hana, one of *The English Patient*'s central characters, concern the desire for homecoming. 'I am sick of Europe, Clara', she writes to her stepmother, 'I want to come home. To your small cabin and pink rock in Georgian Bay. I will take a bus up to Parry Sound. And from the mainland send a message over the shortwave radio out towards the Pancakes. And wait for you, wait to see the silhouette of you in a canoe coming to rescue me from this place we all entered, betraying you' (*EP*, 296). Since the early 1990s Ondaatje's thoughts have been much preoccupied with thoughts of home and the rediscovery of his native Sri Lanka. Six years after *The English Patient* he published *Handwriting*, a collection of poems written in Canada and Sri Lanka between 1993 and 1998. This group of spare, elegiac lyrics explores many aspects of Sri Lanka's history, geography, culture and tradition, offering eloquent evidence of the island's 'traditions of Buddhist and Hindu piety and civilized codes of behaviour'.[28] But not even Ondaatje's pellucid lyrics can escape contamination by the terrible violence of the ongoing civil war. War, indeed, constitutes the volume's prevailing atmosphere and weather: 'To be buried in times of war / in harsh weather, in the monsoon / of knives and stakes' (H, 7). Religious tradition and the ancient forest sanctuaries offer a fragile respite from the 'sects of war', but the 'hundred beliefs' that animate the island are increasingly the material that feeds the conflagration. Time and again lyrics searching for 'dark peace / like a cave of water' are interrupted by appalling bulletins from the world outside (H, 16, 27–8).

In the poem 'The Brother Thief' four men 'steal the bronze / Buddha at Veheragala' and pick out its eyes; in 'Buried 2' the main causes of death in contemporary Sri Lanka are given as 'extra-judicial execution' and 'exemplary killings' (H, 27). Either poem might serve as an introduction to Anil's Ghost, Ondaatje's most recent novel, which explicitly grapples with the terrible history of the Sri Lankan civil war. Set in the early 1990s when the country was torn by a tripartite dispute between the government, Tamil separatists in the North and JVP insurgents in the South, Anil's Ghost tells the story of the return to her homeland of Anil Tissera, a forensic pathologist working for a United Nations Human Rights Commission in order to investigate human rights abuses in Sri Lanka. The novel focuses upon the events that begin to unfold when Anil, forced against her will to collaborate with Sarath, a local archaeologist, discovers a recently buried skeleton in the restricted environs of a government archaeological preserve. Their tortuous effort to restore a name and an identity to the skeleton they call 'Sailor' functions as a metaphor for the need to bind up the wounds of the Sri Lankan body politic and recover the memory of the 'disappeared': the numberless victims of extra-judicial state murder. In the contrast between the modern investigative techniques of forensic pathology and archaeology and Buddhist mysticism Ondaatje once again explores the status of historical truth, a theme central to his work since *Billy the Kid*.[29] The fraught and sometimes elusive relationship between knowledge and truth is an issue that goes straight to the heart of the novel, where Anil and Sarath's very different responses to the trauma of recent Sri Lankan history trace the uncertain ground between ethics and politics in a time of moral darkness.[30]

Michael Ondaatje is a fabulist, a dealer in myths, an inventor of haunting poetic images and uncanny fictional worlds. Reading his work we encounter a series of strange and hallucinatory landscapes that unsettle our historical sense, redraw the boundary between nature and culture, and call into question the moral image of humanity A white European woman staggers into an Australian clearing and confronts the limits of her known world; the identity of an infamous gunslinger dissolves into a chaotic stream of drives and affections; a musician goes berserk in a parade and reinvents the possibilities of jazz; a nun steps off a Toronto bridge into mid-air and enters a subterranean world she never knew existed; a burning man falls from the air stripped of his name, his past and his entire personality. Disturbing, enigmatic and alluring in turn, these images constitute a shock to thought by asking us to suspend our everyday way of seeing the world and perceive life in terms of its modes of becoming rather than its already given forms. In their insistence that we become what we are through a confrontation with forces that exceed us, works like *the man with seven toes*, *The Collected Works of Billy the Kid* and *Coming Through Slaughter* exhort us to extend perception beyond its human home. The same impulse, substantially revisited and redirected, inflects Ondaatje's major fiction of the last twenty years, from *In the Skin of a Lion* onwards, which presents isolated moments from twentieth-century history from the perspective of those abjected social figures – the immigrant, the proletarian worker, the displaced colonial subject – which have done so much to shape our perception of twentieth-century history.

This book offers an overview of the whole of Michael Ondaatje's literary career to date, including detailed discussion of many of his most important poems and all of his published prose fiction up until 2007. Its aim – or at least one of its aims – is to consider the scope and challenge of Ondaatje's work by elucidating some of its major themes and exploring a number of the social, cultural and political contexts that inform his writing. Although Ondaatje has been publishing poetry and prose for forty years, a glance at the 'Books on Ondaatje' section of the bibliography at the end of this volume suggests that his work has still to receive the comprehensive and detailed critical attention it deserves. My hope is that the ensuing pages will contribute to the emergence of a wider debate about the risks and rewards of his writing.

Anyone familiar with *Running in the Family*, Ondaatje's fictionalised memoir of his Ceylonese family history, will find eloquent testimony to the profound, if often ambivalent, connection he feels to his colonial beginnings. This is an important theme in his work that has had considerable influence in defining his image in the public imagination as a 'post-colonial' writer. His receipt of the prestigious Booker Prize in 1992 for *The English Patient*, a novel that imaginatively reworks important elements of the colonial experience, accentuated this trend and his novels are now a familiar presence on university literature courses devoted to subjects like 'Post-Colonial Writing', 'Transnational Identities', 'Diaspora Studies' and their various correlatives. Reflecting in an interview about his childhood as the scion of a Ceylonese family of Dutch-Tamil-Sinhalese origin who was displaced to London at the age of nine, Ondaatje highlighted the effect this experience of dislocation had upon his view of the world. 'I don't feel much of England in me', he explained. 'I *do* feel I have been allowed the migrant's double perspective, in the way, say, someone like Gertrude Stein was "refocused" by Paris'.[31]

The implications of this 'double perspective' will be traced throughout this study. It is by now a critical commonplace that post-colonial theory has given us a language with which to examine the effects of the cultural dislocation and ambivalence Ondaatje describes, and much recent commentary on his work proceeds in precisely these terms. Certainly Ondaatje's representation of himself as a split or doubled subject, a writer who exists in the interstices between cultural allegiances and traditions, chimes with those aspects of contemporary theoretical reflection that emphasise the way such hybrid figures contest the relationship of domination between imperial power and colonial culture. Considering the potential of such hybrid or in-between figures to challenge the dominant representations and stereotypes of imperial discourse, Homi Bhaha famously recast colonial subjectivity as 'a place of hybridity, figuratively speaking, where the construction of a political object that is new, *neither the one nor the other*, properly alienates our political expectations, and changes, as it must, the very form of our recognition of the moment of politics'.[32] Read in these terms, Ondaatje's literary portrait of his own hybrid origins and his fascination with figures like Kip in *The English Patient* who straddle the divide between the First and Third Worlds appears to open up the possibility of what Bhabha calls a 'Third Space of Enunciation' in which the colonial subject might elude the politics of polarity by inhabiting a position between centre and margin where cultural meaning and representation have no primordial unity or fixity.[33]

The readings of Ondaatje that follow are indebted to elements of this post-colonial critique. Yet notwithstanding the many insights afforded by post-colonial theory, it is ultimately unable to account for the power and originality of Ondaatje's writing. One reason for this failure is implicit in Peter Hallward's influential distinction between what he calls singular and specific modes of individuation and differentiation. 'Roughly speaking', Hallward explains, 'a singular mode of individuation proceeds internally, through a process that creates its own medium of existence or expansion, whereas a specific mode operates, through the active negotiation of relations and the deliberate taking of sides, choices and risks, in a domain and under constraints that are external to these takings'.[34] Although the signature concepts mobilised by post-colonial theory – the hybrid, the interstertial, the transnational, the in-between, the liminal, the contingent, the counter-hegemonic and so on –

call into question any absolute idea of subjective coherence or presumed cultural unity, they can only do so by representing experience as a negotiation between already determined poles of distinction like the Same and the Other, centre and margin, or East and West.[35] What these concepts miss, however, is that another experience of life is possible: a singular experience in which our perception of life is not specific to external criteria or imposed frames of reference.[36]

It is one of the wagers of this book that Ondaatje's work is most profitably read between these singular and specific itineraries. Probably the most extraordinary and disquieting feature of Ondaatje's early work is the way it steps back takes from our habitual view of the world to illuminate the movement of perception from which it is composed. Ondaatje achieves this estranging effect by adopting what we might call an 'inhuman' perspective upon worldly experience. Ondaatje's fascination with inhuman life is a staple theme of his early poetry, which bulges with images of suicidal herons and the ravening dreams of dogs. Compelling though these images are, Ondaatje's inhuman art has little in common with atavistic visions of nature red in tooth and claw. Instead his work attempts to break free of the anthropocentric prejudice – the tendency to see 'Man' as the point-of-view or ground from which all other being is determined – by exposing us to the infinitely complex and intense flux of life that flows though and beyond us. By asking that we attend to the way an animal inhabits its world, Ondaatje inducts us into an experience of life irreducible to the organising and purposive viewpoints of conscious experience. This encounter with sensible experience prior to its incorporation into discrete ideas and images offers us in turn a position from which to consider the way we form distinct images of the human from the general flow of life.

Ondaatje's singular vision of life shapes much of his early writing. It is impossible to appreciate the full resonance of works like *The Collected Works of Billy the Kid* or *Coming Through Slaughter* without acknowledging that what distinguishes Billy the Kid and Buddy Bolden is their dissolution of the world around them into singular flows of intensity and affect.[37] Ondaatje's identification of this singular perspective with a musician and an outlaw-artist appears to involve him in a more general claim about the aesthetic: the power of art lies in its ability to disengage experience into the singularities that compose it and alert us to other possible realms of sensibility beyond our known and extended world. Some of Ondaatje's most astonishing literary effects derive from his ability to extend perception beyond its human location, although this liberation of point-of-view is not necessarily in the service of a utopian politics. Indeed, both *Billy the Kid* and *Coming Through Slaughter* have a tragic dimension: Billy lives his life on the edge of madness and Bolden dies in a lunatic asylum. The problem with the unconditional surrender to life their singular vision demands is that it dislocates them from history and leaves them no position from which to contest the field of social and political forces that speak for their experience.[38] In the second half of Ondaatje's literary career to date – the phase that encompasses major novels such as *In the Skin of a Lion*, *The English Patient* and *Anil's Ghost* – he responds to this dilemma by creating panoramic historical fictions that explore the historical determination of our experience while insisting that what we understand as 'history' is always also the effect of a particular perspective or ground. History, for Ondaatje, is a ground but not the limit of being: his work challenges us simultaneously to think ourselves in and out of history and, by so doing, to expand our sense of what an historical 'event' might be.

The Early Poems

The Dainty Monsters

Although Ondaatje has won international renown as a novelist, his first four published books were volumes of poetry. *The Dainty Monsters*, his first book, appeared in 1967, quickly followed by the long poems *the man with seven toes* (1969) and *The Collected Works of Billy the Kid* (1970). A fourth volume, *Rat Jelly*, was published in 1973; six years later Ondaatje made a selection of his poems which appeared under the title *There's a Trick With a Knife I'm Learning to Do*. Unlike many writers, whose careers record a sharp break between the preoccupations of their early and mature work, these volumes immediately introduce a range of themes that resonate throughout Ondaatje's corpus. Three particular themes inflect his early poetry: the schism between nature and culture in modern technological society; the nature and modes of perception of animal and inhuman life; and the disturbing, because perhaps dialectical, relationship between violence and art. Each of Ondaatje's first two books explores and develops these themes; they become in turn the imaginative matrix of his first major achievement *The Collected Works of Billy the Kid* as well as the strongest poems of *Rat Jelly*.

The title *The Dainty Monsters* announces a conflict that haunts the entire volume: the tension between the apparent stability of established cultural norms and values (a sense of order implicit in the associated ideas of daintiness, gentility and social tact) and the emergence of a 'monstrous', inhuman and radically destructuring force lurking just beneath the surface of things. The brooding sense of menace engendered by this apprehension of inhuman monstrosity is reinforced by the lines Ondaatje takes for the volume's epigraph from W. H. Auden's poem 'The Witnesses':

> We've been watching you over the garden wall
> For hours,
> The sky is darkening like a stain,
> Something is going to fall like rain
> And it won't be flowers.

Casually combining a scene of anonymous surveillance with a sense of eschatological portent, Auden's lines are sinister enough in their implication; the shift in historical circumstance between the early 1930s, when 'The Witnesses' was written, and the Cold War paranoia of the 1960s, when Ondaatje's first published poems were composed, imbues them with the contemporary overtones of incipient nuclear catastrophe. Ondaatje's reproduction of these lines, in which 'something' is going to fall 'like rain', but which won't *be* rain, immediately alerts us to one of his key themes: now, in our era of advanced technological rationality, something has happened to disturb the relationship between nature and culture that has potentially catastrophic consequences for our emotional and moral life. To explore this disturbance *The Dainty Monsters* looks out upon a world in which the instruments of technological society have begun to usurp the place of, and speak for, the creative process of the natural world. Here in the clinical spaces of our new technological sublime, bombs 'are shaped like cedars' ('The Inheritors') while 'somewhere in those fields / they are shaping new kinds of women' ('Early Morning, Kingston to Gananoque'). The technological telos of modern culture, these poems seem to suggest, inevitably leads to the devitalisation of nature; but the devitalisation of nature fatally diminishes the scope and quality of human thought and feeling. Ondaatje's poems return continually to this deathly dialectic while seeking a redemptive power that might free us from its terminal embrace. This power will ultimately be found in art: a force capable of constituting an image of the human from a perspective located simultaneously within and beyond its borders, and which, in so doing, transforms the apocalyptic vision of the 'death of man' into the promise of a new beginning.

The tension between the irrefragable alterity of the natural world and an instrumental vision of nature determined to see that world in man's own technological image lies at the heart of the volume's opening poem, 'Birds for Janet – A Heron'. The poem is both a stunning recreation of a 'natural' or pre-reflective mode of life wholly inimical to human experience and a meditation upon the profound limits of the anthropomorphic perspective that lends form to such imaginative projection (DM, 12).

The reader's desire to make sense of the poem and bridge the gap between human and inhuman experience is folded into the poem's mode of disclosure. The spatial isolation of the opening phrase ('The reach') complicates two lines of flight by suggesting both the heron's headlong dive towards the water's surface and our imaginative attempt to apprehend this creature's relation to its world.[1] Meanwhile Ondaatje's fractured syntax and indeterminate verb-phrases ('fingers stretching / backbones') seem to implicate us in the poem's field of reference: do these words describe our movement or the heron's? The poem's angle of vision is continually inflected with this calculated duplicity: 'Reflections make them an hourglass' indicates both the play of light upon water as the heron hurtles towards it and the poetic act of metaphor (or 'reflection') that enables us to locate this inhuman movement within the cultural representations of our own world. The ensuing lines contrast the dynamism of the heron's physical self-expression with its imprisonment within an anthropomorphic perspective that claims to speak for its experience. As the poem progresses, the heron is simultaneously anthropomorphised and denuded of life: his 'hairless ankle / rests on a starved knee', he merely 'fingers his food', his 'soul is jailed' in a sleep from which he will never awaken. Such devitalisation, Ondaatje implies, is the effect of the bird's confinement within the prison-house of language; poetic language makes rudimentary sense of this creature but misses what is essential to its nature in the act of representing it. The heron, we might say, becomes *like* us in the act of being described *by* us; but something vital to its experience is lost in this alignment of language and being. Instead, the heron's existence admits no distinction between the force and *telos* of life; it simply embodies its own nature in the spontaneous act of self-assertion ('Heron is the true king', *DM*, 13).

To be the 'true king' is to affirm the power of one's nature. This aristocratic affirmation of life distinguishes the heron from the subordinate eagles who must depend upon the strength of others for their authority ('only / muscular henchmen / with mad eyes / bedded in black fur'). The heron exists triumphantly amid the competition of forces: its body bisects the plane of a lake to seize upon its prey; a stronger mode of life incorporates a weaker into its domain. Human life, in contrast, transforms the ceaseless flux of life into concepts and values. While this transformation creates a distinction between human and inhuman life, it does so at the expense of sequestering us from the broader interplay of forces from which all life emerges. Language and conceptuality, Ondaatje suggests, seek to account for the infinite variety of existence; but they remain powerless to explain the quality of pre-reflective experience. Rather than illuminating the secret truth of the natural world, the anthropomorphic gaze of poetic language finds only an aporia at the core of inhuman life: a landscape full of 'empty' tracks marking out 'the path / of a heron's suicide'.

The ontological schism between the anthropomorphic gaze and the disposition of inhuman life is a recurring theme of Ondaatje's early poetry. It lies at the heart of 'Pigeons, Sussex Avenue': 'In dark grey or black / they silhouette the vantage points / reconnoitering yards profoundly … ' (*DM*, 14). In the poem's cramped, claustrophobic lines, the life of pigeons is simultaneously revealed and occluded. The birds 'silhouette', rather than occupy, the vantage points; from the perspective available to it the poetic voice cannot even be sure whether their feathers are 'dark grey or black'. So indistinct is Ondaatje's presentation of the image that it is initially unclear whether the poem is describing birds or pieces of statuary ('slight falls of snow betraying their stoneness'). Only when the pigeons spray out a wing and 'break the image' is the nature of their being disclosed. The phrase to 'break the image' captures the paradoxical impulse of Ondaatje's rhetoric, which suggests that poetry, despite its claim to lend us a privileged insight into the truth of experience, can only testify to the abyssal distance between the facts of language and unselfconscious or pre-reflective life. The trajectory of a poem like 'Pigeons' lies, in fact, *through* language towards the *limits* of language where it is no longer apparent what verbs like 'reconnoitering' or adverbs like 'profoundly' tell us about the mode of being of a creature that lives at a crucial distance from self-consciousness: a creature who can only be thought, from an anthropomorphic perspective, as the embodiment of a 'slowly freezing mind'.

Sometimes the schism between language and inhuman life is reviewed in a comic light. A case in point is 'Song to Alfred Hitchcock and Wilkinson', which burlesques poetic language by taking the incommensurability between metaphors and the mode of life they seek to describe as its object of satire:

> Flif flif flif flif very fast
> is the noise the birds make
> running over us.
> A poet would say 'fluttering',
> or
> 'see-sawing with sun on their wings.'
> But all it is
> is flif flif flif flif very fast. (*DM*, 17)

Concepts and metaphors, as Nietzsche knew, create a perspective *upon* the world that does not exist *in* the world.[2] While it is necessary for conceptual thought to employ categories such as 'space', 'time' and 'causality' to render experience thinkable in human terms, the profound anthropomorphism of such acts of imaginative projection is exposed whenever language encounters the inhuman world. We need images and metaphors to make sense of the world; yet these figures help to produce the nature of the experience they purport to describe. A poet might employ metaphor ('see-sawing with sun on their wings') to describe the bodily flight of birds, just as a film director like

Hitchcock might invoke their instinctual life to hint at atavistic human desires or fears, but neither of these representations tells us much about the perceptual world of the creatures themselves. By holding us at an ironic distance from what a 'poet might say', the poem cheerfully accepts the inevitably anthropomorphic and subjective character of poetic designations. At the same time, the ambivalence of Ondaatje's diction ('but all it is') suggests that the reality of inhuman experience is both more and less than language can ever convey. What we can glimpse of the being of inhuman life is in fact revealed to us in the very act of its concealment. The birds, we might say, are open to being, but not to language; the self-subverting logic of Ondaatje's studiously unlyrical song playfully expresses the silence at the heart of this linguistic 'relation'.

A poem like 'Biography' sheds a much darker light upon the same subject (*DM*, 16): a biography confers a self-conscious narrative form upon the chaotic flux of life and then retrospectively invests lived experience with structure and meaning. Biographical narrative is therefore fundamentally at odds with the mode of becoming of animal life which perceives no distinction between an act and its mode of expression. The 'meaning' of an event of animal life, if we may admit so anthropomorphic a term, *is* all that it *does*. For this reason the subject of Ondaatje's poem inhabits a necessarily ambivalent relationship to the form that seeks to accommodate its experience. In a witty move, he expresses this ambivalence by a type of linguistic double exposure whereby a series of metadiscursive phrases call into question the very limits of the textual world in which the poem itself unfolds. The poem's fluctuation between concretion and abstraction is not immediately resolved by the operation of metaphor; the two modes exist side by side, opening the poem to two very different kinds of reading. Key phrases like 'finding no ground' inhabit both registers at once: the dreaming animal can find no ground to act out its fantasmatic pleasures in its world of workaday servitude, while the poem can find no ground in animal life for the distinction between consciousness and self-consciousness upon which biographical narrative depends. Pre-reflective life becomes precisely what cannot be accounted for within the poem's own terms, a failure suggested by the dog's 'unseen eyeballs' and the 'scattering' of its body in sleep. The violence of this act of exclusion is underscored in the poem's closing lines, where the force of inhuman life appears radically distorted in a nightmare vision of torn bulls' heads and the 'loosed / heads of partridges'.

Much of Ondaatje's early work is situated at the border between the human and inhuman worlds. His fascination with inhuman life is motivated by a number of factors. Certainly he shares elements of the romantic commitment to reassert the force of natural, spontaneous and unselfconscious being within a culture of technological rationality that increasingly marginalises any knowledge of life which is not instrumental in function. His work embraces key aspects of the romantic critique of a technocratic culture increasingly less able to understand its relationship with what lies outside itself: both this critique and an uneasy recognition of the forms of irrationalism to which it sometimes leads are distinctive features of his entire oeuvre. This strain of Ondaatje's work is reinforced by another theme that finds its first and perhaps clearest expression in these poems: the realisation that the idea of 'man' that underpins modern humanism is itself constituted by a *division* between human and inhuman life which has had parlous consequences for our relationship to the world around us.

In this sense Ondaatje's poetry chimes with the recent work of the Italian philosopher Giorgio Agamben, who has examined the historical origins of the modern idea of 'man' and its concomitant moral assumption of the 'humanity' of mankind. Writing against the conviction that man is a biologically given species or a substance given once and for all, Agamben suggests that the 'humanity' of man can only be established at the point where man is separated from the animality of nature. 'Man', Agamben argues, 'exists historically only in this tension: he can be human only to the extent that he transcends and transforms the anthropophorous animal which supports him, and only because, through the act of negation, he is capable of mastering, and eventually destroying his own animality'.[3] This is the full and paradoxical import of the idea of *Homo Sapiens:* man can only become himself insofar as he *knows* himself: man, that is, is 'the animal that must recognize itself as human to be human'.[4] Such recognition demands that man transcends himself by lifting himself above his own animal nature. Sapience, or self-knowledge, works remorselessly to 'isolate the non-human within the human'; it becomes a machine that produces the human by severing man from an animal being that is recast as bare, empty and worthless life.[5] Man's nature is defined by this primary act of exclusion; what man has become has historically been determined by the borders he has managed to establish between human and inhuman life.

This is the paradoxical place of inhuman life within modern culture: excluded by means of an inclusion that makes animality fundamental to man's nature; included by means of an exclusion that defines inhuman life as empty, because unselfconscious, being.[6] This paradox explains why inhuman life must simultaneously be subordinated to human needs, since it is less than we are, and continuously brought to light and judged, because we come to a sense of ourselves in our self-conscious distance from everything we transcend. Ondaatje examines precisely this double movement at the core of modern humanism in a series of poems that explore what constitutes 'civilised' modern life. It makes its appearance at the very beginning of 'The Diverse Causes': 'Three clouds and a tree / reflect themselves on a toaster. / The kitchen window hangs scarred, / shattered by winter hunters ...' (*DM*, 22).

Modern life is presented in the poem as an insulated and inward-looking space ruled over by the daylight gods of science and technology and consecrated by the endless reproduction of consumer goods. We live in a 'cell of civilised magic' where 'our milk is powdered' and 'Stravinsky roars at breakfast'. Almost imperceptibly the products of technology have displaced nature from centre stage: 'Three clouds and a tree / reflect themselves on a toaster'. But as so often in these poems the historical triumph of culture over nature appears vulnerable to challenge and reversal: faceless 'winter hunters' shatter the windows of our civilised cell while a capricious god casually manipulates the force of the elements outside. It is crucial that the border between human and inhuman life is perceived to be both established and continually shifting its ground because man constitutes his own image in the very act of division that distinguishes the two spheres.[7] The poem's temporal structure underlines the profound cultural work performed by supposedly natural categories by its late shift from the present towards the future tense. The world disclosed by the poem, Ondaatje concludes, is, like all human worlds, both 'of' and 'not yet' of 'man', projecting itself forward towards an ideological distinction that already precedes it, born to us as it is in the ceaseless separation of our own nature from nature in general.

This idea of inhuman life as a repressed remainder that must constantly renew itself to consciousness is a staple concern of Ondaatje's early work. It declares itself in a number of poems that present the inhuman as not merely other but *monstrously* other to man. This sinister theme is explored in 'Gorillas', a poem which reconsiders the evolution of man from the perspective of the anthropophorous animal that he transcends but which now threatens to displace him (*DM*, 19). The portrait of a bastard genesis, an inhuman and monstrous form of life born of a nature divided violently from itself, is reprised in 'Early Morning, Kingston to Gananoque', where, in a stripped and desolate landscape (a 'land too harsh for picnics'), nature now 'breeds the unnatural' (*DM*, 21). A decisive shift in the 'natural' order of things now appears to have taken place: nature is no longer simply the antithesis of culture; instead it has begun to make itself over in the image of the instrumental rationality that has ravaged it. Out there somewhere, in fields once reserved for pastoral, an anonymous and threatening 'they' are 'shaping new kinds of women'. In poems like 'Early Morning' and 'Eventually the Poem for Keewaydin' nature, for so long an imaginative solace for the instinct of domination embodied in instrumental thought and modern intellectual culture, actively conspires in that culture's destruction. Meanwhile the products of culture, now reified into autonomous objects for our contemplative enjoyment, have begun to usurp the place of nature itself: 'And yet tonight I sat on the steps / and noticed that the cars too with their white eyes / fussed in their circle of space ... their chrome teeth moving among the pith of the night' (*DM*, 39).

The image of inhuman life as the repressed and antagonistic Other of modern culture informs the main conceit of 'The Republic'. So important is this theme to Ondaatje that he gives it an explicitly allegorical formulation: 'This house, exact, / coils with efficiency and style. / A different heaven here, / air even is remade in the basement ... (*DM*, 20). From the beginning the 'house' is overburdened with symbolic significance; suspended uneasily between allegory and anthropomorphism, it defines both the dwelling place and the rational self-image of modern man. If the construction of the house symbolises our ability to give form to the chaotic flux of life, the poem also locates the origins of our modernity in an ideological division between culture and nature. Certainly the internal features of the house flawlessly reproduce aspects of the functional intelligence that devised it: it is 'exact' in proportion, 'efficient' in function, stylish in its transcendence of natural and supernatural forces. At first glance 'The Republic' appears to afford a tantalising glimpse of a technological 'heaven' where even 'air' is 'remade in the basement'. It demarcates its boundaries by pressing nature into service ('The plants fed daily / stand like footmen by the windows') while subjecting it to a moralising vision of life where even the plants are flush with a 'decent' green. Any experience of pleasure which does not serve instrumental ends is bluntly interdicted; there will be 'no dancing with the wind here'. Recast in Nietzschean terms, 'The Republic' might seem to present the triumph of the Apollonian virtues of manifest reason and order over the Dionysian expression of primal forces and ecstatic natural energies. Such a view is, however, profoundly misleading. For Ondaatje is convinced, like Nietzsche, that while we require Apollonian structures – such as art, conceptuality and civic institutions – to prevent primal forces transforming life into a chaos of competing drives, these structures threaten to petrify life within dead forms unless they expose themselves to the renewing force Dionysian energies provide. 'Too much reason', the third stanza of 'The Republic' implies, leads to nothing *but* reason. The responsibility and risk of art is to challenge this restricted vision of experience by opening itself to the force of inhuman life while discovering new forms within which to accommodate its vitality. This challenge begins to emerge in the second half of the poem, where, as day turns to shadowy night, Dionysian forces reassert themselves and 'passions crack the mask in dreams'. Throwing off their 'decent green', the plants 'in frenzy heave doors apart' and reinscribe the trace of nature within the self-enclosed spaces of human culture. Amidst this Dionysian frenzy, the triumph of rational over pre-reflective life is seen as a 'frigid' and devitalising achievement. So vividly rendered is the transfiguring force at work in the third stanza that it compromises the restorative cadence of the final two lines. What can 'decorum' mean, we wonder, in circumstances like these, and how far is its possible to reconcile the antithesis of human and inhuman life in the context of the instrumental rationalisation of nature?

One of the intriguing implications of 'The Republic' is that for modern culture to 'revitalize' itself human and inhuman life must exist in a mutually defining relationship. In saying this we should remain attuned to the Nietzschean aspect of Ondaatje's imagination because the conflict his work presents between human and inhuman experience also sets the scene for an examination of the role of art in transforming a series of pre-reflective drives and investments into images that enable us to reflect upon our place within the general economy of life. This dynamic interplay between different modes of life and the role of art in creating forms capable of accommodating natural energies are dramatised in one of Ondaatje's pivotal early poems, 'King Kong meets Wallace Stevens' from his 1973 collection *Rat Jelly*. It begins:

Take two photographs –
Wallace Stevens and King Kong
(Is it significant that I eat bananas as I write this?) (*RJ*, 61)

'King Kong' offers a dispassionate vision of the shadowy and bestial origins of aesthetic vision in the spirit of W. B. Yeats's dictum that artistic creation has its origins in pre-personal flows of affect or what he calls 'the foul rag and bone shop of the heart'.[8] The poem counterpoints two photographs: one of King Kong, the other of the poet Wallace Stevens. From its opening three stanzas it seems that these photographs are introduced in order to juxtapose the autonomous and elaborately fashioned self-representations of cultural humanism with the chaotic and unregulated drives of pre-reflective 'natural' being. Thus Stevens, the Hartford insurance agent who insisted upon a rigorous distinction between his imaginative and public life, is presented as a 'benign' and self-collected presence separated from his mere animal nature by the quality of the 'thought' in him. Kong, on the other hand, is shown 'staggering' and 'lost' in the maze of the modern metropolis, his 'mind' overwhelmed by the stream of images that flood his vision. Where Stevens's ability to manipulate his own image hints at the impersonal authority of his poetry, Kong's identity is always also an effect of cultural commodity production (he is always 'at the call of Metro-Goldwyn-Mayer'). Yet what begins as the surreal juxtaposition of two modern American cultural icons gradually develops into a metaphor for the act of artistic creation as 'Kong' is unmasked as a repressed aspect of Stevens's own nature. As the poem unfolds Ondaatje slowly begins to realise the suggestiveness of images like 'dark thick hands' and 'naked brain', which trouble the smooth outline of Stevens's public profile by identifying a connection between the mind that creates and the corporeal investments and intensities from which its images are composed. Stevens may still be 'in his suit' but beneath this disguise he 'is thinking chaos is thinking fences' as Ondaatje's equivocal syntax tries to convey the uncanny effect of a poetics situated at a point of indistinction between sensuality and sense. Ondaatje's Nietzschean inheritance is particularly marked during the psychodrama enacted in the poem's two concluding stanzas. In order to create art that has the power to imagine life differently, the artist must expand his notion of experience to include the 'seeds of fresh pain' planted by culture's desolation of nature; but this 'bellow of locked blood' needs also to be 'exorcised' or given imaginative form by the shaping spirit of art. Only the artist who can hold 'blood' and 'brain' in imaginative synthesis can hope to redeem nature upon culture's own ground; to do so we may need to 'pose in the murderer's shadow' and renounce the anthropomorphic privilege conferred upon the sovereign image of 'Man'.

The power of art to create inhuman perspectives upon human experience that expand our notion of what the 'human' can be is the subject of the famous final stanzas of 'The Gate in His Head' (RJ, 62). The poem returns to one of the definitive tropes of Ondaatje's early poetry: the artist reflecting upon the scene of writing. What is remarkable about the scene is its attempt to free sensation and feeling from consciousness and liberate language from the burden of conceptuality. Reflecting upon the process by which poetry translates 'chaos' into 'vision', Ondaatje envisages the poet as a 'blind lover' who does not know 'what I love till I write it out'. Like Roland Barthes's modern *scriptor* the poet's identity is created and ceaselessly reconstituted by the transitive modalities of writing; flows of affect pour across the page without being located within a particular subjectivity or way of seeing.[9] And that, Ondaatje concludes, is all that writing should be: an event that recovers the singularity of perception before it is enclosed with a particular point-of-view. To catch these 'beautiful formed things' at the 'wrong moment' so they are at once 'shapeless' and 'moving to the clear' is to redeem vision from cliché by focusing upon the sequencing of images from which our ideas about life derive. Poetry like this, we might say, does not merely 'represent' a world; it restores language to its active role in the creation of sense by returning us to the singular and specific differences from which life is lived.

'Peter' and the dialectic of enlightenment

'In the anticipatory identification of the wholly conceived and mathematized world with truth', write Adorno and Horkheimer of the 'dialectic of enlightenment' that they find everywhere at work in modern culture, 'enlightenment intends to secure itself against the return of the mythic'.[10] These words might usefully stand as epigraph to 'Peter', one of Ondaatje's most important poems, which extends his meditation upon the idea of the aesthetic by offering a dystopian vision of the fate of the artist in the era of modern instrumental rationality. In the character of Peter, Ondaatje presents his first developed image of 'the romantic artist as tortured artist', an image that will recur, in substantially different forms, in figures like Buddy Bolden and Billy the Kid.[11] Peter's story, which pits the artist against the emergent force of the 'new science', also explores a broader theme by suggesting that the disenchantment of the world intrinsic to enlightenment thought is predicated, in the words of Adorno and Horkheimer, upon 'the extirpation of animism'.[12] What is liquidated in the Enlightenment, they suggest, is any form of knowledge that is not instrumental in its essence. The new science can only uphold its axiomatic principles of the universal calculability of phenomena and the absolute autonomy of ideas by exposing as mystification the truths mankind once discovered in mythology, art and natural religion.[13] But by elevating its own ratiocinative procedures to the status of a universal rule, enlightened thought extirpates in turn the element of critical self-consciousness by which it might examine its own ground and reflect upon its relation to the exterior world.[14] Now the process of enlightenment becomes the subject of its own universal mythology whose regulatory ideal is 'the system from which all and everything follows'.[15] Central to the mythology of 'enlightenment' thinking is the excision of everything that is incommensurable to the identity of thought with the concept; at the same time the potential identity of everything with everything else envisaged in the universal mediation of life by conceptual thought inscribes alienation at the very heart of human experience:

> What was different is equalized. That is the verdict which critically determines the limits of possible experience. The identity of everything with everything else is paid for in that nothing may at the same time be identical with itself.

Enlightenment dissolves the injustice of the old inequality
– unmediated lordship and mastery – but at the same time
perpetuates it in universal mediation, in the relation of
any one existent to any other.[16]

The first two sections of 'Peter' offer an aesthetic analogue
to the experience Adorno and Horkheimer describe by staging a
confrontation between the universal mediation of life by conceptual thought and a poiesis still able to imagine the reconciliation
of nature and culture. Relegated to the bare margin of social
existence in the frozen wastelands beyond the city, Peter labours
to breathe imaginative life into inanimate nature: 'That spring
Peter was discovered, freezing the maze of bones from a dead
cow, skull and hooves glazed with a skin of ice' (DM, 71).

Perhaps the bleakest aspect of the poem's unsparing vision
is that Peter's isolation constitutes the one remaining measure
of freedom in a society dominated by the iron law of rational
computation and conceptual equivalence. Mourning the subordination of sensuous to instrumental modes of knowledge in
cultural modernity, Wordsworth famously wrote in 'The Tables
Turned': 'Sweet is the lore which nature brings; / our meddling
intellect / mis-shapes the beauteous forms of things: / we
murder to dissect'.[17] Ondaatje's nightmarish rendition of this
imaginative schism expresses the same sentiment with more
than comparable physical immediacy. Unwilling to tolerate a
mode of life that does not conform to the rule of computation
and utility, the faceless representatives of social authority first
'snare' Peter like an animal in the wilds then stretch him out
upon the torture-table of the new science:

> They snared him in evening light,
> his body a pendulum
> between the walls of the yard,
> rearing from shrinking flashes of steel
> until they, with a new science,
> stretched his heels and limbs,
> scarred through the back of his knees
> leaving his veins unpinned,
> and him singing in the evening air. (DM, 72)

In these inhuman laboratory conditions the 'new science' transforms a living being into an object for its own contemplation in pursuit of new forms of social domination. As Peter's inspection proceeds his subjectivity is turned into a mere thing among other things: his bound body becomes 'a pendulum / between the walls of the yard'; his shattered feet arc into the air 'like a compass' (*DM*, 73). Ondaatje finds an arresting phrase to encapsulate this vision of damaged life: during his ordeal Peter is 'froze[n] into consciousness' as the objectifying gaze of his antagonists attempts to turn his intuitive openness to the sensuous immediacy of experience into its own mirror image (*DM*, 72). In the first months of his captivity Peter tries to resist thraldom to this new social authority by embracing those abject and asignifying elements of language ('words were growls, meaningless; / disgust in his tone burned everyone') that retain no value within the dissolvent rationality of enlightenment discourse (*DM*, 73). His dissent is met with inhuman ferocity ('After the first year they cut out his tongue'); what cannot be ascribed a value according to the law of computation and utility is simply liquidated. As if to underline the fate awaiting all who challenge the will-to-power of enlightenment rationalism, Peter is placed in a 'hive' at the centre of court and turned into a grisly social spectacle (*DM*, 74). Significantly, his response to this violent negation of his humanity is to reproduce in aesthetic terms the details of his deathly existence. His new carvings reflect in their twisted and fractured forms the atomising force of enlightenment rationality and the splintering of the image of 'man' enforced by its separation of human nature from nature in general (*DM*, 75).

The climax of the poem exemplifies one of the dark truths of the dialectic of enlightenment: 'Domination over nature is paid for with the naturalization of social domination'.[18] The tragic implications of this statement emerge in two juxtaposed scenes. Section six of the poem shows girlish Tara, synecdoche of the social forces that imprison Peter, riding the imprisoned 'court monster' as her personal pet (*DM*, 76). But in section seven Peter dramatically turns the tables by revisiting the violence that holds this society together upon the body of one of its most privileged representatives: 'An arm held her, splayed / its fingers like a cross at her neck / till he could feel fear thrashing at her throat, / while his bent hands tore the sheet of skirt ...' (*DM*, 77).

Ondaatje's use of violence in this scene is precisely (and ironically) calculated. The entire poem has chronicled the relentless objectification and commodification of an aesthetic and animistic comportment to the world; Peter's savage revenge upon his persecutors reproduces exactly the same logic as he turns a living body into an impersonal object of desire and gratification. What is subtracted from this violent encounter is the particularity of individual humanity: Tara's subjectivity is simply synonymous with the feminine pronoun while Peter's complex of motivations is reduced to the 'arm' that holds her fixedly in place. Throughout the rape he 'moulds' her body in a perverse caricature of aesthetic fidelity to the object of perception; but the 'lush oil' in which he now works is 'loathing'. His terrible art of domination eliminates Tara from the human field of vision ('staining / the large soft body like a whale') as surely as the power of the aesthetic is effaced by the conversion of art into a cultural commodity. As the poem's final lines make clear, Peter's violation of Tara represents an obscene parody of freedom rather than a subaltern expression of autonomy: as her tears 'glue' him to her pain he is now utterly indistinguishable from the object of his loathing. Yet although Peter's actions represent in one sense a descent into moral barbarism, they do so by reproducing aspects of the instrumental impulse of cultural modernity which ceaselessly converts the singular and incommensurable into an indifferent object of consumption and exchange. 'With the denial of nature in man', Adorno and Horkheimer suggest in words that bring the central theme of 'Peter' disquietingly into focus, 'not merely the *telos* of the outward control of nature but the *telos* of man's own life is distorted and befogged'.[19]

the man with seven toes

With its abrupt tonal transitions and sharp juxtaposition of narrative perspective, 'Peter' seems in retrospect to be a poem written at the very limit of lyric form. Perhaps with this in mind, Ondaatje began to experiment in the mid-1960s with more extended serial modes of poetic narrative. He took the first steps in this direction in 1966 with the composition of the long poem *the man with seven toes*. The poem was inspired by the Australian artist Sidney Nolan's series of paintings recreating the story of Eliza Fraser, who was shipwrecked off the coast of Queensland in 1836 and compelled to live for several months in an indigenous Australian community. Mrs Fraser was eventually accosted by Bracefell, an escaped convict, who led her to safety through the bush, only to be betrayed back into custody by his companion at the conclusion of their epic journey. Ondaatje had only a sketchy knowledge of the story's precise historical details, relying upon Colin MacInnes's essay 'The Search for an Australian Myth in Painting' for basic background information about the incident. He later appended the following extract from MacInnes's essay as an addendum to the published poem:

> Mrs Fraser was a Scottish lady who was shipwrecked on what is now Fraser Island, off the Queensland Coast. She lived for six months among the aborigines, rapidly losing her clothes, until she was discovered by one Bracefell, a deserting convict who himself had hidden for 10 years among the primitive Australians. The lady asked for the criminal to restore her to civilization, which he agreed to do if she would promise to intercede for his free pardon from the Governor. The bargain was sealed, and the couple set off inland.
>
> At first sight of European settlement, Mrs Fraser rounded on her benefactor and threatened to deliver him up to justice if he did not immediately decamp. Bracefell returned disillusioned to the hospitable bush, and Mrs Fraser's adventures aroused such admiring interest that on her return to Europe she was able to exhibit herself at 6d a showing in Hyde Park.[20]

By the time we come across this brief account of the Fraser story in Ondaatje's poem, we have, of course, already read the thirty-four spare, elliptical fragments that compose the completed sequence. The effect of placing the quotation from MacInnes at the conclusion of the work is inevitably ironic and diminishing; the measured tones of scholarly commentary seem to inhabit a completely different world from the raw, flayed bodies depicted in Ondaatje's poem. This disjunction between content and commentary is crucial to Ondaatje because his aim was to present a series of singular images of bodies in space before they could be organised and recombined into a moral or historical worldview. *the man with seven toes* accords, in this regard, with Ondaatje's conception of the unmediated power of what he calls 'point blank' narrative. Writing about the 'rough-edged' quality of Howard O'Hagan's novel *Tay John* Ondaatje suggests that to realise its implicit mythic power a story should be presented to the reader 'point blank' without any of the 'complex narrative devices' that qualify and contextualise its characters and actions.[21] Only in this way, Ondaatje believes, can the 'raw power of myth' be preserved in an age of acute historical self-consciousness.

Ondaatje preserves the 'point blank' power of his poetic presentation in a number of ways. To begin with, he removes any trace of the story's original historical context, while displacing it from its specifically Australian location and modifying key elements of its plot and characterisation. The poem's central female character steps off a train, rather than enduring a shipwreck; the position of her benefactor as an escaped convict in a penal state is merely implied rather than directly stated; and both the woman's promise to intercede with the authorities upon his behalf and her subsequent betrayal of this pledge – one of the most troubling aspects of the original story – are eclipsed from the narrative. Meanwhile the historical identity of the two principals, along with the psychological motivations and nuances that might enable an understanding of their character, are simply subtracted from the poem: unlike Mrs Fraser, the female protagonist is never named, while Bracefell is rechristened Potter in

Ondaatje's version of the narrative. As a consequence we do not know who these people are, why they behave in the ways that they do, or even what sense they are subsequently able to make of their experiences. The effect of this poetic rewriting is both to weaken the story's historical focus and widen the range of its allegorical and mythic implication. Crucially, it also redirects our attention to the affective quality of the experience they undergo, rather than to the historical, cultural or psychological contexts that might account for its 'meaning' in general terms.

If Ondaatje's poetic recreation of Mrs Fraser's rite of passage is unfaithful to its authentic historical detail, it offers nevertheless a superb imaginative rewriting of Nolan's painterly technique. In plate 19 of Nolan's Mrs Fraser series (1947) the painter creates, in Bryan Robertson's words, 'one of his most alarming, convinced and unforgettable images'. The bestial and exposed form of Mrs Fraser crouching on all fours in an alien and inhospitable landscape

> conveys something of the shock and horror of a white, northern European body flung down in the wild bush of a Pacific island, and forced to fend for itself; a body that has not been exposed to the ravages of strong sun before, straddles horrifically across the land, isolated and lost. Her face is hidden by her hair and this device for anonymity is also employed in all the later paintings of Mrs Fraser. The grey surround makes the scene appear to be caught in the lens of binoculars.[22]

Like Nolan's images, the 'shock' and 'horror' of Ondaatje's poems confront us without an explanatory context that might define their position within a coherent narrative sequence. The opening lyric offers a synoptic introduction to the poem's broader dislocations of time and place, though everything about this strange little poem (*TMWST*, 9) is disconcerting. Who is the woman and what is she doing in a landscape of 'desert and pale scrub'? Where, indeed, is this place, which, defined as it is by the archetypal image of rail tracks extending into seemingly endless space, could just as easily be the North American West as nineteenth-century Australia? For what reason does she step off the

train, and why is she 'too tired' to call it back to her? From the
beginning the woman has no discernible personality or past that
might permit us to identify with her and her situation; at the
same time Ondaatje hollows out the entire level of subjective
interiority or psychological 'depth' that might enable us to bring
her motivations, hopes and fears into focus. Instead he fashions
a type of 'point blank' narrative that presents a succession of
shocking and unaccountable incidents which reproduce, in their
violent and seemingly arbitrary juxtaposition, the disorientation of an individual unable to make sense of her experience in
wholly unfamiliar surroundings. In this way Ondaatje's female
protagonist comes to resemble the archetypal colonial image of
the white outsider adrift in alien space and therefore vulnerable to the play of atavistic forces repressed elsewhere by 'civilised' society. By refusing his readers the fixed coordinates of
time, space and psychological motivation, Ondaatje asks us to
repeat his protagonist's experiences and enter a world for which
we lack the requisite aesthetic vocabulary and interpretative
norms. Certainly no 'temporal, spatial or syntactical continuity'
appears to govern the poem's distribution of scenes and images;
the effect, later developed in *The Collected Works of Billy the
Kid*, resembles the cross-cuttings and jump cuts of cinematic
montage.[23] Some years later Ondaatje described the form of
the sequence as 'a kind of necklace in which each bead-poem
while being related to the others on the string, was, nevertheless, self-sufficient, independent'.[24] The uncanny power generated by these 'bead-poems' is exemplified by the third lyric in
the sequence:

> entered the clearing and they turned
> faces scarred with decoration
> feathers, bones, paint from clay
> pasted, skewered to their skin.
> Fanatically thin,
> black ropes of muscle.
>
> One, whose right eye had disappeared
> brought food on a leaf. (*TMWST*, 11).

These lines present the first meeting of the female protagonist and the indigenous population. Nothing in the woman's
experience prepares her for this encounter; Ondaatje's elliptical
syntax and disordering of the relation between subject and object
captures the raw force of an event that exceeds her imaginative
frame of reference. The appearance of these unimaginable black
bodies saturates her field of vision; by positioning the participle
'entered' at the beginning of the line while suppressing any
sense of the subject who should accompany it, Ondaatje powerfully conveys the way in which the woman's identity begins to
dissolve in these inexplicable new surroundings. Her desperate
attempt to make sense of her situation is reflected in the fragmentary rendition of physical details as her eye slides quickly
from body to body; but her momentary recourse to the aesthetic
vocabulary of European portraiture ('black ropes of muscle')
only reinforces our impression of her disorientation and bewil-
derment. The feeling of extreme cultural dislocation provoked
in the woman by this unsolicited exchange of glances is developed in the next poem in the sequence, which relates the natives'
sudden physical circumscription of the unlikely figure in their
midst: 'they stripped clothes off like a husk / and watched my
white / tugged my breasts ... then threw / the red dress back at
me' (TMWST, 12).

The distinctive feature of these lines is their refusal to
envisage cultural exchange from the sole perspective of white
European eyes. Instead they seek to retrieve a sense of how an
invading white body might be perceived from the point-of-view of
the indigenous inhabitants. The politics of Ondaatje's poem does
not lie in a contrast between the character and ideology of distinct
political groupings – such as the competing interests and territorial claims of 'whites' and 'Aborigines' – but in the way different
modes of perception create different imaginative worlds. Thus
the indigenous Australians perceive space and bodies completely
differently from the European woman: land for them is 'not so
much an object to be named as it is the possibility or potential
for action: a place for walking, dreaming, painting and assem-
bling'.[25] This perception of land as a 'possibility or potential for

action' demands a style of representation that sees the world as an immanent field of forces and affects rather than as a neutral and geographically limited space waiting to be mastered. A line like 'and watched my white' responds to this demand by perceiving whiteness as an intensity or affect instead of an attribute of an extended form. The grammar of the poetic sentence leads us to expect 'white' to function here in the usual way as an adjective qualifying an accompanying noun; but the absence of that noun means that 'whiteness' can no longer be understood as an attribute or quality *of* some thing: it is an image or intensity that exists on its own terms. In their encounter with this anonymous white woman the indigenous Australians are fascinated by the very fact of whiteness irrespective of the 'subject' that it clothes; the effect of Ondaatje's deliberately elliptical syntax is to show how whiteness changes the distribution of forces in their field of vision and creates a new world of sense for them to explore.

The woman's incomprehension of the alien landscape in which she finds herself, and her poignant attempt to bring this landscape into some kind of imaginative focus, is conveyed in the sequence describing her rape at the hands of her tormentors (*TMWST*, 16). The breathless syntax and quicksilver transposition of subject and object positions that mark the passage express the turmoil of a consciousness unable to find descriptive categories for the experience it is enduring. Throughout the scene the indigenous bodies are both terrifyingly inhuman ('black goats' with 'cocks rising like birds flying to you') and also capable of a profound physical poetry (even their semen leaps 'like fountains in your hair'). Ondaatje elsewhere refines this last motif to underscore the sheer horror of the woman's violent incorporation into the indigenous domain; the semen 'tightens your face like a scar'. Her inability to come to terms with the trauma of her assault is movingly indicated by her projection of this experience onto the mutilated body of a dying animal. The savage tears in the goat's flesh leave its body 'open like purple cunts under ribs'; only the frailty of the accompanying syntax, with its tentative and ambiguously reflexive statement 'then tear / like to you' hints at the intolerable reality she cannot bring herself to acknowledge. So complete is the disintegration of her personality during the attack that she can only speak of herself in the form of the second-person pronoun. She cannot begin to readmit her own image into the field of reference until the last two lines of the poem where the phrase 'stringing them out' describes both the shredded nerves of a flayed carcass and the rudiments of her strategy for surviving her ordeal.

Potter, when he appears, is a curiously hybrid figure: he speaks English, but looks like an animal to the woman's eyes in his tattered convict garb: 'his stripes were zebras / cantering from him' (*TMWST*, 18). The journey the pair embarks upon through the swamp towards white settlement appears to slough off the last vestiges of her social consciousness. Instead her subjectivity seems to dissolve to the point where she is no longer an autonomous subject perceiving an independently existing world but rather is continuous with the pure flow of becoming that creates the event of life (*TMWST*, 23). Her experience in the swamp demonstrates once again how perception can be opened beyond itself so that life is freed from the anthropocentric perspective and made one with the flux of becoming. But if this vision of a world composed of intersecting planes of becoming enables us to affirm life beyond its merely human location, Ondaatje never forgets that the power of life is born from the struggle between *stronger* and *weaker* forces. One possible consequence of life lived at the level of an inhuman competition of forces appears in the scene where Potter rapes his helpless companion: 'Stripe arm caught my dress / the shirt wheeling into me / gouging me, ankles manacles, / cock like an ostrich, mouth / a salamander / thrashing in my throat' (*TMWST*, 32).

From the fragments of consciousness left to her, the woman looks out upon a landscape of inhuman forces ('a white world spilling through') rather than recognisable individuals. Humanity now dissolves into the autonomous part-objects that constitute it: Potter simply *is* the 'striped arm' that catches her dress; while it is 'the shirt' not the man who wheels into her. The change wrought upon her is subtly rendered in a late poem describing the final stage of her odyssey:

So we came from there to there
the sun over our shoulders and no one watching
no witness to our pain our broken mouths and bodies.
Things came at us and hit us.
Things happened and went out like matches.

(*TMWST*, 38)

Here Ondaatje work bathos to the point of pathos. 'Things happened and went out like matches' captures the exhaustion of a mind no longer able to find images to describe its experience as poignantly as T. S. Eliot's 'I have measured out my life with coffee spoons' reflects the urban anomie of the affectless suburban iconoclast. This portrait of a life lived at the very limit of representation is then contrasted with the woman's enigmatic reawakening to language in the penultimate poem in the sequence: 'She slept in the heart of the Royal Hotel / Her burnt arms and thighs / soaking the cold off the sheets ...' (*TMWST*, 41).

This penultimate poem offers a deeply ambivalent recoding of the experience the sequence has narrated. Its reference to the woman tracing her 'obvious ribs' hints at an allegorical, indeed possibly edenic, dimension to the narrative, although the adjective also suggests that this interpretation may conceal as much as it reveals about her story. A similar ambiguity haunts the lines 'sensing herself like a map, then / lowering her hands into her body'. At least one critic has been tempted to read them 'positively' as offering support for the assertion that the poem celebrates 'a rediscovery of the instinctual world within the self'.[26] Yet such a reading is obliged to acknowledge that this image echoes an earlier one detailing the woman's glimpse of 'the maps on the soles' of the feet of the indigenous Australians which identifies the 'instinctual world' with elements of amoral violence at the same time as it mobilises the trope of the female body as the map of the land that constitutes one of the staple ideological vehicles of imperial discourse (*TMWST*, 13). With this in mind, it is difficult to support Douglas Barbour's contention that *the man with seven toes* is 'haunted by a 1960s spirit of revolutionary social and sexual idealism' in which 'psychological, social or sexual breakdown leads to breakthrough'.[27] What haunts the poem, in fact, is a pervasive sense of the danger posed to social consciousness by inhuman forces that may lend profound insight into the way different modes of life become what they are, but which also threaten to destroy the psychological foundations upon which 'civilised' society depends. This palpable sense of threat lies at the core of the ballad that concludes the poem, which, with its flickering interplay between 'these people' and the 'you' that form the poem's readership, projects its bitter wisdom out from its time into *our* time:

> Green wild rivers in these people
> running under ice that's calm,
> God bring you all some tender stories
> and keep you all from hurt and harm (*TMWST*, 42)

The unresolved tension in *the man with seven toes* between affective intensity and the demands of social consciousness will subsequently become one of the defining themes of *The Collected Works of Billy the Kid*. Elsewhere Ondaatje explores the same theme at some length in the lyric 'White Dwarfs' from his collection *Rat Jelly* (*RJ*, 70). A 'white dwarf' is what a star becomes when it has exhausted its nuclear fuel. No longer able to burn the carbon at its core, the star collapses inward beneath the weight of gravity. Its outer layers are blown outward to form a shimmering aura or nebula; its inner layers contract into a core of inert and depleted energy. Ondaatje manipulates the image of a ruined yet still resonant star to evoke the life of those outlaw figures who can only exist at the margin of modern society but whose style of perception exposes the hollowness and sterile conformity of social conventions. He is aware of the hypertrophied romanticism of this position, and adopts an ironical attitude to it at key points in the poem; yet his irony also embraces the stalwarts of social orthodoxy who close themselves off from the force of life by subjecting it to a specious and unreflective moralism. What links the otherwise opposed figures of the romantic outlaw and the social conformist is that both ultimately sacrifice the power of life as a force of becoming and change to an *image of life* that restricts its capacity to become other than it is. One figure renounces life and collapses back beneath the dead weight of social gravity; the other is consumed by its own *mythos* of transgression and doomed to burn itself out in the 'ether peripheries'. Both 'disappear' from life by identifying themselves with the 'code' of their own image; both 'shave their moral so raw' that it reduces their experience of the world to a single system of values.

Ondaatje is unflinching in his self-examination here: he is most imaginatively drawn to those outlaw figures who 'sail to that perfect edge / where there is no social fuel'. But the peril of such 'altitude' or transcendence of social norms is that these outlaws can only 'perfect' themselves at the point where life finally collapses into myth: the moment of their own deaths. For Ondaatje to follow their example and 'release' his own 'sand-bags' and expose language to the force of its own becoming would be to risk 'mouthing the silence' by inhabiting 'the perfect white between the words' *(RJ*, 71). What is required instead is an aesthetic form capable of organising the singularities or events of difference from which life flows into recognisable and extended forms. In 'White Dwarfs' this perception defines the ground of a defence of poetry ('this white that can grow') in which 'what we cannot see is growing / in all the colours we cannot see':

> This white that can grow
> is fridge, bed,
> is an egg – most beautiful
> when unbroken, where
> what we cannot see is growing
> in all the colours we cannot see
> there are those burned out stars
> who implode into silence
> after parading in the sky
> after such choreography what would they wish to speak
>   of   anyway *(RJ*, 71).

The concluding lines are both elegiac and resigned, wistfully drawn to those legendary 'burned out stars', ruefully aware that they were swallowed by their own myths. The final line maps the 'choreography' of Ondaatje's art back onto these myths in order to open the poem to an ironic re-reading: after enduring such a rhetorical resurrection, what could Ondaatje's 'heroes' add even if they were here? Only the 'perfect edge' of art, the poem seems to say, can take us beyond an exhausted vision of life – those 'burned out stars' again which continually 'implode in silence' – without destroying life in the process; but to realise this new vision the artist must sometimes be prepared to 'pose in the murderer's shadow'. Ondaatje's acceptance of this melancholy truth took him next to the American West and an imaginative encounter with the 'collected works' of Billy the Kid.

The Collected Works of Billy the Kid

> I knew both men well and, in my opinion, Garrett was just as cold and hard a character as the Kid. The great difference between them was that Garrett had the law on his side and the Kid was outside the law. (Paulita Maxwell)[1]

The publication of Ondaatje's long poem *The Collected Works of Billy the Kid* marked a decisive moment in his writing career. The volume received the Governor General's Award in 1970, bringing Ondaatje's name to a wealth of new readers and establishing him as one of the rising stars of the new generation of Canadian writers who would come to prominence in the ensuing decade. Freely mixing the sketchily known historical facts of Billy the Kid's life and crimes with an imaginative reconstruction of his biography and legend, the poem focuses upon Billy's final outlaw year on the New Mexico frontier and his doomed attempt to evade capture by Sheriff Pat Garrett, his onetime companion and ultimate nemesis. Moving from the concentrated lyric focus of Ondaatje's early poems to an 'open form' created from a collage of textual fragments, *Billy the Kid* combines a range of different registers – 'biographical' writing, oral anecdote, historical romance and singular moments of intense lyrical reflection – in a sometimes bewildering flicker of perspectives. Simultaneously inhabiting Billy's consciousness while maintaining an impersonal and omniscient 'historical' point of view, the poem isolates key moments in the story of Billy's downfall. Beginning with Garrett's systematic destruction of Billy's dwindling band of outlaws, Ondaatje's decentred and synoptic narrative recounts Garrett's relentless pursuit of his retreating quarry, Billy's temporary retreat to the Chisum ranch, his arrest, ride to trial and escape from prison, and the final fateful encounter between lawman and outlaw at Pete Maxwell's ranch in Texas.

To recapitulate the poem's narrative in these bald terms, however, conveys little of the strangeness and visionary power of its rewriting of Billy's history and legend. The volume is entitled the 'collected works', not the 'life' or 'history' of Billy the Kid, and it is clear from its opening pages that Ondaatje's recasting of Billy's story makes little concession to the linear form of historiographical narrative. Instead, Ondaatje's playful rewriting of the struggle between Billy and Pat Garrett reverses the assumed relation between cause and effect, collocates inconsistent and occasionally contradictory evidence, interpolates into the poem apocryphal testimony and 'impossible' points of view, refuses to respect the distinction between 'historical' and 'non-historical' modes of representation, and repeatedly collapses the distance between narrator and the subject of narration. Dead before the narrative even begins, Billy is resurrected by the reader through the act of recomposing the textual traces of him that American history has bequeathed us; meanwhile Ondaatje's ludic superimposition of myth and fantasy upon historical memory underlines our collective responsibility for the present uses to which Billy's image is put. One consequence of the poem's self-conscious fascination with the way memory becomes 'history' and history blurs into myth is to open up the phrase 'collected works' to a multiplicity of possible readings: it comes simultaneously to represent Billy's legacy of murder, the poems that constitute Ondaatje's entire sequence, and the continually renewed labour of interpretation by which each succeeding generation brings a new image of Billy into focus.

Recalling the burst of publicity that attended the poem's publication, Ann Mandel notes the profound, and profoundly volatile, impression made upon its readership by a work that was 'praised by critics and readers and roundly condemned – to [Ondaatje's] delight – by federal MPs for dealing with an *American* hero and outlaw'.[2] This initial ambivalence soon dissipated to the point where, a mere twenty years later, *Billy the Kid* had become one of the most interpreted texts in recent Canadian Literature.[3] One reason for the poem's striking popularity, Douglas Barbour suggests, is that its polyvalent register and decentred form leave it unusually open to reader responses and therefore vulnerable to being pressed into 'a particular critic's ideological needs'.[4] Another reason is that the story already appears deeply familiar to us, recycled as it has been down the years in films, novels, biographies, ballads, 'yellow' journalism and television serials. We think we *know* the story before we *read* the story; such unselfconscious acceptance of the narrative's basic outline enables Ondaatje to play with our generic expectations, leading us in turn to rethink the established relation between law and disorder in the Old West and question our understanding of what we understand an historical event to be. A key component of Ondaatje's revisionist strategy is to emphasise the historically contingent and conditioned character of all our historical knowledge by constructing Billy's story from the same elements of 'prose, prose poem, dime novels, newspaper accounts and interviews' that have always been used to fix his image in the popular imagination.[5] Such exploitation of our prior imaginative investment in Billy's historical drama is made even easier by the fact that his history has undergone mythic revision almost from the moment of his death.[6]

Ondaatje's flamboyantly intertextual version of Billy's legend plays upon our assumed familiarity with the story – a familiarity compounded only three years after the poem's appearance by the release of Sam Peckinpah's movie *Pat Garrett and Billy the Kid*. Although Ondaatje reworks a variety of narrative sources, two intertexts achieve particular prominence. Throughout the poem Ondaatje draws heavily upon Walter Noble Burns's early bestselling historical account of Billy's life. Burns's book, itself a curious amalgam of history, myth-making and oral anecdote, came to exert a considerable influence upon *Billy the Kid*, and Ondaatje's complex rewriting of Burns's narrative is crucial to the poem's development. As we might expect, the genre of Western movies also had a substantial impact upon the text. In the years when Ondaatje was growing up, films like Ray Taylor's *The Son of Billy the Kid* (1949) and Kurt Neumann's *The Kid from Texas* (1950) popularised and reconfigured key elements of Billy's legend; a more direct influence upon Ondaatje's imagination, given the poem's subtitle 'Left Handed Poems', may well have been Arthur Penn's *The Left Handed Gun* (1958), a cinematic version of Gore Vidal's teleplay *The Death of Billy the Kid* (1955). Discussing his admiration for Sergio Leone's *Once Upon a Time in the West*, Ondaatje acknowledged the hold Western films had upon him during his early years: 'Luckily I saw the film after I had finished *Billy the Kid* because here was an Italian film-maker making this Western, in many ways the best Western, where with *Billy the Kid* I was trying to make the film I couldn't afford to shoot, in the form of a book. All those B movies in which strange things that didn't happen but could and should have happened I explored in that book'.[7]

The acute textual self-consciousness of *Billy the Kid* has done much to establish Ondaatje's reputation as a 'postmodern' writer. Certainly Ondaatje's poem has much in common with that vibrant strand of postmodern writing Linda Hutcheon has termed 'historiographic metafiction'. Hutcheon demarcates by this term those radically self-questioning 'historical' texts, such as the novels of Salman Rushdie, E. L. Doctorow and Umberto Eco, which challenge the impersonal and potentially homogenising perspective of traditional historiography by asserting instead the plurality, provisionality and historically constituted character of historical points-of-view.[8] Historiographical metafictions, she argues, are works that are 'intensely self-reflective but that also both re-introduce historical context into metafiction and problematize the entire question of historical knowledge'. Typically these fictions 'problematize' the very nature of historical knowledge by demonstrating that we can have no access to the historical 'real' beyond its textualised remains; they do this by highlighting the inevitable inscription of subjective and ideological points-of-view within the medium of historical narrative.

The similarities between the concerns of historiographical metafiction and the style and form of *Billy the Kid* are striking.

Thus the radical transitivity of Ondaatje's poetics presents a poem groping continually towards an understanding of its historical subject while reproducing, in the elliptical relation between its constituent elements, the hermeneutic problems implicit in every historical judgement. The contingency of historical knowledge is further underscored by Ondaatje's decision to recreate the life of a figure as over-determined as Billy the Kid: a figure who is simultaneously historical and mythic, provincial and international, subaltern and authoritarian, the ceaselessly reconstituted object of a myriad discursive practices. Our problems in understanding Billy's character and motivations, the poem suggests, are partly empirical problems concerning the lack of reliable and incontrovertible historical evidence – a fact Ondaatje emphasises by taking Burns's popular history as his primary source-text – and partly the inevitable consequence of the mediation of the past by multiple layers of historical narrative. *Billy the Kid* explores these questions by recasting the relationship between historicity and history in terms of a distinction between *events*, which Hutcheon reminds us have no intrinsic meaning in themselves, and *facts*, which constitute the explanatory ground of a potentially universal history:

> Historiographic metafiction, like both historical fiction and narrative history, cannot avoid dealing with the problem of the status of their 'facts' and of the nature of their evidence, their documents. And obviously, the related issue is that of how these documentary sources are deployed: can they be objectively, neutrally related? Or does interpretation inevitably enter with narrativization? ... Historiographic metafiction suggests a distinction between 'events' and 'facts' that is one shared by many historians. Events, as I have been suggesting, are configured into facts by being related to 'conceptual matrices within which they have to be imbedded if they are to count as facts' ... Facts are not given but are constructed by the kinds of questions we ask of events.[9]

The formidable artfulness of *Billy the Kid* is to acknowledge that events, to become facts, must be embedded within the conceptual matrix of a narrative history. One problem, of course, with acknowledging the *constructedness* of historical facts is the responsibility one bears to the layers of historical experience from which these facts have been constructed. Rather than explain away the risk of historiographical metafiction's relation to the events and durations beyond narration, Ondaatje's work embraces the problem of the *singular*: those forces that trouble the accepted generalities and narrative consistency of historical discourse. We might refer to this 'problem' as the problem of the *event*, an occurrence 'in' time that calls for a refigured understanding of the very sequence of time or narration. Ondaatje's poetry reflects upon what is lost in the movements of assimilation that constitute collective historical memories, and does this by seeking to establish a point of indiscernibility between the event and a mode of historiography that effaces the specificity of the event in the act of representing it. This subaltern gesture manifests itself in a poetic syntax that explodes linearity into multiple points of perception, which disperses causality into a temporal rhythm with neither beginning nor end, which dissolves the impersonal voice of history into the discordant registers of the subjects for which it claims to speak, which makes no evaluative distinction between wholly incommensurable modes of historical inscription, and obsessively foregrounds the partiality and interestedness of certain historicising judgements. Poetry imagined in these terms, we might say, is not just a way of interpreting or explaining historical experience; it rips a hole in representation by breaking experience down into the singular processes from which it is composed in order to explore the way events become facts and a self comes to conceive of its world.

Yet for all the formal and thematic similarities between *Billy the Kid* and the genre of 'historiographic metafiction', Ondaatje's stubborn emphasis upon the *singularity* of perception also suggests ways in which his work resists the paradigm of an avowedly 'postmodern' poetics. For at work in Hutcheon's idea of the metafictive is an ethics of recuperation: the entire question of apprehending the lost or occluded subject of historical discourse is, for her, always already constituted as a problem of *historical* representation. In these terms, the factors that produce and reconfigure our historical sense – the multiplication of analytical contexts, the imposition of hegemonic narratives or the marginalisation of subaltern voices – are always already historical in their essence. Whilst acknowledging the historically conditioned character of historical knowledge, *Billy the Kid* also asks: what are we to make of the singularity of experience before it is assimilated into a 'subjective' or 'historical' framework? How, indeed, do we open up a world of sense to ourselves and others before we take our place within the historical horizon of discourse? By neglecting these questions and rushing intemperately to a 'postmodern' reading of the poem, we risk effacing its most enigmatic and troubling feature: the sheer *unreadability* of the figure of Billy himself.

The tension the poem creates between a metafictive history and the singularity of the event is evident from its opening pages. The entire question of the construction of the past by the historical context of its reception is typographically focused upon the opening page by Ondaatje's reproduction of an empty photographic frame. The interplay between the frame's black borders and the dazzling whiteness of a space still awaiting its defining image lays stress upon the role representations play in shaping our perception of historical truth. The empty frame is both a provocation and a challenge: make what you will, it invites us, of the fragments that will follow, but accept your responsibility for the version of the past that your interpretation yields. One hundred pages later the poem will conclude by reasserting the abrupt challenge of this empty frame, albeit with one small but highly significant difference: in the bottom right-hand corner of the frame Ondaatje has inserted a tiny photograph of himself as a child dressed in cowboy garb. Playful though this insertion is, it is also a form of confession: Ondaatje will, after all, establish his poetic reputation by inhabiting the voice and persona of Billy the Kid. Beneath the empty frame on the poem's opening page is a terse accompanying note:

> I send you a picture of Billy made with the Perry shutter
> as quick as it can be worked – Pyro and soda developer. I

am making daily experiments now and find I am able to take passing horses at a lively trot square across the line of fire – bits of snow in the air – spokes well defined – some blur on top of wheel but sharp in the main – men walking are no trick – I will send you proofs sometime. I shall show you what can be done from the saddle without ground glass or tripod – please notice when you get the specimens that they were made with the lens wide open and many of the best exposed when my horse was in motion. (*BTK*, 5)

This brief passage provokes more questions than it answers. How, exactly, is this empty frame a 'picture of Billy' and who is the subject of the explanatory text? Recourse to Ondaatje's acknowledgements reveals the note to have been written by 'the great Western photographer L. A. Huffman', a celebrated exponent of frontier photography during Billy's own lifetime. But by detaching Huffman's note from its immediate context and suppressing the identity of its recipient, Ondaatje suspends the text indefinitely between an immediate and a general relevance. It is impossible, from this perspective, to be certain whether the 'I' denoted by the passage is Huffman, Ondaatje or even the impersonal voice of history itself, while the unspecified use of the second-person plural propels these lines beyond their immediate addressee and out towards the historical community of readers. The uncertain relationship established here between text and context is further underscored by the enigmatic phrase 'daily experiments', which extends almost imperceptibly beyond the immediate subject of Huffman's photographs to encompass both Ondaatje's lyrics and our own attempt to make sense of these scattered words and images. Our only path back to the frontier terrain of the nineteenth century, this interplay of frame and commentary implies, lies through this shadowy 'blur' of representations.

These problems of narrative context and address are compounded when we turn the page to read the first poem in the sequence:

These are the killed.

(By me) –

Morton, Baker, early friends of mine.
Joe Bernstein, 3 Indians.
A blacksmith when I was twelve, with a knife.
5 Indians in self-defence (behind a very safe rock).
One man who bit me during a robbery.
Brady, Hindman, Beckwith, Joe Clark,
Deputy Jim Carlyle, Deputy Sheriff J. W. Bell.
And Bob Ollinger. A rabid cat
birds during practice,

These are the killed.

(By them) –
Charlie, Tom O'Folliard
Angela D's split arm,

                    and Pat Garrett
sliced off my head.
Blood a necklace on me all my life. (*BTK*, 6)

Briefly sketching the primary details of Billy the Kid's criminal biography, this lyric introduces us to the curiously hybrid voice of Billy himself. Certainly the emphasis here upon crime outweighs the attention given to biography; with its blunt, affectless air, the poem has the spirit of a police confession. Legal responsibility for the dead is scrupulously adjudicated, while moral responsibility for their deaths is left wholly unexamined, as if somehow beyond the comprehension of the memorialising consciousness. But as the poem steadily accumulates its burden of detail, a nagging doubt makes itself felt concerning the entire question of 'voice' until we are led to the overwhelming question: who is actually speaking these words? The imbrication of the first-person pronoun ('These are the killed. / (By me)') with a list containing many of Billy's actual historical victims suggests these lines represent the authentic speech of Billy the Kid; yet Billy will himself be included within the list of the killed ('and Pat Garrett / sliced off my head'), making it impossible for him to be the sole narrator of this account. Instead, the voice of an exterior and impersonal 'history' speaks *through* Billy at this point; here we receive the first intimation that singular and plural points-of-view are to be seamlessly interwoven throughout the